T0418176

A Special Issue of
Memory

Autobiographical memory and emotional disorder

Guest Editors

Tim Dalgleish
MRC Cognition and Brain Sciences Unit, UK

and

Chris R. Brewin
University College London, UK

Routledge
Taylor & Francis Group

LONDON AND NEW YORK

First published 2007 by Psychology Press

Published 2018 by Routledge
2 Park Square, Milton Park, Abingdon, Oxon OX14 4RN
52 Vanderbilt Avenue, New York, NY 10017

First issued in paperback 2018

Routledge is an imprint of the Taylor & Francis Group, an informa business

British Library Cataloguing in Publication Data
A catalogue record for this book is available from the British Library

Cover design by Design Deluxe
Typeset in Ireland by Datapage International, Dublin

ISSN: 0965-8211

ISBN 13: 978-1-138-87774-0 (pbk)
ISBN 13: 978-1-84169-833-5 (hbk)

Contents*

*This book is also a special issue of the journal *Memory*, and comprises issue 3 of Volume 15 (2007). The page
numbers are taken from the journal and so begin with p. 225.

MEMORY, 2007, 15 (3), 225–226

Editorial

Autobiographical memory and emotional disorder: A special issue of *Memory*

Tim Dalgleish

MRC Cognition and Brain Sciences Unit, Cambridge, UK

Chris R. Brewin

University College London, UK

For those suffering from emotional disorders such as post-traumatic stress disorder (PTSD) or depression, aspects of the personal past can dominate conscious experience in tenacious and toxic ways. Memories of distressing autobiographical experiences can intrude into awareness as thoughts or images, as flashbacks or nightmares, each laden with unwanted and painful affect. These forms of remembering often "feel" very different from memories of less distressing aspects of the personal past, suggesting that they may have a distinct phenomenology. Such emotional disorders are characterised by repertoires of behaviours aimed at dealing with these powerful memories—reminders are avoided, attempts to suppress the intrusions are chronic, and behavioural patterns are adapted to bring about short-term relief in spite of long-term detriment.

For some, this struggle with the autobiographical past seems, on the face of it, to be successful. Specific memories of distressing events become elusive even during effortful recall (J. M. G. Williams et al., 2007). A minority of individuals seem to experience amnesia for highly salient and traumatic events to which objective evidence testifies they have been exposed (e.g., L. M. Williams, 1994). As with the phenomenology, there is a suggestion that such amnesia for salient personal material may be uniquely restricted to such highly emotive experiences.

These issues and questions are at the forefront of current research into the nature of emotional disorder. The purpose behind this special issue of *Memory* is to draw together some of the leading investigators engaged in this endeavour to share recent findings, theories, and opinions about how these issues and questions can be addressed and what some of the answers might be.

This special issue focuses on two broad themes already highlighted in the preamble. The first is the nature of autobiographical remembering of the personal past—what are the characteristics of such memories? And to what extent are they phenomenologically distinct from other types of autobiographical remembering? These questions are addressed directly with respect to trauma memories in the paper by Chris Brewin, which provides an update on the research in this area. The trauma theme is continued by Speckens and colleagues, who investigate different types of remembering in patients with PTSD who have been referred for psychological treatment. Pasupathi considers the interesting question of whether the narrative content of personal memories is different for memories that have been previously disclosed to others in

Address correspondence to : Tim Dalgleish, MRC Cognition and Brain Sciences Unit, 15 Chaucer Rd, Cambridge, CB2 2EF, UK. E-mail: tim.dalgleish@mrc-cbu.cam.ac.uk

http://www.psypress.com/memory   DOI:10.1080/09658210701256399

comparison with memories that are "collaboratively remembered". Finally, Meiser-Stedman and colleagues report the development of a self-report measure—the Trauma Memory Quality Questionnaire (TMQQ)—to assess the distinct phenomenological qualities of trauma memories in children and young people.

The second theme concerns varieties of difficulties in remembering emotional experiences from the personal past. In a target article, Richard McNally presents a provocative critical appraisal of Jennifer Freyd's Betrayal Trauma Theory (Freyd, 1996)—the view that the inability to remember traumatic personal experiences from childhood arises from a betrayal of the child by significant others (prototypically, through abuse), and from the child's need to preserve family relationships in the service of personal survival. The gauntlet thrown down by McNally is picked up in a scholarly and robust reply to his target critique by Freyd and colleagues. These controversial issues regarding amnesia for trauma-related material are also reflected upon in Brewin's review paper.

Three further papers examine the phenomenon of over-general autobiographical memory in PTSD and depression (J. M. G. Williams et al., 2007). Over-general memory refers to the relative difficulty such patients have in recalling specific memories from the past when cued to do so in laboratory settings. Both Crane et al. and Spinhoven et al. explore the idea that this over-general effect may result from the retrieval process for specific memories being hijacked if particular cue words map onto depressed patients' dysfunctional schemas, resulting in a failure to recall specific memories to those cues (Dalgleish et al., 2003). The final paper by Schönfeld and colleagues examines links between attempted suppression of trauma memories and over-general recall in patients with PTSD.

Study of the voluntary and involuntary recall of extremely distressing events is revealing aspects of human memory that are not apparent in standard laboratory studies with healthy volunteers. It is also suggesting new ways of conceptualising psychological therapies in terms of influencing how positive and negative memories compete for retrieval (Brewin, 2006). It seems increasingly likely that many psychological disorders are dependent on how negative life events are encoded and how the resultant memories are brought under control. Understanding why those control processes sometimes fail, and how control can be restored, promises to add greatly to our ability to treat psychological disorder.

REFERENCES

Brewin, C. R. (2006). Understanding cognitive-behaviour therapy: A retrieval competition account. *Behaviour Research and Therapy, 44*, 765–784.

Dalgleish, T., Tchanturia, K., Serpell, L., Hems, S., De Silva, P., & Treasure, J. (2003). Self-reported parental abuse relates to autobiographical memory style in patients with eating disorders. *Emotion, 3*, 211–222.

Freyd, J. J. (1996). *Betrayal trauma theory: The logic of forgetting childhood abuse*. Boston, MA: Harvard University Press.

Williams, J. M. G., Barnhofer, T., Crane, C., Hermans, D., Raes, F., Watkins, E., et al. (2007). Autobiographical memory specificity and emotional disorder. *Psychological Bulletin, 133*, 122–148.

Williams, L. M. (1994). Recall of childhood trauma: A prospective study of women's memories of child sexual abuse. *Journal of Consulting and Clinical Psychology, 62*, 1167–1176.

MEMORY, 2007, 15 (3), 227–248

Autobiographical memory for trauma: Update on four controversies

Chris R. Brewin
University College London, UK

Empirical research since the year 2000 on trauma and autobiographical memory in adults is reviewed and related to four enduring controversies in the field: Whether traumatic memories are inherently different from other types of autobiographical memory; whether memory for trauma is better or worse than memory for non-traumatic events; whether traumas can be forgotten and then recalled later in life; and whether special mechanisms such as repression or dissociation are required to account for any such forgetting. The review concludes that trauma and non-trauma memories differ substantially, but only in clinical and not in healthy populations. Whereas involuntary memory is enhanced in clinical populations, voluntary memory is likely to be fragmented, disorganised, and incomplete. Progress in experimental and neuroimaging research will depend on analysing how task performance is affected by the interaction of voluntary and involuntary memory and by individual tendencies to respond to trauma with increased arousal versus dissociation.

There are four central, but interrelated, controversies concerning autobiographical memory for trauma: Whether traumatic memories are inherently different from other types of autobiographical memory; whether memory for trauma is better or worse than memory for non-traumatic events; whether memories of truly traumatic events can be forgotten and then recalled later in life; and whether special mechanisms such as repression or dissociation are required to account for any such forgetting. These controversies have a long history, but have become a focus of renewed interest recently, particularly since the publication in 1993 of Elizabeth Loftus's article "The reality of repressed memories". Fuelled in part by such questions, but also by research interest in trauma and post-traumatic stress disorder (PTSD), there has been considerable progress in understanding the nature of traumatic memory. The purpose of this article is to summarise research on autobiographical memory for

trauma in adults in which there have been significant developments since the year 2000, and to update conclusions about the four areas of controversy. Research on general memory deficits in PTSD and on memory for non-autobiographical trauma stimuli is reviewed in detail elsewhere (Brewin, 2003; Brewin, Kleiner, Vasterling, & Field, in press; McNally, 2003).

A substantial amount of research on traumatic memory has been conducted in the context of post-traumatic stress disorder (PTSD), a condition that is initiated by exposure to an extremely stressful event. According to the American Psychiatric Association's Diagnostic and Statistical Manual (DSM-IV; APA, 1994), PTSD is characterised by high-frequency, distressing, involuntary memories that individuals are unable to forget and make great efforts to prevent coming to mind. Among these are the traumatic "flashback" memories characterised as being triggered spontaneously by exposure to trauma cues, as being

Address correspondence to: Chris R. Brewin, Subdepartment of Clinical Health Psychology, University College London, Gower Street, London WC1E 6BT, UK. E-mail: c.brewin@ucl.ac.uk

I am grateful to Steve Lindsay for comments on an earlier draft of this article.

http://www.psypress.com/memory   DOI:10.1080/09658210701256423

fragmented, as containing prominent perceptual features, and as involving an intense reliving of the event in the present. Another symptom of PTSD in the DSM-IV is an inability to voluntarily recall important aspects of the trauma (amnesia). However, the diagnostic criteria do not require that re-experiencing and amnesia be present at the same time, and there has been little discussion of whether it is feasible for these two symptoms to co-exist at the same time in the same patient (for an exception see Herman, 1995). Although very influential clinically, these various formulations of trauma-related disorders are relatively silent on whether traumatic memories are thought to differ from memories for other extremely emotional events, whether negative or positive (e.g., non-traumatic bereavement).

The idea that there is a fundamentally distinct type of memory for traumatic events dates back at least as far as Pierre Janet (1904), the French neurologist who distinguished traumatic memory from ordinary or narrative memory. Janet proposed that extremely frightening experiences might be unable to be assimilated into a person's ordinary beliefs, assumptions, and meaning structures, in which case they would be stored in a different form, "dissociated" from conscious awareness and voluntary control. Traumatic memory was inflexible and fixed, in contrast to narrative memory, which was adaptable to current circumstances; traumatic memory involved a constellation of feelings and bodily reactions, whereas narrative memory consisted of independent elements that did not invariably co-exist; traumatic memory was evoked automatically by reminders of the traumatic situation, whereas narrative memory occurred in response to conscious attempts at recollection.

Janet's ideas, involving a dissociative process that simultaneously renders a memory less accessible to voluntary retrieval but more prone to be automatically evoked by reminders, are relevant to what is now a large corpus of clinical observations and continue to be influential among leading trauma therapists and researchers (e.g., Terr, 1990; van der Kolk & van der Hart, 1991). Modern theories of human traumatic memory are beyond the scope of this article and have been reviewed elsewhere (Brewin & Holmes, 2003). It should be noted, however, that commentators such as Jacobs and Nadel (1998; Nadel & Jacobs, 1998) have argued that there are potentially close links between the human literature on traumatic memory and the animal literature with its func-

tional dissociation between (amygdala-dependent) memory for an emotional experience versus (hippocampus-dependent) memory for the spatiotemporal context of the experience. In particular, there is experimental evidence from studies of aversive learning in animals that extremely high levels of stress have opposite effects on the amygdala and hippocampus. These conditions could in humans, Jacobs and Nadel proposed, produce highly accessible intrusive images or conditioned emotional reactions combined with fragmented, incomplete autobiographical memories.

In contrast, Shobe and Kihlstrom (1997) rejected what they called the *trauma-memory argument*, the belief that trauma memories have special properties, can be banished from conscious awareness by processes such as repression or dissociation, and may require specific therapeutic interventions in order to recover them. They argued that research evidence was overwhelmingly in favour of emotion enhancing rather than impairing memory, that reports of amnesia for child sexual abuse were methodologically flawed, and that the arguments for trauma memory being special were at best speculative and unsupported by a solid evidence base. Shobe and Kihlstrom's position, that trauma is extremely well remembered, is frequently cited to contrast with the belief that it is poorly remembered (e.g., Peace & Porter, 2004; Porter & Birt, 2001). Another recent review of the evidence comes to similar conclusions (McNally, 2003).

Similarly, reviewers have been unable to agree on whether the evidence that genuinely traumatic events can sometimes be completely forgotten and then later remembered is positive (Brewin & Andrews, 1998; Brown, Scheflin, & Hammond, 1998; Freyd, 1996; Gleaves, Smith, Butler, & Spiegel, 2004; Lindsay & Read, 1995; Mollon, 1998) or virtually non-existent (McNally, 2003; Pope & Hudson, 1995; Pope, Hudson, Bodkin, & Oliva, 1998). This question has frequently become intertwined with the issue of whether any such forgetting is due to mechanisms such as repression or dissociation. For example, in their review, Pope et al. (1998) specifically considered whether there was any evidence for a failure to recall traumatic events that could *not* be attributed to "ordinary forgetting". Logically, however, the question of whether traumatic events can be forgotten is distinct from the question of why they might be forgotten.

Inevitably, empirical research on autobiographical memory is not equally distributed among, or equally relevant to, the four questions. Some areas of controversy, for example concerning the status of recovered memory, have made little empirical advance since the year 2000, and it may be more profitable to consider whether they are in need of logical or conceptual progress. The empirical research is therefore organised according to other distinctions that have been shown to be important in the study of traumatic memory. One is whether the research has been conducted with healthy volunteers exposed to traumatic events or individuals with PTSD. There is every reason to assume that memory functioning will show group differences, but patterns of similarity and difference may prove informative. Another distinction is whether studies are naturalistic (e.g., concerned with subjective memory characteristics) or experimental. Each may provide different kinds of insights. Where appropriate within these four categories of research, a distinction is also made between voluntary and involuntary memories for trauma. Again, there is no reason to assume that conclusions concerning voluntary and involuntary memories will be similar. I will return to the status of the four controversial questions once the empirical research on autobiographical memory has been reviewed. Where necessary, other areas of relevant research will be briefly touched on at this point.

EMPIRICAL STUDIES SINCE 2000 ON AUTOBIOGRAPHICAL MEMORY FOR TRAUMA

Naturalistic studies of trauma memory in non-clinical groups

Voluntary memory. Previous studies have shown that, in general, memory for negative events tends to be poorer than memory for corresponding positive events (see Walker, Skowronski, & Thompson, 2003, for a review). A more stringent test of clinical theories concerning traumatic memory therefore requires that such non-traumatic negative events be excluded from consideration. Studies that have focused on "most traumatic" or "most stressful" experiences are consequently not reviewed in this section, unless all events would qualify as a trauma according to the American Psychiatric Association's (1994) DSM-IV PTSD Criterion A1 ("The

person experienced, witnessed, or was confronted with an event or events that involved actual or threatened death or serious injury, or a threat to the physical integrity of self or others"). Studies of flashbulb memory for shocking events affecting others and broadcast by the mass media (Conway, 1995) would also not meet these criteria and are likewise excluded. This approach has the disadvantage of excluding a very large and potentially informative literature. The benefit is the more precise focus on events that are likely to have a truly traumatic impact on the individual, and the consequent opportunity to draw stronger conclusions from the data.

Relatively few studies have compared the qualities of memory for highly traumatic versus non-traumatic events in samples not seeking treatment, and those that have returned inconsistent results. A common methodology is to require respondents to rate the qualities of designated memories on Likert scales, estimating factors such as their vividness, amount of detail, emotional components, etc. Earlier work (Koss, Figueredo, Bell, Tharan, & Tromp, 1996) found that rape memories, compared to other unpleasant memories, were rated as being less clear and vivid, less likely to occur in a meaningful order, less well remembered, and were less thought and talked about. Similarly, Bohanek, Fivush, and Walker (2005) found that trauma memories showed few differences from other intense negative memories on variables such as vividness and significance, or narrative structure. Byrne, Hyman, and Scott (2001) reported that their participants rated their trauma memories, relative to positive memories, as having less visual and olfactory detail. One of the few studies to obtain a contrasting result was that of Porter and Birt (2001), who found that memories involving sexual violence were rated as more vivid and contained more sensory components than memories involving other forms of violence.

There has been considerable interest in the consistency of memory for trauma, fuelled by earlier studies indicating that intentionally recalled trauma memories show variability and errors in recall across time, and that increases in reports of trauma exposure are linked to having more PTSD symptoms (Roemer, Litz, Orsillo, Ehlich, & Friedman, 1998; Schwarz, Kowalski, & McNally, 1993; Southwick, Morgan, Nicolaou, & Charney, 1997). King et al. (2000) assessed the trauma exposure of Gulf War veterans shortly after their return home, and found that 2 years later the amount of trauma reported had increased. This was significantly predicted by PTSD symptoms, although the magnitude of the effect was small. Harvey and Bryant (2000) found that greater PTSD symptoms tended to magnify the retrospective reporting of acute stress disorder symptoms following a motor vehicle accident that had occurred 2 years previously.

In contrast, survivors of child sexual abuse were highly accurate in describing traumatic events that had been documented 12 to 21 years earlier, and accuracy was positively associated with greater numbers of PTSD symptoms (Alexander et al., 2005). Bramsen, Dirkzwayer, van Esch, and van der Ploeg (2001) found that reports of trauma exposure among Dutch peacekeepers remained stable over a 9-month period. However, initial measures of trauma exposure were not taken until 3 years after deployment, suggesting that the timing of assessment is a critical factor. Other important factors associated with more consistent combat trauma reports include broader target categories and a focus on traumatic events that meet full DSM criteria, being experienced with a great deal of fear, helplessness, or horror (Krinsley, Gallagher, Weathers, Kutter, & Kaloupek, 2003).

Without comparison data from non-traumatic memories, however, it is hard to evaluate what significance to attach to the inconsistencies that were found. Peace and Porter (2004) compared recall for a traumatic event and a positive event of similar overall emotionality on two occasions 3 months apart. They found that the traumatic event was more consistently recalled whether memories were assessed by free narrative, cognitive interview, guided imagery, or written narrative methods. The quality and vividness of traumatic memories remained constant across measurement periods, whereas that of positive memories declined. However, when traumatised refugees were questioned about a traumatic and a non-traumatic event at two timepoints 3–32 weeks apart, no differences were found in the number of discrepancies involving the two types of event (Herlihy, Scragg, & Turner, 2002).

Another focus of interest has been reports of forgetting. An earlier study (Mechanic, Resick, & Griffin, 1998) had assessed memory in a sample of recent rape victims and found that a minority had a specific problem in remembering the rape that improved over time. More recently, Yovell, Bannett, and Shalev (2003) conducted a pilot study in which just six survivors were required to describe their trauma memories in detail at 7, 20, and 120 days post-trauma. Having collected free narratives, the researchers probed participants to determine whether they could recall additional details. All were screened to rule out head injury, loss of consciousness, or intoxication. All four participants who did not go on to develop PTSD reported brief memory gaps coinciding with the period of greatest emotional intensity. These gaps remained stable over time. Yovell et al. commented that participants were often unaware of gaps in their memory until their recollections were elicited in great detail in the course of the interview. As in the study by Mechanic et al., no comparison memories were targeted to confirm that these findings were specific to traumatic events.

Summary. In non-clinical samples, high-frequency involuntary memories are unlikely to be common, and studies have therefore focused on voluntary memory. Naturalistic studies have had inconsistent results, some supporting the idea that traumatic memory is qualitatively distinct, of unusual clarity, and more consistent over time; some that it is inconsistent, prone to amnesic gaps, and indistinguishable from or even inferior to normal memory. Although knowledge is developing on the factors likely to influence consistency of recall, there is a general lack of well-controlled research that systematically compares traumatic and non-traumatic memory. In particular, detailed interviews to compare recall of traumatic and non-traumatic events over time would be valuable to supplement studies relying on global judgements of memory quality.

Experimental studies of trauma memory in non-clinical groups

Voluntary memory. In experimental studies it is very difficult to arrange for exposure to stressors of the same intensity that are experienced naturally. Nevertheless, even studies conducted with somewhat less intense stressors, providing they share many of the characteristics of traumatic events, may yield results that support clinical observations or suggest important new lines of enquiry. Perhaps the experiment that comes closest to a natural trauma is that of Morgan et al. (2004), who studied servicemen undergoing an extremely harsh survival course that included semi-starvation, sleep deprivation, confinement, lack of control over movement and personal hygiene, and simulated exposure to enemy inter-rogators intent on extracting information. The men were randomly assigned either to a high-stress or to a lower-stress condition. Psychophy-siological measures confirmed that the high-stress conditions produced neurobiological alterations comparable to those produced by actual threat to life. At the conclusion of the course, men exposed to the most extreme stress, compared to those exposed to lower levels of stress, were signifi-cantly poorer at visually identifying their inter-rogator, whether in a live or photo line-up.

Involuntary memory. One previous study (Wells & Papageorgiou, 1995) had found that post-event processing can affect the development of involuntary intrusive memories of the experi-ence of watching a trauma film. More recent studies have focused on the conditions under which films involving traumatic events are en-coded. Halligan, Clark, and Ehlers (2002, Exp. 1) gave participants instructions either to become absorbed in the images and sounds of the film ("data-driven processing") or to focus on the overall story ("conceptual processing"). The data-driven processing group had poorer explicit recall of the film but did not differ in their experience of intrusive film-related memories over the following week. In contrast, participants selected for being high in the general tendency to engage in data-driven processing showed more disorganised explicit memory for the film and more subsequent intrusions than a group selected for high conceptual processing (Halligan et al., 2002, Exp. 2).

In another approach, Brewin and Saunders (2001) and Holmes, Brewin, and Hennessy (2004) had volunteers watch a traumatic film while carrying out a secondary, concurrent task. Sepa-rate measures were taken of recall, recognition, and number of intrusive film-related memories experienced during the following week. In both studies, a concurrent visuospatial tapping task had the effect of reducing later intrusions relative to a control no-task condition. Holmes et al. ruled out a number of explanations of their findings. The effect could not be simply due to distraction since a concurrent verbal task had the opposite effect of increasing subsequent intrusions relative to a control condition. Measures of recall and recog-nition were unrelated to the number of intrusions, and demand characteristics could not account for the pattern of results. A subsequent study (Stuart, Holmes, & Brewin, 2006) replicated the effects of

a concurrent visuospatial task on intrusions using a within-subjects design and an alternative task.

Holmes et al. (2004, Exps. 1 and 2) found that the more participants reported dissociative ex-periences (derealisation and depersonalisation) while they watched the film, the more likely they were to have intrusive memories of the film over the next week. Similar findings using a different film have been noted in two experiments, one measuring intrusions after 4 hours and the other after 1 week, by Kindt, van den Hout, and Buck (2005). The association with intrusions after 4 hours was not significant in a previous experi-ment, however (Kindt & van den Hout, 2003). These results provide an experimental parallel to the many clinical studies showing that reports of dissociation during an actual traumatic event are related to a greater risk of developing subsequent PTSD (Ozer, Best, Lipsey, & Weiss, 2003). Holmes et al. also showed that the lower particip-ants' heart rate while they watched the film, the more likely they were to report later intrusions. Moreover, the specific scenes that intruded for any individual during the following week were associated with a lower heart rate during those sections of the film. Importantly, the measures of involuntary memory (intrusions) were consis-tently unrelated to measures of voluntary mem-ory for the film, such as recall and recognition.

Summary. Experimental studies of analogue trauma experiences must be treated with caution, as their external validity has not been established. Nevertheless, a number of recent findings indi-cate that they are a potentially valuable adjunct to naturalistic studies, and can be used to confirm or refute theoretical predictions under more carefully controlled conditions. A study of objec-tively highly stressed servicemen has suggested that higher levels of stress may be associated with worse rather than better voluntary memory. Films of real traumatic scenes represent an analogue experience that is consistent with the DSM-IV definition of a traumatic event as witnessing serious injury or death. Participants, like actual trauma victims, report increased distress and dissociation, and have increased numbers of intrusive images. Unlike actual victims, levels of distress are comparatively low, and intrusions very rarely last for longer than seven days. These studies have replicated a number of clinical observations about the predictors of intrusions, and have suggested additional hypotheses about the mechanisms involved.

Naturalistic studies of trauma memory in PTSD

Recent studies have confirmed earlier reports (Bremner, Krystal, Southwick, & Charney, 1995; Ehlers & Steil, 1995; van der Kolk & Fisler, 1995) that the trauma memories of PTSD patients are distinguished from the memories of people not suffering from PTSD in terms of them containing prominent perceptual features, being highly emotional, and involving an intense reliving of the event in the present (Berntsen, Willert, & Rubin, 2003; Ehlers et al., 2002; van der Kolk, Hopper, & Osterman, 2001). Compared to individuals without PTSD, their memories are more likely to have an observer perspective in which the events are viewed from outside their body, rather than a field perspective in which events are seen through their own eyes (Berntsen et al., 2003; Reynolds & Brewin, 1999). Those PTSD patients who report field memories recall more emotion and physical sensations, whereas those who report observer memories recall more spatial information, self-observations, and peripheral details (McIsaac & Eich, 2004).

Interestingly, relations between memory characteristics may be different in individuals who do or do not suffer from PTSD, supporting the suggestion that the disorder is accompanied by qualitative differences in memory. For example, the severity of the trauma was strongly related to self-reported memory fragmentation in people with PTSD, but these variables were unrelated in people without PTSD (Berntsen et al., 2003). As noted above, recent studies have attempted to investigate the phenomenology of PTSD in more detail, for example by distinguishing between involuntary memories or memories characterised by reliving, measuring these separately, or comparing them with deliberately retrievable trauma and non-trauma memories.

Voluntary memory. Consistent with the idea that intentional recall of trauma is different from involuntary recall, DSM-IV describes PTSD as being characterised by amnesia for the details of the event. Patients may remember that the traumatic event happened but describe blanks or periods during which their memory for the details of the event is vague and unclear. Apart from the endorsement of this symptom on diagnostic measures, there are hardly any systematic studies of amnesia in PTSD patients. Yovell et al. (2003) compared the trauma memory of their four trauma victims without PTSD to two victims with PTSD. The two PTSD patients reported more initial amnesia, and their memory gaps increased over time. Yovell et al. noted that some of the missing details could be recalled when patients were cued, suggesting a disturbance in retrieval rather than encoding.

Trauma narratives intentionally recalled by individuals with clinical disorders have previously been described as being disorganised and containing gaps (Foa, Molnar, & Cashman, 1995; Harvey & Bryant, 1999). Halligan, Michael, Ehlers, and Clark (2003) confirmed that PTSD patients' trauma memories were rated by experts as much more disorganised than other unpleasant memories, and noted that this was not true of trauma survivors without PTSD. Moreover, they showed that a measure of disorganisation taken at 3 months predicted more PTSD symptoms longitudinally. These findings were extended by Jones, Harvey, and Brewin (2007), who reported that ratings of disorganisation taken 1 week post-trauma predicted the course of PTSD. Individuals diagnosed with ASD or PTSD already had more disorganised narratives 1 week post-trauma, and these differences increased as time went by and the narratives of individuals without ASD or PTSD became more coherent. It should be noted that all these studies have involved detailed analyses of written narratives by independent raters. Asking individuals with PTSD to simply rate the degree of fragmentation of their own memories on single scales, or using computer-based analyses of text complexity, have not produced the same pattern of differences between trauma and non-trauma memories (Brewin & Holmes, 2003; Rubin, Feldman, & Beckham, 2004).

Higher levels of fragmentation in trauma narratives have often been found to be related to self-reported dissociation either during or after the traumatic event (Engelhard, van den Hout, Kindt, Arntz, & Schouten, 2003; Halligan et al., 2003; Harvey & Bryant, 1999; Murray, Ehlers, & Mayou, 2002; Rubin et al., 2004; but see Kindt & van den Hout, 2003; Kindt et al., 2005). During psychotherapy it is common for patients to say that details are returning to them and that they now recall numerous aspects of the event that had been forgotten. However, although there is some suggestion that fragmentation and disorganisation of trauma memories may decrease as patients are treated for PTSD, the results have not been consistent (Van Minnen, Wessel, Dijkstra, &

Roelofs, 2002). Naturalistic follow-up studies have not found any relation between recovery and an improvement in narrative organisation (Halligan et al., 2003; Jones et al., 2007).

Involuntary memories. Previous studies had confirmed that flashbacks, either on their own or in combination with other images and thoughts, were much more common in patients with PTSD than in depressed patients or trauma controls (Reynolds & Brewin, 1998), and that individuals occasionally had intrusive images of scenes that had not actually happened (Merckelbach, Muris, Horselenberg, & Rassin, 1998; Reynolds & Brewin, 1998). More recently, Holmes, Grey, and Young (2005) have shown that intrusive images often correspond to moments of peak emotional distress or "hotspots" in the overall trauma memory.

Hackmann, Ehlers, Speckens, and Clark (2004) assessed involuntary intrusive memories in their sample of PTSD patients. Patients typically described between one and four highly repetitive memories, mainly consisting of sensory experiences of short duration (see also Speckens, Ehlers, Hackmann, Ruths, & Clark, 2007 this issue). Consistent with the observations of Ehlers et al. (2002), only 17% of these corresponded to the worst period of the trauma, the majority consisting of moments signalling that the traumatic event was about to happen or that the meaning of the event had become more threatening. Like Reynolds and Brewin (1998), they also noted a small proportion of images that did not correspond to actual events. Over a small number of reliving sessions, the frequency of the intrusions diminished, as did their vividness, the associated distress, and the sense of how much the events appeared to be happening all over again.

Michael, Ehlers, Halligan, and Clark (2005) extended these findings by showing that there were relatively small differences between samples with and without PTSD in the number of intrusive memories individuals reported and the likelihood that these contained sensory experiences. What did strongly predict PTSD severity was distress associated with the memories, a lack of context, and the sense that the memories were being relived in the present. These intrusion characteristics predicted severity of depression 6 months later over and above initial diagnostic status.

Another recent study compared involuntary trauma and non-trauma memories, using diary methods, in a small sample of 12 individuals with PTSD (Berntsen, 2001, Study 2). Even when the traumatic event had occurred more than 5 years previously, intrusive trauma memories were more vivid and more likely to be accompanied by physical reactions than were non-trauma memories. Trauma memories were also more likely to have the qualities of flashbacks, although Berntsen reported that some experiences similar to flashbacks occurred in relation to highly positive events. Similarly, trauma memories have been found to be more intrusive than other unpleasant memories in PTSD patients, but this difference is much attenuated in trauma survivors without PTSD (Halligan et al., 2003). In contrast, Rubin et al. (2004) did not find that the qualities of intrusive trauma memories differed from non-intrusive trauma memories. Both involved higher degrees of reliving and visceral emotions than did non-trauma memories.

Hellawell and Brewin (2004) described the difference between flashbacks, involving a marked sense of reliving in the present, and ordinary memories to people with PTSD, and then had them write a detailed narrative of their traumatic event. At the completion of the narrative, participants retrospectively identified periods of writing during which they experienced each of the two types of memory. All the participants reported recognising and being able to distinguish between the two types of memory as they wrote about their trauma, but there was great individual variation in how many reliving periods they identified, how long these lasted, and where in the narrative they occurred. Consistent with prediction, during parts of the narrative involving reliving they used more words describing seeing, hearing, smelling, tasting, and bodily sensations, as well as more verbs and references to motion, than they did during ordinary memory sections. Again in line with predictions, fear, helplessness, horror, and thoughts of death were more prominent during the reliving sections, and secondary emotions such as sadness were more prominent during the ordinary memory sections.

Summary. There is now considerable evidence for trauma memories differing from non-traumatic memories in patients with PTSD. Consistent with clinical descriptions, these memories are extremely vivid, contain strong sensory features, and are often re-experienced as happening in the present. Interestingly, in the few examples where direct comparisons have been made, these patterns are weaker or non-existent in trauma victims without PTSD. It is also becoming evident that these characteristics particularly refer to involuntary memories, whereas intentional trauma memories tend to be described as disorganised. Direct comparison of the two using a within-subject design has found differences in terms of content, but this study needs to be replicated and extended to consider other aspects of memory quality.

Previous researchers have observed that some aspects of traumatic events seem to become fixed in the mind, unaltered by the passage of time, being continually re-experienced in the form of images or "video clips" (Ehlers & Steil, 1995; van der Kolk & Fisler, 1995), and this has been confirmed by more recent research (Hackmann et al., 2004). Although this likely represents PTSD patients' own views of their memories, there is as yet little objective evidence that they are unaltered by the passage of time. Nor is it clear that the properties of intrusive memories are unique to PTSD. Involuntary, emotion-laden memories also occur, albeit less often, in response to extremely positive events (Berntsen, 2001, study 4). This is consistent with earlier research indicating that such memories are not unique to PTSD (Pillemer, 1998; Reynolds & Brewin, 1999). Further research is needed to find out what, if anything, is unique about memories associated with PTSD.

Experimental studies of memory in traumatised patients

Voluntary memory. A number of earlier studies focused on the ability of various clinical samples to generate specific autobiographical memories in response to cue words such as "successful" or "lonely". PTSD and ASD patients, like depressed patients, were found to produce an excess of overgeneral memories relating to repeated experiences in their lives (Harvey, Bryant, & Dang, 1998; McNally, Lasko, Macklin, & Pitman, 1995; McNally, Prassas, Shin, & Weathers, 1994). These findings have now been extended to patients diagnosed with ASD following a recent cancer diagnosis (Kangas, Henry, & Bryant, 2005). Even in samples not suffering from PTSD, those with a history of trauma are particularly likely to produce overgeneral memories (Burnside, Startup, Rollinson, & Hill, 2004; de Decker,

Hermans, Raes, & Eelen, 2003; Hermans et al., 2004; Kuyken & Brewin, 1995; Wessel, Merckelbach, & Dekkers, 2002). However, samples with less severe trauma (Wessel, Meeren, Peeters, Arntz, & Merckelbach, 2001) or borderline personality disorder (Arntz, Meeren, & Wessel, 2002; Kremers, Spinhoven, & Van der Does, 2004) may be an exception.

Like many subsequent investigators, Kuyken and Brewin (1995) reported that patients who had high levels of intrusive trauma memories, or were trying to avoid such memories intruding, had the most difficulty retrieving specific autobiographical memories to the cue words. In other words, there appeared to be interference between involuntary and voluntary memory systems. They discussed two possible reasons why traumatic memories might be related to problems in autobiographical recall. One possibility, later elaborated and developed by Williams, Stiles, & Shapiro (1999), is that the occurrence of trauma influences the way memories are organised, with overgeneral recall a strategy to avoid remembering specific distressing incidents. A second possibility, now supported by Dalgleish et al. (2007), is that involuntary intrusions reduce cognitive capacity and lead to a general impairment in task performance.

Involuntary memory. As part of their study comparing flashbacks and ordinary memories during trauma narratives, Hellawell and Brewin (2002) investigated whether the former were predominantly image based, using visuospatial resources, and the latter predominantly verbal. They reasoned that if flashbacks are visuospatial, then they should interfere with performance on other tasks that also made visuospatial demands, but not interfere with unrelated tasks. So, while participants with PTSD were writing their narratives they were stopped on two occasions, once when they were in a reliving phase and once when they were in an ordinary memory phase, and made to carry out two tasks. One task, trail making, involved visuospatial abilities, and the other, counting backwards in threes, involved more verbal abilities. The results showed that trail-making performance was much worse when participants had been halted during a reliving phase of their narrative than when they had been halted during an ordinary memory phase, whereas counting backwards in threes was adversely affected to an equal extent in both phases. This supports the idea that there is a qualitative difference between flashbacks and ordinary memories.

Summary. In contrast to memory for general trauma stimuli such as pictures and words, few studies have looked experimentally at autobiographical memory. A study with PTSD patients, like those with non-clinical participants reviewed above, suggests that the re-experiencing of trauma appears to compete for resources more strongly with visuospatial than with verbal tasks. The occurrence of severe trauma has been repeatedly related to a more general disturbance in autobiographical memory involving a difficulty in intentionally retrieving specific episodes to cue words. Several studies have found an apparent interference between intentional and involuntary remembering, with greater unwanted intrusions linked to more difficulty in the deliberate recall of specific episodes.

CURRENT STATUS OF THE FOUR CONTROVERSIES

We are now in a position to re-evaluate the four interrelated controversies outlined at the beginning of the article.

Are traumatic memories inherently different from other types of autobiographical memory?

The studies reviewed above indicate that consistent differences between trauma and non-trauma memories have been hard to find in the general population, and there is little reason to think that trauma memories differ from those relating to other highly emotional events. The research methods used have most likely only elicited voluntary trauma memories. Although involuntary memories can be provoked in healthy samples, for example by a trauma film, they are shortlived. In contrast, differences between trauma and non-trauma memories in individuals with PTSD are prominent, as are differences between trauma memories in samples with and without PTSD. In clinical samples, traumatic memory is not only quantitatively different but may also be qualitatively different (Berntsen et al., 2003; Halligan et al., 2003). This is consistent with the argument that clinical theories of traumatic memory (e.g., Janet, 1904; Terr, 1990;

van der Kolk & van der Hart, 1991) were not intended to apply to traumatic memories in general, but only to those currently causing significant distress or impairment.

Until recently there have been few attempts to distinguish between the characteristics of voluntary and involuntary trauma memories in clinical samples. Although trauma memories have consistently been found over the years to involve more sensory features and more reliving, it is unclear whether this is equally true of the two types of memory. The only study to directly compare voluntary and involuntary memory for the same event in PTSD patients found that reports of involuntary memories contained significantly more sensory features (Hellawell & Brewin, 2002, 2004). However, Hellawell and Brewin did not require their participants to write a comparable narrative about a non-traumatic event, so could not conclude whether voluntary trauma memories also had additional sensory features. Their study did highlight that asking patients to produce a voluntary narrative is likely to trigger involuntary intrusions that may then be incorporated into the narrative. For this reason, the evidence that trauma narratives consistently reveal greater fragmentation and disorganisation in clinical samples does not necessarily reflect characteristics of voluntary memory. Rather, it may reflect the interaction of voluntary and involuntary memory. It is also possible that the data say less about the nature of the underlying representation and more about the process of converting it into a linguistic account.

Involuntary memories are a widespread and everyday phenomenon (e.g., Berntsen, 1996; Brewin, Christodoulides, & Hutchinson, 1996a). Vivid, emotion-laden memories that spontaneously come to mind may capture highly positive as well as highly negative experiences (Berntsen, 2001; Pillemer, 1998). PTSD samples are distinguished from the healthy population by the distress, lack of context, and extent of reliving associated with these involuntary memories (Michael et al., 2005). Intrusive memories for other kinds of negative event are also a reasonably common feature of depression, in which they may involve the activation of bodily sensations and a degree of reliving (Reynolds & Brewin, 1998, 1999). There is clearly a much greater overlap than had been appreciated between intrusive memories of trauma and other aversive events in clinical samples. What differences there are may involve dissociative characteristics

(Reynolds & Brewin, 1999). Other rare presentations described by clinicians, for example dissociative flashbacks involving complete loss of contact with the current environment, have also not been described in relation to non-traumatic experiences.

Summary. Differences between trauma and non-trauma memories appear largely restricted to clinical samples. Do these findings mean that clinical observations have no relevance to individuals not diagnosable with a disorder such as PTSD? Such a conclusion is premature. Current conceptualisations of PTSD emphasise that the symptoms are not in themselves pathological, but represent a failure of adaptation (Brewin, 2003; Shalev, 2003). That is, PTSD consists of normal reactions to a traumatic event that have failed to recover spontaneously. If this is true, clinical observations should apply to normal individuals in the very early stages of their response to a traumatic event, before recovery is complete. This could be tested with detailed longitudinal studies conducted in the hours and days post-trauma. Like most of the questions covered in this section, it is likely to yield to empirical study.

Is memory for trauma better or worse than memory for non-traumatic events?

Contrary to the belief that high levels of emotion only serve to enhance memory (McNally, 2003; Shobe & Kihlstrom, 1997), there is persistent evidence that emotion can have detrimental effects as well. The view that emotion tended to impair memory was widely held until comparatively recently (e.g., Kassin, Ellsworth, Smith, 1989), and was supplanted with the intuitively appealing thesis that, in an emotional context, memory for central details was enhanced at the expense of memory for peripheral details (Christianson, 1992). A recent study has confirmed that both enhanced memory for an emotional stimulus and impaired memory for an adjacent stimulus appear to be linked to the same adrenergic mechanisms (Strange, Hurlemann, & Dolan, 2003). The problem is that an objective distinction between central and peripheral information that is easy to define in the laboratory becomes impossible in the real world of complex, often extended traumatic events engaging multiple senses. Thus, it is hard to identify what in real life would be the central

experiences that everyone would agree should be recalled better.

This problem is relevant to the strategy of comparing reports about traumatic experiences collected at two points in time. Studies have yielded inconsistent results, with accuracy related in part to the breadth of the question asked. More importantly, the failure of all but a few studies to compare stability of recall for a traumatic and a non-traumatic event has limited the conclusions that can be drawn. Recall of trauma clearly shows some inconsistency, but we cannot say with any confidence whether this is more or less than for everyday events.

Certainly there are repeated suggestions that deliberate attempts to remember even central aspects of traumatic events do not invariably produce clear recall. Both clinical and non-clinical samples have at times described misidentifications, amnesic gaps, and a lack of sensory details in their traumatic recall (Byrne et al., 2001; Koss et al., 1996; Mechanic et al., 1998; Morgan et al., 2004; Yovell et al., 2003). Also, as noted above, fragmentation and disorganisation are characteristic of trauma recall in PTSD, and even predict the course of disorder. One explanation for this has been that extreme levels of stress impair brain structures (e.g., the hippocampus) responsible for the encoding of a coherent, explicit, contextually situated memory, while simultaneously enhancing the encoding of images or the formation of conditioned emotional reactions (e.g., Brewin, 2001, 2003; Metcalfe & Jacobs, 1998; Nadel & Jacobs, 1998; van der Kolk & Fisler, 1995).

The evidence that supports this view comes mainly from animal studies, which have produced broad agreement that the effects of stress on memory correspond to a U-shaped curve, with moderate levels of stress enhancing certain kinds of memory and severe or chronic stress impairing them (Kim & Diamond, 2002; Sapolsky, 2003). The adverse effects of stress have mainly been reported to affect memory that is dependent on the hippocampus, a medial temporal lobe structure particularly associated with the formation of declarative memories in humans and spatial or contextual memory in animals. On an electrophysiological level, stress (and particularly uncontrollable stress) has been found to impair synaptic plasticity in the hippocampus by reducing long-term potentiation (LTP) or primed burst potentiation (a low threshold form of LTP) (e.g., Mesches, Reshner, Heman, Rose, &

Diamond, 1999; Shors, Gallegos, & Breindl, 1997; Shors, Seib, Levine, & Thompson, 1989) or increasing long-term depression (e.g., Xu, Anwyl, & Rowan, 1997).

There are numerous processes that are potentially implicated in these effects, of which most attention has been paid to the role of corticosteroid stress hormones (e.g., Alderson & Novack, 2002; Roozendaal, 2000). The hippocampus has an extremely high concentration of corticosteroid receptors, consisting of mineralocorticoid and glucocorticoid receptors, and it is heavy occupation of the latter that appears to be associated with the adverse effects of stress. However, stress-induced impairment in hippocampal LTP may still occur in the absence of high levels of corticosteroids (Foy, Fory, Levine, & Thompson, 1990; Shors, Levine, & Thompson, 1990). Other processes that may mediate the adverse effects of stress include the activation of NMDA (N-methyl-D-aspartate) receptors, and the availability of stress-induced opioid peptides and serotonin (Kim & Diamond, 2002).

Summary. There is persistent evidence that memory for trauma can be both better and worse than non-trauma memory, and this has been related to the existence of multiple memory systems that behave in different ways under extreme stress. These observations suggest that human laboratory research on stress and memory, in which mild levels of stress are induced or moderate doses of psychoactive drugs administered, may be limited in what it can tell us about responses to trauma. They also suggest that asking respondents to make global judgements of the vividness or completeness of their trauma memories is unlikely to yield sufficiently detailed information. Progress will depend, therefore, on separately measuring different types of memory, such as conditioned emotional responses, voluntary recall, and involuntary intrusions. It must be anticipated that traumatic recall may be both better and worse, depending on the measures. More generally, there is a need for well-controlled investigations that probe in detail individuals' ability to recall traumatic and non-traumatic events over time. The kind of methodology used by Yovell et al. (2003) has the potential to uncover important distinctions between failures of encoding and failures of retrieval. In addition, the type of study conducted by Morgan et al. (2004) will be valuable in bringing stress effects under experimental control. In principle, this too

is a controversy that promises to yield to focused empirical study.

Can memories of truly traumatic events be forgotten and then recalled later in life?

There have been many observations that some individuals are unable to remember traumatic events for long periods, only for them to be involuntarily retrieved at a later date. The evidence, including surveys, legal cases, and detailed single case studies, has been exhaustively reviewed elsewhere, and I will not detail the studies again (see Brewin & Andrews, 1998; Freyd, 1996; Gleaves et al., 2004; Lindsay & Read, 1995; McNally, 2003, for reviews). It is worth noting, however, that these observations encompass a wide variety of traumatic events not restricted to child abuse, that memory recovery frequently occurs outside any therapeutic setting, and that various degrees of corroborative evidence for the recovered memories is sometimes, but not always, available. This has led to the widely adopted conclusion that "recovered memories" sometimes correspond to verifiable events and are sometimes objectively false.

Since 2000 new empirical work relevant to this question has largely involved attempts to produce an experimental analogue of this process by comparing memory for non-autobiographical trauma stimuli in women who think they have been abused but have no memory of it (the "repressed memory" group), women who have recovered memories of abuse (the "recovered memory" group), and women who have always known they were abused (the "continuous memory" group). Based on a study by Clancy, Schacter, McNally, and Pitman (2000), Geraerts, Smeets, Jelicic, van Heerden, and Merckelbach (2005) showed participants a list of trauma-related words and tested if they would later falsely remember having seen another trauma-related word that was highly associated to all of them but was never actually shown. The experiment was designed to test whether individuals reporting recovered or repressed autobiographical memories were prone to falsely recall non-autobiographical stimuli.

Similar to Clancy et al.'s findings with non-trauma stimuli, Geraerts et al. reported that the recovered memory group was more prone than the other groups to agree they had seen the non-presented word, but the repressed memory group did not differ from the controls. Proneness to false recall and recognition was related to fantasy proneness rather than to self-reported trauma or dissociative tendencies. However, as Freyd and Gleaves (1996) have pointed out, it is hazardous to draw inferences from this kind of word experiment with its compelling associative cues to the situation of people with recovered memories of actual incidents of abuse, especially since other techniques have failed to show that they are any more suggestible than non-abused women (Leavitt, 1997).

McNally and his colleagues have also investigated the proposition that traumatised individuals may be able to forget their distressing experiences by testing whether they are particularly good at forgetting non-autobiographical trauma-related material. Despite using various versions of a directed forgetting task, they found no evidence that people with PTSD related to child sexual abuse, or people with repressed or recovered memories of abuse, were any more able to forget trauma-related words than people who had not been abused (McNally, Clancy, Barrett, & Parker, 2004; McNally, Clancy, & Schacter, 2001; McNally, Metzger, Lasko, Clancy, & Pitman, 1998).

It is unclear, however, whether one would expect to find an enhanced ability to forget in individuals with active PTSD, in individuals who have now remembered forgotten trauma, or in individuals who willingly come forward to take part in research on abuse memories. The idea that trauma can be forgotten has mainly been applied to young people faced with intolerable family stresses who are isolated and have nobody in whom they can safely confide, or who have been betrayed by attachment figures (see Freyd, De-Prince, & Gleaves, 2007 this issue, and McNally, 2007 this issue, for contrasting evaluations of betrayal trauma theory). Forgetting is thought to provide a way of coping with their situation, and it is the breakdown in this strategy, when distressing thoughts and images can no longer be prevented from reaching consciousness, that results in PTSD. These results emphasise the need for more longitudinal studies that investigate changes in cognitive processing as post-traumatic disorders unfold.

Despite the many studies in which individuals reported having had periods when they did not recall their traumatic experiences, there is still considerable doubt over how to interpret these findings. McNally (2003), for example, outlined three major objections to these studies. The first is that people can easily be mistaken about the presence of gaps in their memory for childhood, and may simply be wrong when they claim they could not remember. It has been argued (Belli, Winkielman, Read, Schwarz, & Lynn, 1998; Read & Lindsay, 2000) that when assessing the integrity of their memory for childhood, people rely partly on the ease or difficulty with which they can bring instances to mind. In the experiment by Belli et al., participants were asked to report four, eight, or twelve events from when they were 5–7 and 8–10 years old, after which they had to evaluate the adequacy of their childhood memory. Those who were instructed to retrieve more events paradoxically rated their childhood memory as worse than the groups who had to retrieve fewer events, presumably because they attributed the difficulty of the task to deficiencies in their memory. On the basis of these reports, both Belli et al. (1998) and Winkielman, Schwarz, and Belli (1998) suggested that psychotherapy patients' reports of incomplete childhood memory might be a mistaken consequence of difficulty in trying to recall large numbers of events, rather than reflecting genuine problems with memory. Schooler (2001) has also presented some interesting cases suggesting that memory recovery may involve changes in meta-awareness of trauma. For example, people may sometimes confuse the gaining of a new understanding of a traumatic experience with the recovery of memory for it.

Despite this evidence that memory judgements may sometimes be mistaken, there is also reason to think that they are sometimes accurate. Brewin and Stokou (2002) investigated whether ordinary individuals who judge themselves to have a bad memory for their childhood do in fact score more poorly on a standardised test of autobiographical memory. They found that a group who thought they had poor memory for childhood did in fact score worse than a control group on tests of memory for both the facts and events of their own life. Using the same test of autobiographical memory, Hunter and Andrews (2002) found that women with recovered memories of childhood abuse found it harder to recall facts about their childhoods, such as home addresses and names of teachers, friends, and neighbours, than did women who had never been abused. Similar results have been obtained with traumatised adolescents by Meesters, Merckelbach, Muris, and Wessel (2000).

McNally's second objection is the absence of corroboration that the events people with recovered memories claim to have remembered ever occurred. There are a few well-documented case studies that he regards as exceptions and agrees provide stronger evidence for genuine recovered memories (Schooler, 2001). In addition, however, over 100 documented and verifiable cases from legal, clinical, scientific, and other sources have been collected by Professor Ross Cheit, the director of Brown University's Recovered Memory Archive (http://www.brown.edu/Departments/Taubman_Center/Recovmem/Archive.html). To be included in this archive, the recovered memory at issue had to be corroborated by at least one of the following sources: (a) confession, guilty plea, or self-incriminatory statement; (b) testimony from other victims (or from an eyewitness to the abuse) or corroborative documentary evidence that was vitally relevant to the charges at issue; (c) corroboration of significant circumstantial evidence. Most cases have more than one kind of corroboration.

Comments on the archive's website rebut McNally's (2003) suggestion that many of these cases are compromised by the need on the part of complainants to present memories as recovered in order to overcome the statute of limitations. Moreover, in many of the cases no financial claim was apparently involved.

The literature contains a substantial amount of other corroborative evidence, but it is mainly based on self-report, and relatively little has been formally seen or tested by a third, independent party (see Brewin & Andrews, 1998, for a review). Nevertheless, the fact that over 40% of samples consisting of both therapists and clients have regularly reported corroboration cannot be easily dismissed, even though some individual reports may be unreliable. The work of Schooler (as well as Dalenberg, 1996) has shown that the testing of corroborative evidence, although time consuming, is often feasible. In other words, reviewers do not need to make a value judgement about the plausibility of this evidence but can expect the answer to yield to empirical enquiry.

McNally's third major objection is that when people agree they had periods when they could not remember the trauma, they may not have forgotten the events but simply not thought about them. He argues that for their statement to make sense they *must* have tried to think about the trauma but failed. However, there is an alternative view. When people make such a statement, they may be referring to a failure of memory for the *fact* that the trauma happened, and that the trauma represents an important aspect of their life that they would expect always to retain in semantic memory, even if they did not actively think about specific episodic memories. For example, most people would expect to remain aware of whether or not they had ever made a parachute jump or visited Paris, even if they had not tried to recall the specific occasion for a long time. Several studies based on detailed questioning or knowledge of the individual have clarified that most people claiming recovered memories do not mean that they retained knowledge for the fact that the trauma happened (e.g., Joslyn, Carlin, & Loftus, 1997). Moreover, if individuals knew about the traumatic event all along there would be no reason for the shock and surprise that is often described as accompanying memory retrieval (e.g., Andrews et al., 1999; Hunter & Andrews, 2002; Schooler, 2001).

Summary. There do not appear to be compelling empirical or conceptual objections to accepting at least a proportion of the thousands of accounts of recovered memories that are now in the literature. Although little progress has been made in specifying the processes by which traumas may be forgotten, it has been established that judgements about memory can be consistent with performance on objective tests, that many recovered memory accounts are corroborated, and that individuals do genuinely believe they have had periods when their trauma memories have been completely forgotten. Accounts of recovered memories include the testimony of many different kinds of people, including mental health professionals, involve many different kinds of plausible events, and report recovery in a variety of different circumstances inside and outside therapy. The conclusion that some of these recovered memories are genuine is entirely compatible with the view that some people make mistaken judgements about their memory for traumas, and that some recovered memory experiences are not veridical.

Are special mechanisms such as repression or dissociation required to account for forgetting of trauma?

The *ordinary memory argument* (e.g., Loftus & Ketcham, 1994) suggested that there was no need to propose special mechanisms of forgetting of trauma. Trauma might sometimes be forgotten, but this could be attributed to well-established processes such as the gradual decay of memory traces or blocking by subsequent learning. From the simple assumption that memories are encoded at variable strengths depending on the intensity of the experience and decay with time, one can derive the prediction that memories recovered after a period of years should be of relatively weak intensity. Moreover, they should be weaker the less traumatic the event, and the younger the age of the victim. Are the data consistent with this "ordinary memory" view?

Most of the detailed accounts of recovered memory experiences confirm that they are often, but not always, exceptionally strong and emotion-laden. The individuals described by Schooler (2001) used words and phrases like "stunned", "complete chaos in my emotions", "just this extreme emotion of fear and disbelief", "it was literally like a brick wall just hit me . . . I just started crying and screaming uncontrollably". Andrews et al. (2000) found that recovered memories were described by therapists as having numerous characteristics, such as reliving the event in the present, that suggested a highly vivid and emotional recall experience such as is commonly found in patients suffering from post-traumatic stress disorder.

From the "ordinary memory" argument, it should also follow that the more distressing the event, the harder it would be to forget. However, Elliott (1997) found the opposite in her community study of a wide range of traumatic events. Focusing on child abuse, we would similarly predict that the less violent or threatening the experience, or the less the events were interpreted as sexual at the time, the easier the abuse should be to forget. Almost every study (see Goodman et al., 2003, for an exception) that has examined the influence of threats and violence has found the opposite, with greater forgetting being associated with more violence (Briere & Conte, 1993; Herman & Schatzow, 1987), with more threats of harm (Elliott & Briere, 1995), and with a trend towards greater use of force

(Williams, 1994). In contrast, the prediction that the younger the age at which the trauma occurred, the greater should be the forgetting, has been confirmed in most studies that have examined the question (Briere & Conte, 1993; Goodman et al., 2003; Herman & Schatzow, 1987; Elliott, 1997; Williams, 1994), with a nonsignificant trend in the same direction reported by Feldman-Summers and Pope (1994).

Other findings relevant to the "ordinary memory" position involve child sexual abuse. For example, it has been argued that if abusive acts were not accompanied by violence and their significance was not fully appreciated by the child at the time, they may have been forgotten in the ordinary way. Recall of the events in adulthood may then be accompanied by intense emotion, not because these emotions were present at the time the abusive acts occurred, but because the adult came belatedly to a full realisation of the significance of what had happened to them (McNally, 2003). Consistent with this, Joslyn, Carlin, and Loftus (1997) reported that events that were not thought about or were forgotten were less likely to have been interpreted as sexual at the time. This appears to be a perfectly reasonable explanation for some examples of recovered memories, but it would struggle to account for the recovery of memories of death, violent abuse, and other more extreme traumatic events.

The data, then, are only partly consistent with a simple version of the "ordinary memory" argument. But a lot depends on what "ordinary memory" is. In addition to processes such as decay and blocking, many contemporary theorists regard active inhibition as a part of everyday memory, with individuals constantly engaged in the business of retrieving desired information and preventing unwanted or inappropriate information from coming to mind (e.g., Anderson & Green, 2001; Anderson & Spellman, 1995). From this perspective, repression, in at least one of the two major senses employed by Freud (Erdelyi, 1990), is not a "special mechanism" at all but an integral part of everyday memory. Further conceptual and theoretical progress is therefore necessary if the "ordinary memory" argument is to be properly evaluated.

At present, the idea that repression and dissociation are involved in amnesia for traumatic incidents remains a largely untested clinical theory, although there is a variety of evidence that suggests it cannot be too readily dismissed.

Previous research has shown that healthy volunteers with a repressive coping style, despite having histories involving greater adversity, are superior at selectively suppressing and forgetting non-traumatic negative material (Barnier, Levin, & Maher, 2004; Myers & Brewin, 1995; Myers, Brewin, & Power, 1998). More recent evidence, reviewed above, indicates that dissociative reactions at the time of the trauma are linked both with a disturbance in voluntary trauma memories and with an increased risk of involuntary trauma memories. Individuals with high levels of dissociative symptoms are less likely to disclose previously documented abuse in their childhoods (Goodman et al., 2003), and are superior at forgetting trauma words (Moulds & Bryant, 2002, 2005).

DePrince and Freyd (2001, 2004) conducted directed forgetting experiments with healthy volunteers who were low or high in trait dissociation, requiring them to forget neutral and trauma-related words. They reported that the high dissociators were superior at forgetting trauma words, but only when they were distracted by having a secondary cognitive task. McNally, Ristuccia, and Perlman (2005) conducted a similar experiment with groups of individuals reporting continuous memories of sexual abuse, recovered memories of abuse, or no abuse, but failed to support the prediction that the recovered memory group would be better at forgetting trauma words under divided attention conditions. However, it is not clear whether McNally et al.'s recovered memory group reported more betrayal trauma or were more highly dissociative, the two factors identified as critical by DePrince and Freyd.

Summary. The results of investigations utilising healthy samples of repressors and dissociators are significant because they contradict the common-sense view that individuals with more negative experiences in life must be better able to recall negative stimuli. Both these groups are more likely to have experienced trauma or adverse parenting, and yet it appears that both are better able to forget negative than neutral or positive stimuli, at least under certain conditions. These results are consistent with clinical views about the importance of defensive mental processes that affect attention and memory. Although there is little firm evidence yet to link these processes to the forgetting of trauma, there is ample reason to believe they are clinically relevant and will repay additional clinical and experimental investigation.

PROSPECTS FOR THE FUTURE

In addition to providing an update on enduring controversies surrounding trauma and memory, this review has also highlighted promising areas for future research. Two sets of findings, concerning dissociation and involuntary memories, appear likely to yield valuable insights.

The reporting of dissociative experiences such as depersonalisation and derealisation has been linked to the forgetting of trauma words, to the formation of incoherent and fragmented declarative trauma memories, and to an increased risk for involuntary memories of a trauma film. The latter finding is consistent with retrospective and prospective clinical studies that have repeatedly shown that high levels of peritraumatic dissociation are an important predictor of later PTSD symptoms (Ozer et al., 2003). However, attempts to manipulate dissociation experimentally have so far been ineffective in altering rates of involuntary memories, suggesting that it may represent a relatively stable aspect of cognitive style.

In previous studies, victims reporting dissociative responses have been found to have lowered heart rate when describing their traumatic event (e.g., Griffin, Resick, & Mechanic, 1997; Koopman et al., 2004), in contrast to the raised heart rate that is commonly found among samples with PTSD (Pitman, Shalev, & Orr, 2000). This has been explained by equating dissociation with the freezing response to threat, a pattern that is behaviourally and physiologically distinct from the more widely studied fight–flight response (Nijenhuis, Vanderlinden, & Spinhoven, 1998). Consistent with these findings, experimental studies have found that lowered heart rate while watching a trauma film predicts both the probability and the content of later intrusive memories, firmly identifying physiological variability as at least in part responsible for the development of intrusive memories (Holmes et al., 2004). In these studies, self-reported dissociation was not correlated with heart rate but still predicted the development of intrusive memories in its own right. These various findings suggest that dissociation is an important topic for future research, and support recent attempts to provide greater conceptual and terminological clarity in this field

(Holmes et al., 2005; van der Hart, Nijenhuis, Steele, & Brown, 2004).

There are several sources of evidence that involuntary trauma memories draw heavily on sensory and spatial processes. Apart from the relatively greater numbers of sensory and motion words associated with involuntary versus deliberately recalled trauma memories (Hellawell & Brewin, 2004), involuntary memories appear to interfere more with visuospatial than with verbal tasks (Hellawell & Brewin, 2002). Visuospatial, but not verbal, tasks interfere with the development of involuntary memories (Holmes et al., 2004). These findings are consistent with recent research showing that the vividness and emotionality of emotional imagery is related to the visuospatial scratchpad slave system of working memory described by Baddeley, but not to the phonological loop (Baddeley & Andrade, 2000). In results that paralleled the trauma studies reviewed, Baddeley and Andrade showed that a concurrent tapping task interfered with emotional imagery, whereas counting did not.

These data are broadly supportive of theories of trauma and memory that distinguish different types of processing operating during the critical event. For example, the dual representation theory of PTSD (Brewin, 2003; Brewin, Dalgleish, & Joseph, 1996b) explicitly distinguishes between image-based and verbal forms of memory, discussing in some detail their characteristics and how they interact. In this theory, the extent of encoding into the two memory systems is critical for the development of intrusions as well as for the quality of intentional recall. Involuntary intrusive images are believed to be driven by a lower-level, sensory memory system, and can be inhibited by higher-level, voluntarily retrievable memories of the traumatic event. In PTSD, however, it is thought that these higher-level memories do not contain sufficient information about critical retrieval cues and hence are unable to inhibit the intrusions.

Ehlers and Clark's (2000) cognitive model distinguishes between episodic memories and associative processes, and has also suggested that encoding processes (specifically, "data-driven" versus "conceptual" processing) are important for the development of intrusions. It draws on Conway and Pleydell-Pearce's (2000) model of autobiographical memory, which is arranged hierarchically and distinguishes between more general autobiographical knowledge and event-specific knowledge consisting largely of sensory information. Both the dual representation and cognitive models readily account for the fact that voluntary memory is impaired in PTSD, while at the same time there are vivid and detailed intrusions of specific scenes. Both theories are generating novel findings (e.g., enhanced perceptual priming for trauma-related material in PTSD: Michael, Ehlers, & Halligan, 2004) and are currently providing a stimulus to ask new questions and use new methods in the quest to understand traumatic memory.

It is likely that neuroimaging methods will further assist the understanding of trauma and memory. Existing functional imaging studies of PTSD patients have often used a provocation technique, "script-driven imagery", in which patients are presented with brief scripts they have previously generated about their own trauma and are asked to imagine the events as vividly as possible while they listen to the script being played. PET and fMRI studies have suggested that the retrieval of trauma memories in PTSD patients, compared to controls, is characterised by increased activity of limbic and paralimbic areas, including the amygdala (Hull, 2002; Shin, Rauch, & Pitman, 2005). Other replicated findings include deactivation of medial prefrontal areas and Broca's area (Hull, 2002; Shin et al., 2005). Two PET studies have found reduced hippocampal activity in PTSD patients when they processed emotional rather than neutral material (Bremner et al., 1999, 2003). As noted by Hull (2002), the findings are not consistent across all studies. One problem is that patients normally react in a variety of ways to reminders of their trauma, and these are likely to be replicated in a scanning context: Some experience flashbacks (e.g., Osuch et al., 2001; Shin et al., 1999), while others have strong dissociative reactions (e.g., depersonalisation) associated with a different pattern of neuronal responses (Lanius et al., 2002).

It is important to distinguish between the effect of processing information that is specific to the trauma versus that of processing any information that has been encoded in an emotional context. Bremner et al. (2003) and Lanius et al. (2003) have shown that in PTSD neural processing differs not just for traumatic memories but also for sad and anxious memories and for emotional words likely to be high in personal relevance. Other work by Maratos and Rugg (2001) and Maratos, Dolan, Morris, Henson, and Rugg (2001) shows that in normal participants neural responses are affected by the emotional context of a word even when this context is retrieved incidentally. What is not known is whether there is a more fundamental disturbance in PTSD, such that an emotional context is processed differently even when the stimuli are neutral and uncontaminated by personal meanings. Investigations of this kind are needed to appropriately interpret the results of neuroimaging studies using specific trauma reminders.

To date most techniques for eliciting trauma memories, such as script-driven imaging, have not been designed to directly compare neural responses to the retrieval of ordinary autobiographical memories of trauma and involuntary flashbacks, even though they may have a different anatomical basis. Conscious autobiographical memories are widely regarded as dependent on hippocampal processing. Brewin (2001, 2003) suggested that high levels of neurotransmitters and neurohormones released during traumatic experiences interfere with the normal operation of the hippocampus, resulting in the trauma being poorly represented in the autobiographical memory system. In contrast, lower-level representations of sensory (primarily visuospatial or image-based) information about the trauma remain intact since they depend on processing that has little hippocampal involvement but relies instead on pathways that link other cortical and subcortical areas directly to the amygdala. These lower-level representations are informationally encapsulated, encode temporal information poorly, and when triggered are experienced as flashbacks.

To summarise, a wide range of new findings and methodological approaches are now beginning to shape the study of traumatic memory and to provide empirical answers to enduring controversies. Phenomenological enquiries, experimental methods, and neuroimaging all have an important part to play and are already yielding significant new insights. What is clear, however, is that the questions are subtle and complex. Effective research will be based on the understanding gained from all these methods, and no one approach on its own is likely to be sufficient.

REFERENCES

Alderson, A. L., & Novack, T. A. (2002). Neurophysiological and clinical aspects of glucocorticoids and memory: A review. *Journal of Clinical and Experimental Neuropsychology, 24*, 335–355.

Alexander, K. W., Quas, J. A., Goodman, G. S., Ghetti, S. G., Edelstein, R. S., Redlich, A. D., et al. (2005). Traumatic impact predicts long-term memory for documented child sexual abuse. *Psychological Science, 16*, 33–40.

American Psychiatric Association. (1994). *Diagnostic and statistical manual* (4th ed.). Washington, DC: APA.

Anderson, M. C., & Green, C. (2001). Suppressing unwanted memories by executive control. *Nature, 410*(6826), 366–369.

Anderson, M. C., & Spellman, B. A. (1995). On the status of inhibitory mechanisms in cognition: Memory retrieval as a model case. *Psychological Review, 102*, 68–100.

Andrews, B., Brewin, C. R., Ochera, J., Morton, J., Bekerian, D. A., Davies, G. M., et al. (1999). The characteristics, context, and consequences of memory recovery among adults in therapy. *British Journal of Psychiatry, 175*, 141–146.

Andrews, B., Brewin, C. R., Ochera, J., Morton, J., Bekerian, D. A., Davies, G. M., et al. (2000). The process of memory recovery among adults in therapy. *British Journal of Clinical Psychology, 39*, 11–26.

Arntz, A., Meeren, M., & Wessel, I. (2002). No evidence for overgeneral memories in borderline personality disorder. *Behaviour Research and Therapy, 40*, 1063–1068.

Baddeley, A. D., & Andrade, J. (2000). Working memory and the vividness of imagery. *Journal of Experimental Psychology: General, 129*, 126–145.

Barnier, A., Levin, K., & Maher, A. (2004). Suppressing thoughts of past events: Are repressive copers good suppressors? *Cognition and Emotion, 18*, 513–531.

Belli, R. F., Winkielman, P., Read, J. D., Schwarz, N., & Lynn, S. J. (1998). Recalling more childhood events leads to judgments of poorer memory: Implications for the recovered false memory debate. *Psychonomic Bulletin and Review, 5*, 318–323.

Berntsen, D. (1996). Involuntary autobiographical memories. *Applied Cognitive Psychology, 10*, 435–454.

Berntsen, D. (2001). Involuntary memories of emotional events: Do memories of traumas and extremely happy events differ? *Applied Cognitive Psychology, 15*, S135–S158.

Berntsen, D., Willert, M., & Rubin, D. C. (2003). Splintered memories or vivid landmarks? Qualities and organization of traumatic memories with and without PTSD. *Applied Cognitive Psychology, 17*, 675–693.

Bohanek, J. G., Fivush, R., & Walker, E. (2005). Memories of positive and negative emotional events. *Applied Cognitive Psychology, 19*, 51–66.

Bramsen, I., Dirkzwager, A. J. E., van Esch, S. C. M., & van der Ploeg, H. M. (2001). Consistency of self-reports of traumatic events in a population of Dutch peacekeepers: Reason for optimism? *Journal of Traumatic Stress, 14*, 733–740.

Bremner, J. D., Krystal, J. H., Southwick, S. M., & Charney, D. S. (1995). Functional neuroanatomical correlates of the effects of stress on memory. *Journal of Traumatic Stress*, *8*, 527–553.

Bremner, J. D., Narayan, M., Staib, L. H., Southwick, S. M., McGlashan, T., & Charney, D. S. (1999). Neural correlates of memories of childhood sexual abuse in women with and without posttraumatic stress disorder. *American Journal of Psychiatry*, *156*, 1787–1795.

Bremner, J. D., Vythilingam, M., Vermetten, E., Southwick, S. M., McGlashan, T., Nazeer, A., et al. (2003). MRI and PET study of deficits in hippocampal structure and function in women with childhood sexual abuse and posttraumatic stress disorder. *American Journal of Psychiatry*, *160*, 924–932.

Brewin, C. R. (2001). A cognitive neuroscience account of posttraumatic stress disorder and its treatment. *Behaviour Research and Therapy*, *39*, 373–393.

Brewin, C. R. (2003). *Posttraumatic stress disorder: malady or myth?*. New Haven, CT: Yale University Press.

Brewin, C. R., & Andrews, B. (1998). Recovered memories of trauma: Phenomenology and cognitive mechanisms. *Clinical Psychology Review*, *18*, 949–970.

Brewin, C. R., Christodoulides, J., & Hutchinson, G. (1996). Intrusive thoughts and intrusive memories in a nonclinical sample. *Cognition and Emotion*, *10*, 107–112.

Brewin, C. R., Dalgleish, T., & Joseph, S. (1996). A dual representation theory of post traumatic stress disorder. *Psychological Review*, *103*, 670–686.

Brewin, C. R., & Holmes, E. A. (2003). Psychological theories of posttraumatic stress disorder. *Clinical Psychology Review*, *23*, 339–376.

Brewin, C. R., Kleiner, J. S., Vasterling, J. J., & Field, A. P. (in press). Memory for emotionally neutral information in posttraumatic stress disorder: A meta-analytic investigation. *Journal of Abnormal Psychology*.

Brewin, C. R., & Saunders, J. (2001). The effect of dissociation at encoding on intrusive memories for a stressful film. *British Journal of Medical Psychology*, *74*, 467–472.

Brewin, C. R., & Stokou, L. (2002). Validating reports of poor childhood memory. *Applied Cognitive Psychology*, *16*, 509–514.

Briere, J., & Conte, J. (1993). Self-reported amnesia for abuse in adults molested as children. *Journal of Traumatic Stress*, *6*, 21–31.

Brown, D., Scheflin, A. W., & Hammond, D. C. (1998). *Memory, trauma treatment, and the law*. New York: Norton.

Burnside, E., Startup, M., Rollinson, L., & Hill, J. (2004). The role of overgeneral autobiographical memory in the development of adult depression following childhood trauma. *British Journal of Clinical Psychology*, *43*, 365–376.

Byrne, C. A., Hyman, I. E, & Scott, K. L. (2001). Comparisons of memories for traumatic events and other experiences. *Applied Cognitive Psychology*, *15*, S119–S133.

Christianson, S. A. (1992). Emotional stress and eyewitness memory: A critical review. *Psychological Bulletin*, *112*, 284–309.

Clancy, S. A., Schacter, D. L., McNally, R. J., & Pitman, R. K. (2000). False recognition in women reporting recovered memories of sexual abuse. *Psychological Science*, *11*, 26–31.

Conway, M. A. (1995). *Flashbulb memories*. Hove, UK: Lawrence Erlbaum Associates Ltd.

Conway, M. A., & Pleydell-Pearce, C. W. (2000). The construction of autobiographical memories in the self-memory system. *Psychological Review*, *107*, 261–288.

Dalenberg, C. J. (1996). Accuracy, timing, and circumstances of disclosure in therapy of recovered and continuous memories of abuse. *Journal of Psychiatry and Law*, *24*, 229–275.

Dalgleish, T., Williams, J. M. G., Perkins, N., Golden, A. J., Barnard, P. J., Auyeung, C., et al. (2007). Reduced specificity of autobiographical memory and depression: The role of executive processes. *Journal of Experimental Psychology: General*, *136*, 23–42.

de Decker, A., Hermans, D., Raes, F., & Eelen, P. (2003). Autobiographical memory specificity and trauma in inpatient adolescents. *Journal of Clinical Child and Adolescent Psychology*, *32*, 22–31.

DePrince, A. P., & Freyd, J. J. (2001). Memory and dissociative tendencies: The roles of attentional context and word meaning. *Journal of Trauma and Dissociation*, *2*, 67–82.

DePrince, A. P., & Freyd, J. J. (2004). Forgetting trauma stimuli. *Psychological Science*, *15*, 488–492.

Ehlers, A., & Clark, D. M. (2000). A cognitive model of posttraumatic stress disorder. *Behaviour Research and Therapy*, *38*, 319–345.

Ehlers, A., Hackmann, A., Steil, R., Clohessy, S., Wenninger, K, & Winter, H. (2002). The nature of intrusive memories after trauma: The warning signal hypothesis. *Behaviour Research and Therapy*, *40*, 995–1002.

Ehlers, A., & Steil, R. (1995). Maintenance of intrusive memories in posttraumatic stress disorder: A cognitive approach. *Behavioural and Cognitive Psychotherapy*, *23*, 217–249.

Elliott, D. M. (1997). Traumatic events: Prevalence and delayed recall in the general population. *Journal of Consulting and Clinical Psychology*, *65*, 811–820.

Elliott, D. M., & Briere, J. (1995). Posttraumatic stress associated with delayed recall of sexual abuse: A general population study. *Journal of Traumatic Stress*, *8*, 629–647.

Engelhard, I. M., van den Hout, M. A., Kindt, M., Arntz, A., & Schouten, E. (2003). Peri-traumatic dissociation and posttraumatic stress after pregnancy loss: A prospective study. *Behaviour Research and Therapy*, *41*, 67–78.

Erdelyi, M. H. (1990). Repression, reconstruction, and defense: History and integration of the psychoanalytic and experimental frameworks. In J. L. Singer (Ed.), *Repression and dissociation* (pp. 1–31). Chicago, IL: University of Chicago Press.

Feldman-Summers, S., & Pope, K. S. (1994). The experience of forgetting childhood abuse: A national survey of psychologists. *Journal of Consulting and Clinical Psychology*, *62*, 636–639.

Foa, E. B., Molnar, C., & Cashman, L. (1995). Change in rape narratives during exposure to therapy for posttraumatic stress disorder. *Journal of Traumatic Stress*, *8*, 675–690.

Foy, M. R., Fory, J. G., Levine, S., & Thompson, R. F. (1990). Manipulation of pituitary-adrenal activity affects neural plasticity in rodent hippocampus. *Psychological Science*, *3*, 201–204.

Freyd, J. J. (1996). *Betrayal trauma: The logic of forgetting childhood abuse*. Cambridge, MA: Harvard University Press.

Freyd, J. J., DePrince, A. P., & Gleaves, D. H. (2007). The state of betrayal trauma theory: Reply to McNally (2006), Conceptual issues, and future directions. *Memory*, *15*, 295–311.

Freyd, J. J., & Gleaves, D. H. (1996). "Remembering" words not presented in lists: Relevance to the current recovered/false memory controversy. *Journal of Experimental Psychology: Learning, Memory and Cognition*, *22*, 811–813.

Geraerts, E., Smeets, E., Jelicic, M., van Heerden, J., & Merckelbach, H. (2005). Fantasy proneness, but not self-reported trauma is related to DRM performance of women reporting recovered memories of childhood sexual abuse. *Consciousness and Cognition*, *14*, 602–612.

Gleaves, D. H., Smith, S. M., Butler, L. D., & Spiegel, D. (2004). False and recovered memories in the laboratory and clinic: A review of experimental and clinical evidence. *Clinical Psychology: Science and Practice*, *11*, 3–28.

Goodman, G. S., Ghetti, S., Quas, J. A., Edelstein, R. S., Alexander, K. W., Redlich, A. D., et al. (2003). A prospective study of memory for child sexual abuse: New findings relevant to the repressed-memory controversy. *Psychological Science*, *14*, 113–118.

Griffin, M. G., Resick, P. A., & Mechanic, M. B. (1997). Objective assessment of peritraumatic dissociation: Psychophysiological indicators. *American Journal of Psychiatry*, *154*, 1081–1088.

Hackmann, A., Ehlers, A., Speckens, A., & Clark, D. M. (2004). Characteristics and content of intrusive memories in PTSD and their changes with treatment. *Journal of Traumatic Stress*, *17*, 231–240.

Halligan, S. L., Clark, D. M., & Ehlers, A. (2002). Cognitive processing, memory, and the development of PTSD symptoms: Two experimental analogue studies. *Journal of Behavior Therapy and Experimental Psychiatry*, *33*, 73–89.

Halligan, S. L., Michael, T., Ehlers, A., & Clark, D. M. (2003). Posttraumatic stress disorder following assault: The role of cognitive processing, trauma memory, and appraisals. *Journal of Consulting and Clinical Psychology*, *71*, 419–431.

Harvey, A. G., & Bryant, R. A. (1999). A qualitative investigation of the organization of traumatic memories. *British Journal of Clinical Psychology*, *38*, 401–405.

Harvey, A. G., & Bryant, R. A. (2000). Memory for acute stress disorder symptoms-A two-year prospective study. *Journal of Nervous and Mental Disease*, *188*, 602–607.

Harvey, A. G., Bryant, R. A., & Dang, S. T. (1998). Autobiographical memory in acute stress disorder. *Journal of Consulting and Clinical Psychology*, *66*, 500–506.

Hellawell, S. J., & Brewin, C. R. (2002). A comparison of flashbacks and ordinary autobiographical memories of trauma: Cognitive resources and behavioural observations. *Behaviour Research and Therapy*, *40*, 1139–1152.

Hellawell, S. J., & Brewin, C. R. (2004). A comparison of flashbacks and ordinary autobiographical memories of trauma: Content and language. *Behaviour Research and Therapy*, *42*, 1–12.

Herlihy, J., Scragg, P., & Turner, S. (2002). Discrepancies in autobiographical memories: Implications for the assessment of asylum seekers: Repeated interviews study. *British Medical Journal*, *324*, 324–327.

Herman, J. L. (1995). Crime and memory. *Bulletin of the American Academy of Psychiatry and the Law*, *23*, 5–17.

Herman, J. L., & Schatzow, E. (1987). Recovery and verification of memories of childhood sexual trauma. *Psychoanalytic Psychology*, *4*, 1–14.

Hermans, D., Van den Broeck, K., Belis, G., Raes, F., Pieters, G., & Eelen, P. (2004). Trauma and autobiographical memory specificity in depressed inpatients. *Behaviour Research and Therapy*, *42*, 775–789.

Holmes, E. A., Brewin, C. R., & Hennessy, R. G. (2004). Trauma films, information processing, and intrusive memory development. *Journal of Experimental Psychology: General*, *133*, 3–22.

Holmes, E. A., Brown, R. J., Mansell, W., Fearon, R. P., Hunter, E. C. M., Frasquilho, F., et al. (2005). Are there two qualitatively distinct forms of dissociation? A review and some clinical implications. *Clinical Psychology Review*, *25*, 1–23.

Holmes, E. A., Grey, N., & Young, K. A. D. (2005). Intrusive images and "hotspots" of trauma memories in Posttraumatic Stress Disorder: An exploratory investigation of emotions and cognitive themes. *Journal of Behavior Therapy and Experimental Psychiatry*, *36*, 3–17.

Hull, A. M. (2002). Neuroimaging findings in posttraumatic stress disorder: Systematic review. *British Journal of Psychiatry*, *181*, 102–110.

Hunter, E. C. M., & Andrews, B. (2002). Memory for autobiographical facts and events: A comparison of women reporting child sexual abuse and nonabused controls. *Applied Cognitive Psychology*, *16*, 575–588.

Jacobs, W. J., & Nadel, L. (1998). Neurobiology of reconstructed memory. *Psychology, Public Policy, and Law*, *4*, 1110–1134.

Janet, P. (1904). L'amnesie et la dissociation des souvenirs par l'emotion. *Journal de Psychologie*, *1*, 417–453.

Jones, C., Harvey, A. G., & Brewin, C. R. (2007). The organisation and content of trauma memories in survivors of road traffic accidents. *Behaviour Research and Therapy*, *45*, 151–162.

Joslyn, S., Carlin, L., & Loftus, E. F. (1997). Remembering and forgetting childhood sexual abuse. *Memory*, *5*, 703–724.

Kangas, M., Henry, J. L., & Bryant, R. A. (2005). A prospective study of autobiographical memory and posttraumatic stress disorder following cancer. *Journal of Consulting and Clinical Psychology, 73*, 293–299.

Kassin, S. M., Ellsworth, P. C., & Smith, V. L. (1989). The "general acceptance" of psychological research on eyewitness testimony: A survey of the experts. *American Psychologist, 44*, 1089–1098.

Kim, J. J., & Diamond, D M. (2002). The stressed hippocampus, synaptic plasticity, and lost memories. *Nature Reviews Neuroscience, 3*, 453–462.

Kindt, M., & van den Hout, M. (2003). Dissociation and memory fragmentation: Experimental effects on meta-memory but not on actual memory performance. *Behaviour Research and Therapy, 41*, 167–178.

Kindt, M., van den Hout, M., & Buck, N. (2005). Dissociation related to subjective memory fragmentation and intrusions but not to objective memory disturbances. *Journal of Behavior Therapy and Experimental Psychiatry, 36*, 43–59.

King, D. W., King, L. A., Erickson, D. J., Huang, M. T., Sharkansky, E. J., & Wolfe, J. (2000). Posttraumatic stress disorder and retrospectively reported stressor exposure: A longitudinal prediction model. *Journal of Abnormal Psychology, 109*, 624–633.

Koopman, C., Carrion, V., Butler, L. D., Sudhakar, S., Palmer, L., & Steiner, H. (2004). Relationships of dissociation and childhood abuse and neglect with heart rate in delinquent adolescents. *Journal of Traumatic Stress, 17*, 47–54.

Koss, M. P., Figueredo, A. J., Bell, I., Tharan, M., & Tromp, S. (1996). Traumatic memory characteristics: A cross-validated mediational model of response to rape among employed women. *Journal of Abnormal Psychology, 105*, 421–432.

Kremers, I. P., Spinhoven, P., & Van der Does, A. J. W. (2004). Autobiographical memory in depressed and non-depressed patients with borderline personality disorder. *British Journal of Clinical Psychology, 43*, 17–29.

Krinsley, K. E., Gallagher, J. G., Weathers, F. W., Kutter, C. J., & Kaloupek, D. G. (2003). Consistency of retrospective reporting about exposure to traumatic events. *Journal of Traumatic Stress, 16,* 399–409.

Kuyken, W., & Brewin, C. R. (1995). Autobiographical memory functioning in depression and reports of early abuse. *Journal of Abnormal Psychology, 104*, 585–591.

Lanius, R. A., Williamson, P. C., Boksman, K., Densmore, M., Gupta, M., Neufeld, R. W. J., et al. (2002). Brain activation during script-driven imagery induced dissociative responses in PTSD: A functional magnetic resonance imaging investigation. *Biological Psychiatry, 52*, 305–311.

Lanius, R. A., Williamson, P. C., Hopper, J., Densmore, M., Boksman, K., Gupta, M. A., et al. (2003). Recall of emotional states in posttraumatic stress disorder: An fMRI investigation. *Biological Psychiatry, 53*, 204–210.

Leavitt, F. (1997). False attribution of suggestibility to explain recovered memory of childhood sexual abuse following extended amnesia. *Child Abuse and Neglect, 21*, 265–272.

Lindsay, D. S., & Read, J. D. (1995). "Memory work" and recovered memories of childhood sexual abuse: Scientific evidence and public, professional, and personal issues. *Psychology Public Policy and Law, 1*, 846–908.

Loftus, E. F. (1993). The reality of repressed memories. *American Psychologist, 48*, 518–537.

Loftus, E. F., & Ketcham, K. (1994). *The myth of repressed memory.* New York: St. Martin's Press.

Maratos, E. J., Dolan, R. J., Morris, J. S., Henson, R. N. A., & Rugg, M. D. (2001). Neural activity associated with episodic memory for emotional context. *Neuropsychologia, 39*, 910–920.

Maratos, E. J., & Rugg, M. D. (2001). Electrophysiological correlates of the retrieval of emotional and non-emotional context. *Journal of Cognitive Neuroscience, 13*, 877–891.

McIsaac, H. K., & Eich, E. (2004). Vantage point in traumatic memory. *Psychological Science, 15*, 248–253.

McNally, R., Clancy, S., Barrett, H., & Parker, H. (2004). Inhibiting retrieval of trauma cues in adults reporting histories of childhood sexual abuse. *Cognition and Emotion, 18*, 479–493.

McNally, R. J. (2003). *Remembering trauma.* Cambridge, MA: Harvard University Press.

McNally, R. J. (2007). Betrayal trauma theory: A critical appraisal. *Memory, 15*, 280–294.

McNally, R. J., Clancy, S. A., & Schacter, D. L. (2001). Directed forgetting of trauma cues in adults reporting repressed or recovered memories of childhood sexual abuse. *Journal of Abnormal Psychology, 110*, 151–156.

McNally, R. J., Lasko, N. B., Macklin, M. L., & Pitman, R. K. (1995). Autobiographical memory disturbance in combat-related posttraumatic stress disorder. *Behaviour Research and Therapy, 33*, 619–630.

McNally, R. J., Metzger, L. J., Lasko, N. B., Clancy, S. A., & Pitman, R. K. (1998). Directed forgetting of trauma cues in adult survivors of childhood sexual abuse with and without posttraumatic stress disorder. *Journal of Abnormal Psychology, 107*, 596–601.

McNally, R. J., Prassas, A., Shin, L. M., & Weathers, F. W. (1994). Emotional priming of autobiographical memory in posttraumatic stress disorder. *Cognition and Emotion, 8*, 351–367.

McNally, R. J., Ristuccia, C. S., & Perlman, C. A. (2005). Forgetting of trauma cues in adults reporting continuous or recovered memories of childhood sexual abuse. *Psychological Science, 16*, 336–340.

Mechanic, M. B., Resick, P. A., & Griffin, M. G. (1998). A comparison of normal forgetting, psychopathology, and information-processing models of reported amnesia for recent sexual trauma. *Journal of Consulting and Clinical Psychology, 66*, 948–957.

Meesters, C., Merckelbach, H., Muris, P., & Wessel, I. (2000). Autobiographical memory and trauma in adolescents. *Journal of Behavior Therapy and Experimental Psychiatry, 31*, 29–39.

Merckelbach, H., Muris, P., Horselenberg, R., & Rassin, E. (1998). Traumatic intrusions as 'worse case scenarios'. *Behaviour Research and Therapy*, *36*, 1075–1079.

Mesches, M., Fleshner, M., Heman, K., Rose, G., & Diamond, D. (1999). Exposing rats to a predator blocks primed burst potentiation in the hippocampus *in vitro*. *Journal of Neuroscience*, *19*, RC18.

Metcalfe, J., & Jacobs, W. J. (1998). Emotional memory: The effects of stress on "cool" and "hot" memory systems. In D. L. Medin (Ed.), *The psychology of learning and motivation* (Vol. 38, pp. 187–222). New York: Academic Press.

Michael, T., Ehlers, A., & Halligan, S. L. (2004). Enhanced priming for trauma-related material in posttraumatic stress disorder. *Emotion*, *5*, 103–112.

Michael, T., Ehlers, A., Halligan, S. L., & Clark, D. M. (2005). Unwanted memories of assault: What intrusion characteristics are associated with PTSD? *Behaviour Research and Therapy*, *43*, 613–628.

Mollon, P. (1998). *Remembering trauma: A psychotherapist's guide to memory and illusion*. Chichester, UK: Wiley.

Morgan, C. A. III, Hazlett, G., Doran, A., Garrett, S., Hoyt, G., Thomas, P., et al. (2004). Accuracy of eyewitness memory for persons encountered during exposure to highly intense stress. *International Journal of Law and Psychiatry*, *27*, 265–279.

Moulds, M. L., & Bryant, R. A. (2002). Directed forgetting in acute stress disorder. *Journal of Abnormal Psychology*, *111*, 175–179.

Moulds, M. L., & Bryant, R. A. (2005). An investigation of retrieval inhibition in acute stress disorder. *Journal of Traumatic Stress*, *18*, 233–236.

Murray, J., Ehlers, A., & Mayou, R. (2002). Dissociation and posttraumatic stress disorder: Two prospective studies of motor vehicle accident survivors. *British Journal of Psychiatry*, *180*, 363–368.

Myers, L. B., & Brewin, C. R. (1995). Repressive coping and the recall of emotional material. *Cognition and Emotion*, *9*, 637–642.

Myers, L. B., Brewin, C. R., & Power, M. J. (1998). Repressive coping and the directed forgetting of emotional material. *Journal of Abnormal Psychology*, *107*, 141–148.

Nadel, L., & Jacobs, W. J. (1998). Traumatic memory is special. *Current Directions in Psychological Science*, *7*, 154–157.

Nijenhuis, E. R. S., Vanderlinden, J., & Spinhoven, P. (1998). Animal defensive reactions as a model for trauma-induced dissociative reactions. *Journal of Traumatic Stress*, *11*, 243–260.

Osuch, E. A., Benson, B., Geraci, M., Podell, D., Herscovitch, P., McCann, U. D., et al. (2001). Regional cerebral blood flow correlated with flashback intensity in patients with posttraumatic stress disorder. *Biological Psychiatry*, *50*, 246–253.

Ozer, E. J., Best, S. R., Lipsey, T. L., & Weiss, D. S. (2003). Predictors of posttraumatic stress disorder and symptoms in adults: A meta-analysis. *Psychological Bulletin*, *129*, 52–73.

Peace, K. A., & Porter, S. (2004). A longitudinal investigation of the reliability of memories for trauma and other emotional experiences. *Applied Cognitive Psychology*, *18*, 1143–1159.

Pillemer, D. B. (1998). *Momentous events, vivid memories*. Cambridge, MA: Harvard University Press.

Pitman, R. L., Shalev, A. Y., & Orr, S. P. (2000). Posttraumatic stress disorder: Emotion, conditioning, and memory. In M. S. Gazzaniga (Ed.), *The new cognitive neurosciences* (2nd ed, pp. 1133–1147). Cambridge, MA: MIT Press.

Pope, H. G., & Hudson, J. I. (1995). Can memories of childhood sexual abuse be repressed? *Psychological Medicine*, *25*, 121–126.

Pope, H. G., Hudson, J. I., Bodkin, J. A., & Oliva, P. (1998). Questionable validity of 'dissociative amnesia' in trauma victims: Evidence from prospective studies. *British Journal of Psychiatry*, *172*, 210–215.

Porter, S., & Birt, A. R. (2001). Is traumatic memory special? A comparison of traumatic memory characteristics with memory for other emotional life experiences. *Applied Cognitive Psychology*, *15*, S101–S117.

Read, J. D., & Lindsay, D. S. (2000). "Amnesia" for summer camps and high school graduation: Memory work increases reports of prior periods of remembering less. *Journal of Traumatic Stress*, *13*, 129–147.

Reynolds, M., & Brewin, C. R. (1998). Intrusive cognitions, coping strategies and emotional responses in depression, post-traumatic stress disorder, and a non-clinical population. *Behaviour Research and Therapy*, *36*, 135–147.

Reynolds, M., & Brewin, C. R. (1999). Intrusive memories in depression and posttraumatic stress disorder. *Behaviour Research and Therapy*, *37*, 201–215.

Roemer, L., Litz, B. T., Orsillo, S. M., Ehlich, P. J., & Friedman, M. J. (1998). Increases in retrospective accounts of war-zone exposure over time: The role of PTSD symptom severity. *Journal of Traumatic Stress*, *11*, 597–605.

Roozendaal, B. (2000). Glucocorticoids and the regulation of memory consolidation. *Psychoneuroendocrinology*, *25*, 213–238.

Rubin, D. C., Feldman, M. E., & Beckham, J. C. (2004). Reliving, emotions, and fragmentation in the autobiographical memories of veterans diagnosed with PTSD. *Applied Cognitive Psychology*, *18*, 17–35.

Sapolsky, R. M. (2003). Stress and plasticity in the limbic system. *Neurochemical Research*, *28*, 1735–1742.

Schooler, J. W. (2001). Discovering memories of abuse in the light of meta-awareness. *Journal of Aggression, Maltreatment and Trauma*, *4*, 105–136.

Schwarz, E. D., Kowalski, J. M., & McNally, R. J. (1993). Malignant memories: Posttraumatic changes in memory in adults after a school shooting. *Journal of Traumatic Stress*, *6*, 545–553.

Shalev, A. Y. (2003). Psycho-biological perspectives on early reactions to traumatic events. In R. Ørner & U. Schnyder (Eds.), *Reconstructing early intervention after trauma* (pp. 57–64). Oxford, UK: Oxford University Press.

Shin, L. M., McNally, R. J., Kosslyn, S. M., Thompson, W. L., Rauch, S. L., Alpert, N. M., et al. (1999). Regional cerebral blood flow during script-driven imagery in childhood sexual abuse-related PTSD: A

PET investigation. *American Journal of Psychiatry*, *156*, 575–584.

Shin, L. M., Rauch, S. L., & Pitman, R. L. (2005). Structural and functional anatomy of PTSD. In J. J. Vasterling & C. R. Brewin (Eds.), *The neuropsychology of PTSD: Biological, clinical, and cognitive perspectives* (pp. 59–82). New York: Guilford Press.

Shobe, K. K., & Kihlstrom, J. F. (1997). Is traumatic memory special? *Current Directions in Psychological Science*, *6*, 70–74.

Shors, T. J., Gallegos, R. A., & Breindl, A. (1997). Transient and persistent consequences of acute stress on long-term potentiation (LTP), synaptic efficacy, theta rhythms, and bursts in area CA1. *Synapse*, *26*, 209–217.

Shors, T. J., Levine, S., & Thompson, R. F. (1990). Effect of adrenalectomy and demedullation on the stress-induced impairment of long-term potentiation. *Neuroendocrinology*, *51*, 70–75.

Shors, T. J., Seib, T. B., Levine, S., & Thompson, R. F. (1989). Inescapable versus escapable shock modulates long-term potentiation in the rat hippocampus. *Science*, *244*, 224–226.

Southwick, S. M., Morgan, A. C., Nicolaou, A. L., & Charney, D. S. (1997). Consistency of memory for combat-related traumatic events in veterans of Operation Desert Storm. *American Journal of Psychiatry*, *154*, 173–177.

Speckens, A. E. M., Ehlers, A., Hackmann, A., Ruths, F. A., & Clark, D. M. (2007, this issue). Intrusive memories and rumination in patients with posttraumatic stress disorder: A phenomenological comparison. *Memory*, *15*, 249–257.

Strange, B. A., Hurlemann, R., & Dolan, R. J. (2003). An emotion-induced retrograde amnesia in humans is amygdala- and beta-adrenergic-dependent. *Proceedings of the National Academy of Sciences of the USA*, *100*, 13626–13631.

Stuart, A. D. P., Holmes, E. A., & Brewin, C. R. (2006). The influence of a visuo-spatial grounding task on intrusive images of a traumatic film. *Behaviour Research and Therapy*, *44*, 611–619.

Terr, L. (1990). *Too scared to cry*. New York: Basic Books.

van der Hart, O., & Brom, D. (2000). When the victim forgets: Trauma-induced amnesia and its assessment in Holocaust survivors. In A. Y. Shalev, R. Yehuda, & A. C. McFarlane (Eds.), *International handbook of human response to trauma* (pp. 233–248). New York: Kluwer Academic/Plenum Publishers.

van der Hart, O., Nijenhuis, E., Steele, K., & Brown, D. (2004). Trauma-related dissociation: Conceptual clarity lost and found. *Australian and New Zealand Journal of Psychiatry*, *38*, 906–914.

van der Kolk, B. A., & Fisler, R. (1995). Dissociation and the fragmentary nature of traumatic memories:

Overview and exploratory study. *Journal of Traumatic Stress*, *8*, 505–525.

van der Kolk, B. A., Hopper, J. W., & Osterman, J. E. (2001). Exploring the nature of traumatic memory: Combining clinical knowledge with laboratory methods. *Journal of Aggression, Maltreatment and Trauma*, *4*, 9–31.

van der Kolk, B. A., & van der Hart, O. (1991). The intrusive past: The flexibility of memory and the engraving of trauma. *American Imago*, *48*, 425–454.

Van Minnen, A., Wessel, I., Dijkstra, T., & Roelofs, K. (2002). Changes in PTSD patients' narratives during prolonged exposure therapy: A replication and extension. *Journal of Traumatic Stress*, *15*, 255–258.

Vasterling, J. J., & Brewin, C. R. (Eds.). (2005). *The neuropsychology of PTSD: Biological, clinical, and cognitive perspectives*. New York: Guilford Press.

Walker, W. R., Skowronski, J. J., & Thompson, C. P. (2003). Life is pleasant – and memory helps to keep it that way! *Review of General Psychology*, *7*, 203–210.

Wells, A., & Papageorgiou, C. (1995). Worry and the incubation of intrusive images following stress. *Behaviour Research and Therapy*, *33*, 579–583.

Wessel, I., Meeren, M., Peeters, F., Arntz, A., & Merckelbach, H. (2001). Correlates of autobiographical memory specificity: The role of depression, anxiety and childhood trauma. *Behaviour Research and Therapy*, *39*, 409–421.

Wessel, I., Merckelbach, H., & Dekkers, T. (2002). Autobiographical memory specificity, intrusive memory, and general memory skills in Dutch-Indonesian survivors of the World War II era. *Journal of Traumatic Stress*, *15*, 227–234.

Williams, J. M. G., Stiles, W. B., & Shapiro, D. A. (1999). Cognitive mechanisms in the avoidance of painful and dangerous thoughts: Elaborating the assimilation model. *Cognitive Therapy and Research*, *23*, 285–306.

Williams, L. M. (1994). Recall of childhood trauma: A prospective study of women's memories of child sexual abuse. *Journal of Consulting and Clinical Psychology*, *62*, 1167–1176.

Winkielman, P., Schwarz, N., & Belli, R. F. (1998). The role of ease of retrieval and attribution in memory judgments: Judging your memory as worse despite recalling more events. *Psychological Science*, *9*, 124–126.

Yovell, Y., Bannett, Y., & Shalev, A. Y. (2003). Amnesia for traumatic events among recent survivors: A pilot study. *CNS Spectrums*, *8*, 676–685.

Xu, L., Anwyl, R., & Rowan, M. (1997). Behavioural stress facilitates the induction of long-term depression in the hippocampus. *Nature*, *387*, 497–500.

MEMORY, 2007, 15 (3), 249–257

Psychology Press
Taylor & Francis Group

Intrusive memories and rumination in patients with post-traumatic stress disorder: A phenomenological comparison

Anne E. M. Speckens and Anke Ehlers
Institute of Psychiatry, London, UK

Ann Hackmann
Warneford Hospital, Oxford, UK

Florian A. Ruths
Centre for Anxiety Disorders and Trauma, London, UK

David M. Clark
Institute of Psychiatry, London, UK

The aim of the study was to investigate the phenomenological differences between intrusive memories and rumination in PTSD. The study population consisted of 31 patients with PTSD referred for cognitive behavioural therapy to specialist services. A semi-structured interview was used to examine the characteristics of the most prominent intrusive memory and rumination. Intrusive memories were predominantly sensory experiences of short duration, whereas rumination was predominantly a thought process of longer duration. Shame was associated more with rumination than with intrusive memories. Anxiety, helplessness, numbness, and threat were greater at the time of the trauma than when experiencing the intrusive memory. In contrast, feelings like anger and sadness were greater when experiencing intrusive memories than at the time of the event. The distinction between intrusive memories and rumination is of clinical importance as intrusive memories usually decrease with imaginal reliving of the trauma, whereas rumination may require different therapeutic strategies, such as rumination-focused or mindfulness-based cognitive therapy.

Recurrent and intrusive distressing recollections of the traumatic event, including images, thoughts, or perceptions, are among the key features of post-traumatic stress disorder (PTSD) (American Psychiatric Association, 1994). Research in both student and clinical populations has shown that intrusive memories of traumatic events differ in important ways from other autobiographical memories. In students who met criteria for PTSD, Berntsen (2001) found that trauma memories were more vivid than non-traumatic memories, had more impact on current mood, and were more often accompanied by a physical reaction at retrieval. In a further study, they found that traumatic memories of students who met criteria for PTSD involved

Address correspondence to: Anne E. M. Speckens, Department of Psychiatry (966), UMC St Radboud, Postbus 9101, 6500 HB Nijmegen, The Netherlands. E-mail: a.speckens@psy.umcn.nl

The study was supported by a grant from the Wellcome Trust. At the time of the study, Anne Speckens was supported by a scholarship of the Netherlands Organization for Scientific Research.

http://www.psypress.com/memory   DOI:10.1080/09658210701256449

more emotion, smell/taste, bodily sensations, and feeling of travelling in time, and tended to involve more visual aspects and sounds, than traumatic memories of those who did not (Berntsen, Willert, & Rubin, 2003). In patients with PTSD who were assessed for treatment, Ehlers et al. (2002) also found that intrusive memories were distressing, had a vivid perceptual content, and appeared to be happening in the "here and now". With imaginal reliving of the traumatic event, the frequency, vividness, distress, and nowness of the intrusive memories gradually faded (Hackmann, Ehlers, Speckens, & Clark, 2004).

Theorists of PTSD have suggested that these intrusive memories are functionally distinct from intrusive thoughts about the trauma that do not represent re-experiencing (DeSilva & Marks, 1999; Ehlers, Hackmann, & Michael, 2004; Joseph, Williams, & Yule, 1997). The latter include evaluative thoughts about the trauma (Reynolds & Brewin, 1998, 1999) and rumination. Rumination has been defined as passively focusing one's attention on a negative emotional state like depression, its symptoms, and thinking repetitively about the causes, meanings, and consequences of that state (Nolen-Hoeksema, 1991). Rumination has been shown to predict the onset (Just & Alloy, 1997; Spasojevic & Alloy, 2001), severity (Muris, Roelofs, Rassin, Franken, & Mayer, 2005; Nolen-Hoeksema & Morrow, 1993) and maintenance of depression (Kuehner & Weber, 1999; Nolen-Hoeksema, 2000). In a recent study, Cheung, Gilbert, and Irons (2004) showed that rumination was also significantly correlated with shame, and that rumination partially mediated a link between shame and depression. Other researchers have developed a model for anger rumination (Sukhodolsky, Golub, & Cromwell, 2001) and established its negative association with forgiveness (Barber, Maltby, & Macaskill, 2005).

Apart from its importance in depressed subjects, several studies have now established the importance of rumination in subjects who experienced traumatic events. In normal subjects, Wells and Papageorgiou (1995) showed that ruminative activity following exposure to a stressor led to significantly more intrusions in the next 3 days than a settle-down control condition. Watkins (2004) demonstrated that conceptual-evaluative writing about an induced failure experience (e.g. "Why did you feel this way?") was associated with a more depressed mood and more intrusions about the failure in high trait ruminators than

experiential writing ("How did you feel moment-by-moment?"). Rumination has also been shown to be linked to subsequent depressive symptoms following negative life events such as an earthquake (Nolen-Hoeksema & Morrow, 1991) and bereavement (Nolen-Hoeksema, Parker, & Larson, 1994). In victims of road traffic accidents, rumination is one of the strongest predictors of the subsequent PTSD symptoms (Holeva, Tarrier & Wells, 2001; Murray, Ehlers, & Mayou, 2002).

The above empirical findings of different types of emotions that are associated with intrusive memories and ruminations are in accordance with the dual representation theory of post-traumatic stress disorder of Brewin, Dalgleish, and Joseph (1996). They argued that traumatic experiences are processed in both conscious and non-conscious ways. Sensory (visual, auditory, olfactory etc.), physiological, and motor aspects of the traumatic experience are processed non-consciously and represented in situationally accessible knowledge. In contrast, autobiographical memories that are processed consciously are represented in verbally accessible knowledge. Consequently, emotional processing of traumatic events will involve different kinds of emotional reactions. First, there will be conditioned emotional reactions corresponding to the activation of specific emotional states experienced during the trauma, as represented in the person's situationally accessible memories of the event. In conjunction with these, secondary emotions such as sadness, anger, guilt, and shame, may follow from the conscious processing of the consequences and implications of the trauma.

The aim of this study was to conduct a direct comparison between intrusive memories and rumination, using the phenomenological characteristics that Hackmann et al. (2004) used in their previous research of intrusive memories of patients with PTSD. By definition and methodology, intrusive memories were expected to involve more sensory experiences, whereas rumination was expected to be more of a thought process. In accordance with the dual representation theory, we hypothesised that intrusive memories are more associated with emotions like anxiety, helplessness, numbness, and threat, and that rumination is more associated with secondary emotions such as sadness, guilt, shame, and anger. We also expected that emotions like anxiety, helplessness, numbness, and threat are less intense at the time of assessment than at the time of the trauma, but that secondary emotions like sadness, guilt, shame, and anger may be more intense at the time of assessment than at the time of the trauma.

METHOD

Study population

The study population comprised patients with PTSD who had been referred for cognitive behavioural treatment to the University Department of Psychiatry, Warneford Hospital, Oxford, UK, or the Centre for Anxiety Disorders and Trauma, Maudsley Hospital, London. To be included in the study, patients had to meet the following criteria: age between 18 and 65 years; meeting diagnostic criteria for PTSD as determined by the Structured Clinical Interview for DSM-IV (First, Spitzer, Gibbon, & Williams, 1995); PTSD being the main problem; and the current episode of PTSD being due to a single event trauma. Exclusion criteria were: having been unconscious for more than 15 minutes or having no memory of the traumatic event; a history of psychosis; current alcohol or drug dependence; borderline personality disorder; severe depression needing immediate treatment in its own right (i.e., suicide risk); and the need of an interpreter to conduct assessment or treatment sessions.

The study population consisted of 15 male and 16 female subjects. Their mean age was 38.3 (SD 11.0) years. The majority of the patients were Caucasian ($N = 21$, 68%), nine (29%) were Afro-Caribbean, and one (4%) was Asian. A total of 15 (48%) of the patients were married or co-habiting, 10 (32%) were divorced, and six (19%) were single. The majority of the patients were working ($N = 20$, 65%), seven (23%) were on disability allowance, and two (7%) were unemployed; nine (29%) were working in professional jobs, seven (23%) in white collar, and thirteen (42%) in blue-collar jobs.

A total of 13 patients (42%) suffered from PTSD after a road traffic accident, 11 (36%) patients had been assaulted, and seven (22%) had experienced other accidents. Nine (29%) patients had a comorbid depressive disorder and nine (29%) a comorbid anxiety disorder, i.e., panic disorder ($N = 4$), specific phobia ($N = 4$), and social phobia ($N = 1$). At the start of treatment, the mean scores on the PDS (see next section) were 32.2 (SD 8.6), on the BDI 23.7 (SD 10.3), and on the BAI 22.7 (SD 11.4).

Measures

Post-traumatic Diagnostic Scale (PDS)

The PDS is a self-report measure of PTSD (Foa, 1995; Foa, Cashman, Jaycox, & Perry, 1997). Patients are asked to rate how much they were bothered by each of the PTSD symptoms specified in the DSM-IV in the past month. The PDS has good internal consistency and test–retest reliability.

Beck Depression Inventory (BDI)

The BDI is a 21-item self-report measure of depression that has been shown in previous research to have good reliability and validity (Beck, Ward, Mendelsohn, Mock, & Erbaugh, 1961).

Beck Anxiety Inventory (BAI)

The BAI is a 21-item scale that measures the severity of self-reported anxiety (Beck & Steer, 1993). The BAI has a high internal consistency, test–retest reliability, and convergent validity.

Intrusion and Rumination Interview

Intrusion section. This semi-structured interview was developed for the purpose of the study and was modelled after the interviews used in earlier work of Ehlers et al. (2002), Hackmann et al. (2004), and Michael (2005). The interviewer introduced the section on intrusive memories as follows:

Many people have recollections of things that happened in the trauma when they do not want them. These are usually from particular moments from before, during, or after the event that somehow "got stuck" in memory and keep coming back. For example, memories of the headlights of a car coming towards you in people who had a road traffic accident, or memories of the knife in someone who was assaulted.

The interviewer then asked whether the patient had such unwanted memories that kept coming back, and if so, whether they could describe them. The content of the memories was noted. Patients were asked to classify whether the memory was about something that happened before or during the traumatic event, or of fantasies about what might have happened but had not. They were then asked what meaning the memory had for them, both at the time and at present. If patients reported more than one intrusive memory, they were asked to describe them all in the above manner, after which they were asked to identify which intrusive memory was troubling them most.

The interviewer then asked "Could you tell me a bit more about how you experience this most prominent memory? What is it like?" and prompted "Is it more like a thought (please describe)? ... like a feeling (please describe)? ... or like a sensory experience?". The responses were not mutually exclusive.

If patients chose sensory experience, they were asked whether visual aspects, sounds, smells, tastes, or bodily sensations were part of the experience. If patients indicated bodily sensations were part of the experience, they were asked whether they consisted of part of the anxiety response during the trauma, part of sensations during the trauma (e.g., touch on shoulder), pain like during the trauma, or part of actions, movement, or posture during the trauma. The frequency with which the most prominent intrusive memory had occurred in the previous week was noted, and its usual duration was rated using the following categories: 1–10 seconds, 20–30 seconds, 30–60 seconds, 1–2 minutes, 2–5 minutes, 5–15 minutes, 15–60 minutes, 1–2 hours, more than 2 hours.

Patients then rated which emotions accompanied the part of the event represented by the memory at the time of the trauma, and at present, each on a scale from 0 (not at all), 1 (a little), 2 (moderately), 3 (very), to 4 (extremely). Patients were asked to indicate on a scale from 0 (never), 1 (rarely), 2 (sometimes), 3 (often), to 4 (always) how often intrusive memories were elicited by dwelling on the event.

Rumination section. The rumination section of the interview introduced the concept of rumination as follows:

Besides the unwanted recollections of things that happened in the trauma that we already talked about, many people cannot help repeatedly going over in their mind parts of the experience and what it meant to them. For example, they think about what could have happened or how the trauma has affected their life.

The interviewer then asked whether this happened to the patient, and if so, whether they could tell a bit more about what parts they went over, over and over again. If patients reported more than one rumination, they were asked to identify what part was most significant to them. They also rated on a 5-point scale from 0 (never) to 4 (always) how often they ruminated about a list of themes based on earlier work by Michael (2002), such as "why it happened to me" or "what else might have happened". They indicated to what extent their ruminations concerned the past, the present, and the future. The patients were then asked about the quality, frequency, duration, and accompanying emotions of the most prominent rumination in the same way as they had been asked about the most prominent intrusive memory. They were also asked what their thoughts were like when they were dwelling on the event, and to indicate, on a scale from 0 (never) to 4 (always), to what extent they had images of the event or of the consequences of the event while they were ruminating. Finally, they were asked to indicate, on a scale from 0 (never) to 4 (always), how often rumination was elicited by intrusive memories of the event.

Classification of the content of the intrusive memories. Two raters independently classified the content of each memory using the following classification system that was based on the earlier work of Hackmann et al. (2004), and on further observations of the authors when treating PTSD patients.

1. Stimulus that was present shortly before the traumatic event began and signalled its onset (e.g., "Perpetrator standing by my bed with a knife" before stabbing).
2. Stimulus that occurred in the course of the event, and signalled a moment when the meaning of the event became more traumatic (e.g., "Paramedics touching my shoulder" – which preceded them asking whether the patient was all right, a moment when the patient suddenly felt pain and realised she was injured).
3. Moment before the trauma when everything still seemed OK (e.g., images of a pleasant day before the accident happened).
4. Moment when patient later wished he/she had done something differently (e.g., inter-

action with another person after the event – patient regretted later that she had not been friendlier at the time).

5. Intrusion of elements from previous traumatic event when experiencing the present trauma (e.g., sound of previous accident in which mother was killed).

6. Intrusion of fantasies of what might have happened, but did not.

Categories 1 and 2 both represent "warning signals", and can be considered two examples of the same concept. They were distinguished for the purposes of the study, as the onset of the trauma can be determined more unambiguously than later time points. Interrater reliability was Kappa = .84. A consensus rating was agreed for the few cases of discrepancy between raters (all of these were between categories 1 and 2).

Procedure

In the assessment interview, information was gathered on sociodemographic variables and the traumatic event. PTSD and comorbid psychiatric disorders were diagnosed with the Structured Clinical Interview for DSM-IV (First et al., 1995). In addition, the PDS, BDI, and BAI were administered. Patients were offered 12 sessions of cognitive behavioural treatment for PTSD. The treatment was based on the cognitive model for PTSD as described by Ehlers and Clark (2000). The Intrusion and Rumination Interview usually took place between the assessment and the first treatment session or after the first treatment session.

Data analysis

As the distribution of the number and frequency of intrusive memories and ruminations were skewed, and the duration was assessed in categories, we chose to analyse the difference in these characteristics by means of Wilcoxon signed ranks tests. Proportions of patients who experienced intrusive memories or rumination like a thought, feeling, or sensory experience were compared by means of a chi-square test. Differences in emotions were tested by paired t-tests. As specific predictions were involved, the t-tests were one-tailed.

RESULTS

Phenomenology of intrusive memories and rumination

All patients had intrusive memories, and all but one patient reported ruminations. Table 1 compares the characteristics of intrusive memories and ruminations. Although the number and frequency of intrusive memories and ruminations did not differ, ruminations took significantly longer than intrusive memories ($z = 4.56$, $p < .001$).

As expected, the most prominent intrusive memories were more often like a sensory experience ($z = 3.46$, $p = .001$), while the most prominent ruminations were more often like a thought process ($z = 4.12$, $p < .001$). All but one patient reported intrusive memories to be like a sensory experience. Visual aspects were part of it for all of them ($N = 24$), sounds for 17 (71%), smells for four (17%), and taste for three (12%). For the majority ($N = 19$, 79%), bodily sensations were

TABLE 1
Phenomenology of most prominent intrusive memory and rumination

	Intrusive memory	Rumination	p value
Quantitative features (MD, range)			
number	3 (1–11)	3 (2–5)	0.746
frequency	3 (0–25)	4 (1–35)	0.108
duration	30–60s (1s – 15m)	5–15m (1m –2hr)	0.000
Quality (N =25%)			
like a thought	6 (24)	23 (92)	0.000
like a feeling	17 (68)	17 (68)	1.000
like a sensory experience	24 (96)	12 (48)	0.001

N = 30.

part of the memory. In 17 (90%) these were like the anxiety response, in eight (42%) like actions, movement, or posture, in four (21%) like sensations, and in two (10%) like pain during the trauma.

However, 12 patients reported sensory experiences to be part of the most prominent rumination as well as the most prominent intrusive memory. For these patients, the sensory modalities involved in ruminations were very similar to *those* involved in intrusive memories: visual aspects were present for all, sounds were present for six (50%), and smells for one (8%). If bodily sensations were present ($N = 5$, 42%), they most often consisted of the anxiety response during the trauma ($N = 4$, 80%) and, for one patient (20%), also of sensations during the trauma.

When asked what their thoughts were like when dwelling on the event, even more of the patients reported that images of the event were often ($N = 14$, 45%) or always ($N = 11$, 36%) part of the experience. Similar proportions of the patients reported to often ($N = 12$, 39%) or always ($N = 9$, 29%) have images of the consequences of the event while dwelling on the event. In 18 (58%) of the patients, dwelling on the event was often a trigger for intrusive memories. Conversely, 22 (73%) patients reported that intrusive memories were often triggers for ruminations about the traumatic event.

With regard to the accompanying emotions, rumination was associated with greater shame than intrusive memories (see Table 2).

Table 3 compares the intensity of emotions that patients described during their traumatic experience with those they reported for their

most prominent intrusive memory. Anxiety, helplessness, numbness, and perceived threat were stronger at the time of the traumatic event than when having the intrusive memory. In contrast, anger and sadness were stronger when having the intrusive memory than at the time of the trauma.

Content of intrusive memories and rumination

The classification of the content of the main intrusive memory and all intrusive memories together is shown in Table 4. The majority (90%) of the main intrusive memories and all intrusive memories (84%) were classified as warning signals that signalled either the onset of the trauma or the beginning of a moment when the meaning became more traumatic. One pa-

TABLE 3
Emotions at the time of the trauma and when having intrusive memory

Emotions	At the time of trauma (Mean, SD)	When having intrusive memory (Mean, SD)	t value	p value
Anxiety	3.1 (1.3)	2.5 (1.3)	2.34	0.013
Anger	1.8 (1.7)	2.6 (1.4)	−2.25	0.016
Sadness	1.4 (1.6)	2.1 (1.4)	−1.92	0.032
Guilt	0.7 (1.4)	0.9 (1.3)	−0.71	0.242
Shame	0.9 (1.4)	0.6 (1.2)	1.16	0.127
Helplessness	3.1 (1.3)	2.2 (1.5)	3.02	0.002
Numbness	2.0 (1.6)	1.3 (1.4)	2.61	0.007
Threat	3.1 (1.4)	1.9 (1.5)	3.11	0.002

$N = 30$.

TABLE 2
Associated emotions of most prominent intrusive memory and rumination

Emotions	Intrusive memory (Mean, SD)	Rumination (Mean, SD)	t value	p value (one-sided)
Anxiety	2.6 (1.2)	2.5 (1.2)	0.33	0.372
Anger	2.7 (1.3)	2.8 (1.2)	−0.17	0.434
Sadness	2.2 (1.4)	2.6 (1.3)	−1.69	0.051
Guilt	1.0 (1.4)	1.4 (1.6)	−1.58	0.062
Shame	0.7 (1.2)	1.2 (1.4)	−3.25	0.002
Helplessness	2.3 (1.4)	2.5 (1.3)	−0.61	0.272
Numbness	1.5 (1.5)	1.7 (1.2)	−1.23	0.114
Threat	2.0 (1.5)	2.2 (1.4)	−0.90	0.188

$N = 30$.

TABLE 4
Classification of intrusive memories

	Main intrusive memory ($N = 31$) N (%)	All intrusive memories ($N = 97$) N (%)
Warning signal of onset	14 (45)	25 (26)
Warning signal of more traumatic meaning	14 (45)	56 (58)
Everything still OK		2 (2)
Done something differently	1 (3)	3 (3)
Earlier trauma	1 (3)	7 (7)
Fantasies of what might have happened	1 (3)	4 (4)

TABLE 5
Themes of rumination

	Mean (SD)
About the long-term consequences of the event	3.3 (0.9)
What life would be like if the event had not happened	3.0 (1.2)
About what else might have happened	2.7 (1.1)
How unfair it is	2.4 (1.5)
About my relationship to other people	2.3 (1.3)
How things would have been, if only I had done something differently	2.2 (1.6)
About why it happened to me	2.1 (1.5)
About what I would like to say or do to the person who caused the trauma	2.1 (1.4)
About other bad things that may happen in the future	2.1 (1.3)
Things that I do not understand	2.1 (1.3)
About the kind of person I am	1.9 (1.4)
Things I cannot remember	1.5 (1.4)

$N = 30$.

tient, for example, had intrusive memories of his mouth being cut with a knife and the taste of blood, and the sound of his wrist being broken and the pain. At the time of the attack, at both these moments the patient thought that he would be killed and that his wife and children would be killed.

With regard to rumination, patients appeared to ruminate most often about the past ($N = 22$, 73%), and slightly less often about the future ($N = 18$, 60%) or the present ($N = 15$, 50%). The patient mentioned above, for example, ruminated about why the attack had happened, about how it had affected his life, and about the fact that he had to protect his wife and children from something bad happening to them. Table 5 shows the frequency with which patients ruminated about the range of themes provided to them. The most important themes were the long-term consequences of the traumatic event, what life would be like if the event had not happened, what else might have happened, how unfair it was, and the patient's relationship to other people.

DISCUSSION

Characteristics of intrusive memories and rumination

As expected, the most prominent intrusive memories and rumination appeared to be phenome-

nologically different. Intrusive memories were predominantly sensory experiences, whereas rumination was mainly described as a thought process. Intrusive memories were mostly of short duration, less than a minute, as opposed to rumination, which could take hours.

In the light of the definitions and examples that participants were supplied with, it is striking that almost half of the group reported the predominant rumination to be like a sensory experience as well. In fact, when asked what their thoughts were like when dwelling on the event, the majority of the patients indicated that they often had images of the event itself or of the consequences of the event. Part of the explanation for the high prevalence of sensory experiences while ruminating might be that intrusive memories and rumination take place simultaneously. In a high proportion of patients, intrusive memories triggered rumination and vice versa. However, as rumination is often assumed to be a verbal process, imagery might also be an underestimated and understudied part of the ruminative process.

Emotional reactions

In accordance with our hypothesis, shame was associated more with rumination than with intrusive memories, and sadness and guilt tended to be so, although these differences did not reach significance.

Feelings such as anxiety, helplessness, numbness, and threat were reported to be stronger at the time of the trauma than at the time of the assessment. In contrast, feelings like anger and sadness were greater at the time of assessment than at the time of the trauma. This is in accordance with the dual representation theory of post-traumatic disorder, which suggests that some emotions (such as fear) tend to be most intense during the trauma, whereas secondary emotions (such as anger) tend to be more intense post-trauma.

Rumination might be an important mediating factor between the traumatic event, the increase of feelings like sadness, shame, and anger, and the subsequent onset or maintenance of PTSD symptoms. This is in accordance with the study of Cheung et al. (2004), who also showed that rumination was correlated with shame, and that rumination partially mediated a link between shame and depression.

Limitations of the study

Obviously, the definitions and examples of intrusive memories and rumination provided to the patients may partly account for the difference in the sensory versus verbal ratings between the two types of thinking. In addition, the study sample was relatively small and non-consecutive in nature. Both of these were determined by the availability of an experienced clinician (AS), who conducted most of the interviews. Furthermore, the lack of a comparison or control group makes it difficult to judge whether the nature of intrusive memories and rumination observed here is specific to PTSD, or might apply to other populations as well.

Clinical implications

The distinction between intrusive memories and rumination may have important clinical implications. Reliving of traumatic memories and cognitive restructuring of appraisals and beliefs emerging from trauma experiences have demonstrated to be effective in reducing the frequency and associated distress of intrusive memories (Hackmann et al., 2004).

However, rumination might require additional therapeutic interventions. In a preliminary study, Wells and Sembi (2004) described a new brief treatment for PTSD—metacognitive therapy, involving elements such as analysing the advantages and disadvantages of rumination, and training patients to respond to their symptoms by acknowledging that the symptoms are occurring and reminding themselves that ruminating about them is unhelpful.

In a recent study, Ramel, Goldin, Carmona, and McQuaid (2004) reported on the effects of mindfulness-based stress reduction on rumination. Mindfulness is defined as "paying attention in a particular way: on purpose, in the present moment, and non-judgmentally" (Kabat-Zinn, 1994. p. 4), which has similarities to the experiential mode of self-focused attention that Watkins (2004) showed to be adaptive in emotional processing of upsetting events. Mindfulness-based cognitive therapy has been shown to be effective in preventing relapse in patients with recurrent depression in two separate randomised controlled trials (Ma & Teasdale, 2004; Teasdale et al., 2000). The results of Ramel et al. (2004) suggested that mindfulness practice primarily led to decrease in ruminative thinking, even after controlling for reductions in affective symptoms. This might make mindfulness-based interventions an interesting new approach, also for patients with PTSD in whom rumination plays an important role.

REFERENCES

American Psychiatric Association. (1994). *Diagnostic and Statistical Manual of Mental Disorders (4th ed.) (DSM-IV)*. Washington, DC: American Psychiatric Association.

Barber, L., Maltby, J., & Macaskill, A. (2005). Angry memories and thoughts of revenge: The relationship between forgiveness and anger rumination. *Personality and Individual Differences, 39*, 253–262.

Beck, A. T., & Steer, R. A. (1993). *Beck Anxiety Inventory: Manual*. San Antonio, TX: The Psychological Corporation.

Beck, A. T., Ward, D. H., Mendelsohn, M., Mock, J., & Erbaugh, J. (1961). An inventory for measuring depression. *Archives of General Psychiatry, 4*, 561–571.

Berntsen, D. (2001). Involuntary memories of emotional events: Do memories of traumas and extremely happy events differ? *Applied Cognitive Psychology, 15*, S135–S158.

Berntsen, D., Willert, M., & Rubin, D.C. (2003). Splintered memories or vivid landmarks? Qualities and organization of traumatic memories with and without PTSD. *Applied Cognitive Psychology, 17*, 675–683.

Brewin, C. R., Dalgleish, T., & Joseph, S. (1996). A dual representation theory of post-traumatic stress disorder. *Psychological Review, 103*, 670–686.

Cheung, M. S. P., Gilbert, P., & Irons, C. (2004). An exploration of shame, social rank and rumination in relation to depression. *Personality and Individual Differences, 36*, 1143–1153.

DeSilva, P., & Marks, M. (1999). Intrusive thinking in post-traumatic stress disorders. In W. Yule (Ed.), *Post-traumatic stress disorder: Concepts and therapy* (pp. 161–175). New York: Wiley.

Ehlers, A., & Clark, D. M. (2000). A cognitive model of post-traumatic stress disorder. *Behaviour Research and Therapy, 38*, 319–345.

Ehlers, A., Hackmann, A., & Michael, T. (2004). Intrusive re-experiencing in post-traumatic stress disorder: Phenomenology, theory, and therapy. *Memory, 12*, 403–415.

Ehlers, A., Hackmann, A., Steil, R., Clohessy, S., Wenninger, K., & Winter, H. (2002). The nature of intrusive memories after trauma: The warning signal hypothesis. *Behaviour Research and Therapy, 40*, 1021–1028.

First, M. B., Spitzer, R. L., Gibbon, M., & Williams, J. B. W. (1995). *Structured Clinical Interview for DSM-IV Axis I Disorders – Patient Edition (SCID-I/*

P, Version 2.0). New York: New York State Psychiatric Institute.

Foa, E. B. (1995). The Post-traumatic Diagnostic Scale (PDS) manual. Minneapolis, MN: National Computer Systems.

Foa, E. B., Cashman, L., Jaycox, L. H., & Perry, K. (1997). The validation of a self-report measure of PTSD: The PTSD Diagnostic Scale (PDS). Psychological Assessment, 9, 445–451.

Hackmann, A., Ehlers, A., Speckens, A., & Clark, D. M. (2004). Characteristics and content of intrusive memories in PTSD and their changes with treatment. Journal of Traumatic Stress, 17, 231–240.

Holeva, V., Tarrier, N., & Wells, A. (2001). Prevalence and predictors of acute stress disorder and PTSD following road traffic accidents: Thought control strategies and social support. Behavior Therapy, 32, 65–83.

Joseph, S., Williams, R., & Yule, W. (1997). Understanding post-traumatic stress. A psychosocial perspective on PTSD and treatment. Chichester, UK: Wiley.

Just, N., & Alloy, L. B. (1997). The response styles theory of depression: Tests and an extension of the theory. Journal of Abnormal Psychology, 106, 221–229.

Kabat-Zinn, J. (1994). Wherever you go, there you are. New York: Hyperion.

Kuehner, C., & Weber, I. (1999). Responses to depression in unipolar depressed patients: An investigation of Nolen Hoeksema's response styles theory. Psychological Medicine, 29, 1323–1333.

Ma, S. H., & Teasdale, J. D. (2004). Mindfulness-based cognitive therapy for depression: Replication and exploration of differential relapse prevention effects. Journal of Consulting and Clinical Psychology, 72, 31–40.

Michael, T. (2000). The nature of trauma memory and intrusive cognitions in post-traumatic stress disorder. D.Phil. thesis, Oxford University, UK.

Muris, P., Roelofs, J., Rassin, E., Franken, I., & Mayer, B. (2005). Mediating effects of rumination and worry on the links between neuroticism, anxiety and depression. Personality and Individual Differences, 39, 1105–1111.

Murray, J., Ehlers, A., & Mayou, R. A. (2002). Dissociation and post-traumatic stress disorder: Two prospective studies of motor vehicle accident survivors. British Journal of Psychiatry, 180, 363–368.

Nolen-Hoeksema, S. (1991). Responses to depression and their effects on the duration of depressive episodes. Journal of Abnormal Psychology, 100, 569–582.

Nolen-Hoeksema, S. (2000). The role of rumination in depressive disorders and mixed anxiety/depressive symptoms. Journal of Abnormal Psychology, 109, 504–511.

Nolen-Hoeksema, S., & Morrow, J. (1991). A prospective study of depression and post-traumatic stress symptoms after a natural disaster: The 1989 Loma Prieta earthquake. Journal of Personality and Social Psychology, 61, 115–121.

Nolen-Hoeksema, S., & Morrow, J. (1993). Effects of rumination and distraction on naturally occurring depressed mood. Cognition and Emotion, 7, 561–570.

Nolen-Hoeksema, S., Parker, L. E., & Larson, J. (1994). Ruminative coping with depressed mood following loss. Journal of Personality and Social Psychology, 67, 92–104.

Ramel, W., Goldin, P. R., Carmona, P. E., & McQuaid, J. R. (2004). The effects of mindfulness meditation on cognitive processes and affect in patients with past depression. Cognitive Therapy and Research, 28, 433–455.

Reynolds, M., & Brewin, C. R. (1998). Intrusive cognitions, coping strategies and emotional responses in depression, post-traumatic stress disorder and a non-clinical population. Behaviour Research and Therapy, 36, 135–147.

Reynolds, M., & Brewin, C. R. (1999). Intrusive memories in depression and post-traumatic stress disorder. Behaviour Research and Therapy, 37, 201–215.

Spasojevic, J., & Alloy, L. B. (2001). Rumination as a common mechanism relating depressive risk factors to depression. Emotion, 1, 25–37.

Sukhodolsky, D. G., Golub, A., & Cromwell, E. N. (2001). Development and validation of the anger rumination scale. Personality and Individual Differences, 31, 689–700.

Teasdale, J. D., Segal, Z. V., Williams, J. M. G., Ridgeway, V. A., Soulsby, J. M., & Lau, M. A. (2000). Prevention of relapse/recurrence in major depression by mindfulness-based cognitive therapy. Journal of Consulting and Clinical Psychology, 64, 615–623.

Watkins, E. (2004). Adaptive and maladaptive ruminative self-focus during emotional processing. Behaviour Research and Therapy, 42, 1037–1052.

Wells, A., & Papageorgiou, C. (1995). Worry and the incubation of intrusive images following stress. Behaviour Research and Therapy, 33, 579–583.

Wells, A., & Sembi, S. (2004). Metacognitive therapy for PTSD: A preliminary investigation of a new brief treatment. Journal of Behavior Therapy and Experimental Psychiatry, 35, 307–318.

MEMORY, 2007, 15 (3), 258–270

Telling and the remembered self: Linguistic differences in memories for previously disclosed and previously undisclosed events

M. Pasupathi

University of Utah, Salt Lake City, UT, USA

Prior work suggests that disclosing experiences may provide people with more distance, more positive emotion, greater cognitive elaboration, and greater certainty regarding those experiences. Two studies ($n = 58$ undergraduates and $n = 123$ community-living adults) examined linguistic indicators of such differences between previously disclosed and previously undisclosed memories elicited on subsequent, solitary occasions using the LIWC text analysis program (Pennebaker & Francis, 1999). Disclosure was associated with differences in the linguistic features of subsequent memories. Potential mechanisms and implications of those differences are discussed.

The conceptual self has received the bulk of attention from empirical researchers in psychology. However, life story researchers (Hooker & McAdams, 2003; McAdams, 1996), those interested in self-defining memories (Moffitt & Singer, 1994; Singer, 2004), and autobiographical memory researchers (Conway & Pleydell-Pearce, 2000) have all highlighted the importance of the remembered self for a more comprehensive account of self-development (Neisser, 1988). The studies presented below explore whether the nature of that remembered self varies depending on whether memories have previously been disclosed.

I first consider how disclosure might influence the remembered self, including existing evidence on disclosure. I then present two studies suggesting that previously disclosed and undisclosed experiences are remembered with different language on subsequent occasions. In the discussion, I consider both potential explanations and implications of those differences.

WHAT DISCLOSURE MIGHT DO FOR THE REMEMBERED SELF

We disclose experiences to others frequently (Rimé, Finkenauer, Luminet, Zech, & Phillipot, 1998; Rimé, Phillipot, Boca, & Mesquita, 1992), which implies that disclosure serves important psychological functions. Proposed functions of disclosure include self-regulatory and social goals, such as finding meaning in experiences, integrating experiences with the self, recovering from emotions induced by an experience, and connecting with important others (Baumeister & Newman, 1994; Conway & Pleydell-Pearce, 2000; Pasupathi, 2001; Pennebaker & Seagal, 1999; Rimé et al., 1998; Schank & Abelson, 1995; Thorne, 2000). Generally, telling others about experiences is believed to make those experiences less immediate, less intrusive, more a part of the remembered self, and less a part of the individual's current working sense of self (Conway & Pleydell-Pearce,

Address correspondence to: Monisha Pasupathi, Department of Psychology, University of Utah, 390 S. 1530 E. BEH-S 502, Salt Lake City, UT 84109, USA. E-mail: Pasupath@psych.utah.edu

Data collection was supported by Faculty Research and Proposal Initiative grants from the University of Utah, and writing by NIMH R03MH64462-01A1. Other data from these studies are reported elsewhere (Pasupathi, 2003; Pasupathi & Carstensen, 2003). Thanks are due to Pasupathi Laboratory Research Assistants for their help with data collection and data management. Frank Drews and Kate McLean provided helpful comments on earlier versions of the manuscript.

http://www.psypress.com/memory   DOI:10.1080/09658210701256456

2000; Finkenauer & Rimé, 1998; Pennebaker & Keough, 1999). Other possible effects of disclosure are thought to be greater positive and reduced negative emotion regarding an experience (Pasupathi, 2003; Rimé et al., 1998), and possibly more sophisticated understandings of the experience (Baumeister & Newman, 1994; Pennebaker & Seagal, 1999).

Remembering to others requires language and an audience, in contrast to solitary remembering. Listeners require a remember to take into account the listener's need for additional information about the event, including characters, the temporal ordering of sub-events, the reason they should listen, and the interpretation they should hold (Clark, 1996; Grice, 1957). These requirements are derived from the Gricean maxims of Quantity (provide sufficient information) and Clarity (be orderly in that provision), said to describe rules of conduct for speakers in conversation.

Remembering to and with listeners elicits different memories from other recall contexts (Edwards & Middleton, 1986, 1988; Gould & Dixon, 1993; Pasupathi, 2001; Pasupathi, Stallworth, & Murdoch, 1998). In social contexts, memory is negotiated in conversations, including agreement to hear a story as well as disputing details and interpretations (Hirst, Manier, & Apetroaia, 1997; Manier, Pinner, & Hirst, 1996; Ross, 1997; Ross & Holmberg, 1990; Weldon, 2000; Weldon & Bellinger, 1997). Listeners elicit more opinions, evaluations, and summaries than solitary writing contexts, and this may be especially true for friends and family as listeners (Hyman, 1994). Speakers also place events in temporal context for listeners (Skowronski & Walker, 2004), and provide a balance between information about their own personal reactions and those of others. People may also selectively present positive and de-emphasise negative aspects of events in relating them to others, to regulate emotion and follow assumed conversational norms (Pasupathi, 2003; but see Skowronski & Walker, 2004). However, despite much theorising (Baumeister & Newman, 1994; Greenwald, 1980), recent empirical evidence suggests that people are equally likely to disclose positive and negative experiences to others (Rimé et al., 1998; Skowronski, Gibbons, Vogl, & Walker, 2004). Finally, people feel more certain about collaborative recollections than solitary ones (Weldon & Bellinger, 1997).

Taken together, this work suggests that remembering to listeners may produce a less egocentric perspective, a clearer delineation of past and present, greater elaboration, and greater certainty about the remembered event. Such remembering may also change the positivity of memories for an event. If such differences have lasting effects, then remembering events to listeners may change the nature of the remembered self in important ways.

LONG-TERM EFFECTS OF DISCLOSURE ON THE REMEMBERED SELF

Because remembering of an event involves re-encoding that event, differences in recall to listeners have implications for how events are remembered subsequently. Distracted or uncooperative listeners elicit shorter and less coherent event tellings than do attentive listeners, and this lack of detail is reflected in later memory deficits for experiences (Dickinson & Givon, 1995; Pasupathi et al., 1998). Speakers who retell events with a particular goal later recall those events with the same goal-related bias (Dudukovic, Marsh, & Tversky, 2004; McGregor & Holmes, 1999; Tversky & Marsh, 2000), even under instructions to be unbiased in their remembering (Tversky & Marsh, 2000).

However, such work has not examined the types of outcomes (egocentricity, temporal context, elaboration, emotion, or certainty) addressed above. Further, research examining such long-term effects typically contrasts different listeners or goals for disclosure, not disclosure versus no disclosure. One study that explicitly did the latter found that narrated memories were equally likely to contain lessons and insights regardless of their disclosure history (Thorne, McLean, & Lawrence, 2004).

SUMMARY AND OVERVIEW OF THE PRESENT STUDIES

In sum, disclosure to listeners results in greater distance, certainty, positive emotion, and cognitive elaboration *on the disclosure occasion*. These effects should be evident in subsequent memory for the disclosed event. The specific hypothesis tested in the studies below is that prior disclosure is associated with greater distance, elaboration, po-sitivity, *and* certainty in *subsequent* remembering.

The present studies compare written memories for disclosed and non-disclosed events drawn from participants' everyday lives. To provide measures of distance, certainty, cognitive elabora-tion, and emotion in memories, I employed indices from the Linguistic Inquiry and Word Count program (LIWC; Pennebaker & Francis, 1999). Linguistic indicators are believed to reflect aspects of representation that are less deliberative (Pennebaker & Graybeal, 2001; Pennebaker & Keough, 1999; Pennebaker & Seagal, 1999), and thus less susceptible to demand characteristics or self-presentational concerns than self-reported ratings. I examined two different indicators of distance: egocentricity, or the extent to which events were recalled with a self-related language or other-related language (counts of self pronouns and other-related pronouns); and temporal dis-tance (counts of the use of present tense and past tense). These two types of "distance" may be conceptually related, as suggested by the work of Ross and colleagues (Ross & Wilson, 2002; Wilson & Ross, 2003). Certainty was indicated by counts of certain and tentative words. Emotion was indicated by counts of positive and negative emotion words, and cognitive elaboration by counts of insight words and causal words. These indices were chosen for face validity, but prior work on health and disclosure links them to personality and health (Pennebaker & Graybeal, 2001; Pennebaker & Keough, 1999; Pennebaker & King, 1999; Pennebaker, Mayne, & Francis, 1997).

Importantly, differences between disclosed and non-disclosed events from participants' lives in-volve three facets: (1) differences in the types of events that are, versus are not, disclosed; (2) encoding of events into language; and (3) the needs of listeners. The studies below do not address which of these three differences is key to producing subsequent differences. However, the issue of event type is partially examined by looking at events involving interpersonal and achievement themes, basic dimensions in person-ality research that have broad applicability across different life domains (e.g., McAdams, Hoffman, Mansfield, & Day, 1996). Interpersonal and achievement events may involve differences in self and other pronouns, one of the indicators used to reflect distance. Thus, the extent to which interpersonal versus achievement events were recalled by participants across the two disclosure conditions was an important control for the particular language indicators used.

Study 1 employed a between-subjects design with a sample of college students, with the primary goal of comparing LIWC-based indica-tors of distance, certainty, cognitive elaboration, and emotion in written memories for previously disclosed and previously undisclosed experiences.

STUDY 1

Method

Participants

A total of 60 introductory psychology students, Age M $(SD) = 20$ (3), range 17–38, participated for course credit. Of these participants, 43% were male, and 75% European-American. Two parti-cipants' data were excluded, one for concerns about event veridicality and one due to a pre-existing relationship with the experimenter; the final sample size was 58.

Procedure

Participants were randomly assigned to one of two conditions,[1] "disclosed" ($n = 38$) and "undi-sclosed" ($n = 20$). Those in the "disclosed" con-dition were asked to think of a recent (in the last 2 weeks) experience that they had told to others. Those in the "undisclosed" condition were asked to think of a recent experience they had never told anyone about. Both groups wrote a detailed account of the experience, and rated their emo-tional reactions to the initial event on 19 emo-tions (Anger, Guilt, Pride, Sadness, Happiness, Fear, Accomplishment, Shame, Amusement, An-xiety/Worry, Joy, Contentment, Irritation, Frus-tration, Disgust, Interest, Embarrassment, Boredom, Excitement) on 7-point Likert-type scales. Participants in the disclosed condition were also asked questions about times they had told the event. Most participants required ap-proximately 30 minutes to complete the study, with the maximum time needed being 1 hour.

---

[1] The random assignment ensured that one-third of participants were in the "undisclosed" condition, and two-thirds in the "disclosed" condition. The "disclosed" condition involved additional counterbalancing of the order in which participants were asked about the event, and its disclosure. Order was irrelevant to the results reported here and is not discussed further.

Reported events ranged from bereavement to minor traffic violations or receiving praise from a professor, with the majority being everyday emotional experiences like receiving a good grade or a minor conflict with a friend.

Measures

Linguistic characteristics. Participants' handwritten narratives were typed into text files, and subjected to a computer-based microanalytic linguistic analysis system—Linguistic Inquiry and Word Count (LIWC; Pennebaker & Francis, 1999; Pennebaker et al., 1997). LIWC indexed five features of participants' narrative recollections in percentages of total words: *distance from self* (the percentage of words involving self-references and references to other people), *temporal distance* (percentage of past tense and present tense),[2] *certainty* (the percentage of words reflecting certainty, and tentativeness), *cognitive elaboration* (percentage of causal words and insight words), and *emotion* (percentage of positive and negative emotion words).

Thematic coding. Two coders coded events as reflecting primarily interpersonal (concerned with relationships) or agency (concerned with issues of agency, control, performance) concerns (80% agreement, $K = .59$, $p < .001$), using an adaptation of McAdams' coding criteria (McAdams et al., 1996). Disagreements were resolved by discussion, and analyses are based on a consensus classification.

Emotions. Participants' ratings of the positive and negative emotions elicited by the events were averaged to create single indices of positive emotion (Cronbach's $\alpha = .89$), and negative emotion ($\alpha = .88$).

Results and discussion

Were disclosed and undisclosed events similar?

Table 1 presents means, standard deviations, and univariate F values by disclosure condition. The small percentages are consistent with research using LIWC indicators (e.g., Pasupathi, Henry, & Carstensen, 2002; Pennebaker & King, 1999). A MANOVA of all included variables by gender indicated no significant gender differences,

$F(17, 40) < 1, p > .50$.[3] Disclosed and undisclosed events did not differ significantly in overall length, $F(1, 56) < 1$, $p > .70$, M (SD) disclosed = 107.8 (48.7), M (SD) undisclosed = 113.1 (71.4), or emotion. A chi-squared test suggested that told events were as likely to concern interpersonal themes as not-told events ($\chi^2 = 2.5$, $p = .11$), although descriptively such themes were more prevalent among told events.

Is prior disclosure associated with linguistic features of written narratives?

Indicators of distance. A MANOVA examined the percentage of other and self references with condition (disclosed versus undisclosed) as an independent variable, and yielded a main effect of condition, $F(2, 55) = 3.7$, $p < .05$, $\eta^2 = .12$. Univariate tests showed that this effect was primarily due to the fact that disclosed event memories had more other references than undisclosed memories. A second MANOVA examined the percentage of past versus present tense constructions as a function of time (past vs present) and condition (disclosed vs undisclosed), revealing an interaction of time and condition, $F(1, 56) = 11.1$, $p < .01$, $\eta^2 = .17$. Disclosed events contained a greater percentage of past tense verbs and a smaller percentage of present tense verbs than did undisclosed events.

Certainty. A MANOVA comparing the use of tentative words and certain words as a function of condition revealed a significant main effect of condition, $F(2, 55) = 6.9$, $p < .01$, $\eta^2 = .20$. Undisclosed events were more tentative than disclosed events, but not less certain.

Cognitive elaboration. A MANOVA comparing the percentage of causal and insight-related words in narratives of disclosed and undisclosed events revealed no effect of disclosure on this aspect of participants' narratives, $F(2, 55) = 1.1$, $p > .30$.

Positivity. A MANOVA of positive and negative emotion in the narratives as a function of condition revealed no differences in disclosed and undisclosed events in terms of the emotion included in the narrative, $F(2, 55) < 1$.

---

[2] Future tense verbs were rare in these memory narratives.

[3] One univariate F-value was significant. Males tended to use more words reflecting tentativeness than did females, $F(1,56) = 6.1$, $p < .02$, but including gender in the relevant analysis resulted in no changes to the findings ($Fs < 1.5$, $ps > .10$).

TABLE 1
Means and SD for all variables, Study 1

	Disclosed		Undisclosed			
	M	SD	M	SD	F	η^2
Characteristics of events						
Rated positive emotion	3.5	1.7	2.8	1.5	2.4	–
Rated negative emotion	2.8	1.5	3.3	1.5	1.5	–
Guilt	1.9	1.8	2.4	2.0	<1	–
Shame	1.9	1.8	2.4	2.1	<1	–
Interpersonal themes	N = 27		N = 10			
Agentic themes	N = 11		N = 10			
LIWC indicators Distance						
Self-references	10.9	3.9	11.5	3.4	<1	–
Other-references	6.4	3.0	3.9	3.9	7.4**	.12
Past	11.8	2.7	10.0	3.5	5.0 *	.08
Present	4.5	2.6	7.1	3.9	9.6**	.15
Certainty						
Certain	1.2	1.0	1.3	1.2	<1	
Tentative	1.1	1.1	2.4	1.4	14.0**	.20
Positivity						
Positive language	2.4	1.6	2.1	1.3	<1	–
Negative language	1.7	1.4	1.4	1.2	<1	–
Elaboration						
Insight language	1.8	1.8	1.2	1.2	<1	–
Causal language	1.0	1.1	1.0	1.2	2.1	–

**p < .01, *p < .05.

These findings suggest that disclosure results in more distance and certainty about a memory—consistent with prior theoretical and empirical work (Conway & Pleydell-Pearce, 2000; Pennebaker & Seagal, 1999; Pillemer, 1998; Weldon, 2000; Weldon & Bellinger, 1997)—but do not suggest disclosure differences in emotion or elaboration. However, the small and homogeneous sample, the emphasis on recent and therefore largely insignificant events, and the limited ability to examine differences in what is and is not disclosed and to address potential individual variability in language use (Pennebaker & King, 1999), all constrain the generality of the findings. Further, Study 1 did not address how disclosure goals affect the nature of both concurrent and subsequent remembering, an issue raised by existing findings (McLean, 2005).

Study 2 replicates Study 1 in a larger and more heterogeneous sample of individuals and events. Further, a within-subjects design permitted control of individual variability in language use (Pennebaker & King, 1999), and the thematic content of the events was experimentally manipulated. Finally, participants were asked about their goals for disclosing.

DISCLOSURE GOALS AND THE REMEMBERED SELF

People engage in remembering for many reasons (Baumeister & Newman, 1994; Bluck, Levine, & Laulhere, 1999; Hyman & Faries, 1992; Norrick, 1997; Pasupathi, Lucas, & Coombs, 2002; Webster & McCall, 1999), and these goals affect both current and subsequent recall (Dudukovic et al., 2004; Marsh & Tversky, 2004; McGregor & Holmes, 1999; Tversky & Marsh, 2000). I examined three broad goals for disclosure, derived from diary research (Marsh & Tversky, 2004) and personality/self perspectives on autobiographical remembering (McLean, 2005): *meaning-seeking*, *information-sharing*, and *entertaining others*.

Seeking meaning involves a search for insight, understanding, and positive effects of even highly negative experiences (McAdams, Diamond, de St. Aubin, & Mansfield, 1997; Murray, Lamnin, & Carver, 1989; Murray & Segal, 1994) and may lead to more elaboration of subsequent memories. Disclosure for *meaning-seeking* has been shown to lead to more insights in subsequent memories for the disclosed event when compared to *entertainment* goals (McLean, 2005). The goal to *share information* may also be associated with increased elaboration as it involves the repetition and transmission of meanings that people have already derived (Dudukovic et al., 2004; Hyman & Faries, 1992; Webster & McCall, 1999). Finally, the goal of *entertaining* has been shown to involve more emotion language, and more distortion in subsequent remembering than accuracy-oriented remembering (Dudukovic et al., 2004; Marsh & Tversky, 2004). Thus, goals for finding meaning or sharing information may be associated with more cognitive elaboration, and goals for entertainment may result in heightened emotional content. Because goals for disclosure may vary across occasions, Study 2 asked participants to focus on the first time they disclosed the events. Early findings by Bartlett (1932/1995) suggested that initial and early rehearsals of memories constrained subsequent ones, and thus held more influence over later recall.

STUDY 2

Method

Participants

A total of 123 individuals—*M* (*SD*) Age = 42.9 (19.1), range 18–89—were recruited via flyers, newspaper advertisements, and radio announcements for participation in a "study of life experiences". Of these, 64% were female. A total of 66% had not completed a bachelor's degree, 17% had done so, and 17% had gone on to graduate or professional training; 44% were single, 20% married, 24% divorced, and 8% widowed. The majority (79%) were European-American, with Native Americans the next largest group (7%). Individuals were compensated at 10$ per hour of study time, usually between 1 and 2 hours. The maximum time required was 3 hours by one older adult, due to arthritis.

Procedure

Individuals participated at the laboratory as well as in community settings. They were randomly assigned to one of three different event-type conditions: interpersonal (*n* = 40), achievement (*n* = 33), or a control condition (*n* = 36). The interpersonal event instructions read "we are interested in events that involve other people and our relationships" and listed examples of feeling connected to or distanced from others. The achievement event instruction read "we are

interested in events involving successes and failures" and listed experiences such as making errors or performing really well at some task. The control condition told participants we were interested in all types of events from their lives, and provided two examples of each type.

Participants completed two questionnaires: one about a previously disclosed event, and one about a previously undisclosed event. Both questionnaires first asked participants to write a narrative describing the past experience as completely as possible. Participants were then asked how long ago the experience occurred, and to rate, on 7-point Likert-type scales, how important the event was, how self-revealing it was, to what extent they gained insight from it, and the extent to which they felt the 19 emotions rated in Study 1. Following those questions, the *disclosed event questionnaire* asked participants to describe the first time they talked about the event and to rate their goals for doing so along single-item, 7-point Likert-type scales. Additional questions about the retelling context and reasons for not disclosing events were asked, but are not reported here.

Order of completion was counterbalanced, and both questionnaires asked for the same type of event (interpersonal or achievement). Order was unrelated to the results and is not further discussed.

Measures

Features of the events. As in Study 1, ratings of the positive and negative emotion elicited by the events were averaged to create indices of positive and negative emotion (Cronbach's α = .92 and .87, respectively). Items assessing insight, importance, and self-revealingness were moderately intercorrelated (.63 < rs > .37, ps < .05) and were averaged to create two indices of event salience, one for disclosed (Cronbach's α = .65) and one for undisclosed events (Cronbach's α = .79). Reports of the time of the event were converted to indicate how long ago, in years, the event occurred.

Features of the narratives. LIWC analyses of participants' narratives yielded the same variables used in Study 1.

Speaker's motives during retelling. Single-item ratings of the extent to which participants told about the event in order to entertain others, share information, or better understand the meaning of the experience served as measures of goals.

Results and discussion

Preliminary analyses: Do disclosed and non-disclosed events differ?

Means and standard deviations for all variables as a function of disclosure status are shown in Table 2. In this study, narratives for previously undisclosed events involved fewer words, M $(SD) = 130.2$ (101.5), than did narratives for previously disclosed events, M $(SD) = 153.6$ (98.3), $F(1, 110) = 4.3$, $p < .04$, $\eta^2 = .04$. This difference does not affect the results below, but does suggest more detailed narratives for previously disclosed events. We examined differences between disclosed and non-disclosed events across the three different event-type conditions (interpersonal, achievement, unspecified) for positive emotion, negative emotion, salience, and the age of the event using a multivariate repeated measures analysis of variance. There were no interactions of event-type and disclosure, $F(8, 196) = 1.3$, $p = .26$, and no overall effects of event-type, $F(8, 196) = 1.7$, $p = .09$.[4] However, differences by disclosure did emerge, $F(4, 97) = 5.6$, $p < .01$, $\eta^2 = .19$. As shown in Table 2, disclosed events, regardless of type, were rated as more emotionally positive and more salient than undisclosed events. Including these two variables as covariates in the analyses did not change any results. Descriptively, participants recalled a wide range of events, from returning items to a store to experiencing child abuse. Most of the experiences were everyday emotional events similar to Study 1.

Do features of participants' narratives differ depending on whether an event is disclosed or undisclosed?

Indicators of distance. A repeated measures MANOVA examined the percentage of other and self-references with disclosure status as a within-subjects factor and event-type as a between-subjects factor. The results indicated a significant overall effect of disclosure, $F(2, 109) = 6.4$, $p < .01$, $\eta^2 = .11$, and no effects or interactions involving the type of event, $Fs(4, 220) < 1.4$, $ps > .20$. As can be seen in Table 2, narratives

of previously disclosed events contained significantly fewer self-references, and descriptively more other references, in comparison to narratives of previously undisclosed events.

A second MANOVA examined past versus present tense as a function of time (past vs present), disclosure status, and event-type (between-subjects). The results revealed a significant main effect of time $F(1, 110) = 146.4$, $p < .001$, $\eta^2 = .57$, because past tense predominates in memory narratives, and a significant interaction of time and status, $F(1, 110) = 6.4$, $p < .01$, $\eta^2 = .06$. As seen in Table 2, disclosed events, compared to undisclosed events, were recalled with significantly more past tense and significantly less present tense.

Certainty. A repeated measures MANOVA examining the percentage of tentative and certain words as a function of disclosure status and event-type revealed no significant effects.

Cognitive elaboration. A repeated measures MANOVA comparing the percentage of causal and insight-related words as a function of disclosure status and event-type yielded no significant effects.

Positivity. A repeated measures MANOVA of positive and negative emotion as a function of disclosure status and event-type revealed a significant interaction of disclosure status and event type, $F(4, 220) = 3.7$, $p < .01$, $\eta^2 = .06$, with no other significant effects, $ps > .3$. Univariate tests suggested the interaction was attributable primarily to differences in positive emotion language, $F(2, 110) = 6.8$, $p < .01$, $\eta^2 = .11$. Simple effects tests examining the impact of disclosure separately within each type of event suggested that disclosure was significantly related to differences in positive emotion for interpersonal events, $p < .03$, and for the control condition, $p < .01$, but not for achievement events, $p > .25$. However, the direction of the difference in these conditions was reversed. For interpersonal events, disclosed events contained lower percentages of positive emotion language, M $(SD) = 1.9$ (1.6), than did non-disclosed events, M $(SD) = 2.8$ (2.3). In contrast, in the control condition, disclosed events contained more positive emotion language, M $(SD) = 2.4$ (1.7), than did non-disclosed events, M $(SD) = 1.5$ (1.7). Descriptively, the achievement condition followed this latter pattern, with disclosed events being narrated with more positive emotion language, M $(SD) = 2.4$

---

[4] This near-significant result is due to differences in the age of the event; events in the control condition were older, M $(SD) = 12.4$ (14.8), than those in the interpersonal, M $(SD) = 6.6$ (12.9) or achievement, M $(SD) = 7.4$ (13.1). All conditions were highly skewed towards recent events.

TABLE 2
Means and SD for all variables by disclosure condition, Study 2

	Disclosed		Undisclosed			
	M	SD	M	SD	F	η^2
Characteristics of events						
Rated positive emotion	3.4	1.9	2.6	1.6	18.2**	.15
Rated negative emotion	3.3	1.6	3.4	1.7	<1	–
Salience	5.8	1.3	5.4	1.6	9.5**	.09
Age of event	7.6	15.0	9.1	14.7	1.2	–
LIWC Indicators Distance						
Self-references	9.9	3.5	11.2	3.1	10.9**	.09
Other-references	5.1	3.4	4.4	3.7	2.1	–
Past	10.4	3.5	9.5	3.8	5.1*	.05
Present	4.7	2.8	5.5	3.7	4.8*	.04
Certainty						
Certain	1.1	1.2	1.0	1.0	<1	–
Tentative	1.7	1.5	2.1	2.2	2.1	–
Positivity						
Positive language	2.2	1.8	2.1	2.0	<1	–
Negative language	1.6	1.7	1.6	1.6	<1	–
Elaboration						
Insight language	1.9	1.6	2.1	1.9	2.8+	.03
Causal language	0.7	1.0	0.8	0.9	< 1	–

$**p < .01$, $*p < .05$, $+p < .10$.

(2.0), than non-disclosed events, M $(SD) = 1.9$ (1.7), though not significantly so.

Disclosure of interpersonal events can involve substantial negative emotion without having negative implications for the speaker—this may have been less true for the events recalled in the achievement condition and the control condition. For interpersonal experiences, people may complain about others, with the negativity retained in subsequent remembering. This would be particularly true for experiences of victimisation (Baumeister, Stilman, & Wotman, 1990), and may in part account for the lack of evidence for a positivity norm in work on memory telling (Skowronski & Walker, 2004). Because this finding requires replication (and is not consistent with Study 1), it is not discussed further.

Can features of later memory be predicted by speaker motives at the initial disclosure?

Pearson's correlations between ratings of the extent to which participants talked about the experience to find meaning, share information, or entertain others, and the LIWC indices, suggested that entertainment goals were not associated with any of the narrative features. Information-sharing goals were associated with

increased causal language, $r(111) = .22$, $p < .05$, and decreased negative emotion language, $r(111) = -.34$, $p < .05$, while meaning seeking goals were associated with increased insight language, $r(113) = .19, p < .05$.[5,6]

---

[5] Controlling for the age of the event decreased the magnitude of the latter correlation, $r(112) = .17$, $p < .08$, but resulted in no other changes to the findings; controlling for the initial positive and negative emotions elicited by an event resulted in no changes.

[6] In Study 1, participants in the "disclosed" condition were divided into four groups based on their reported disclosure goals: meaning seeking $(n = 5)$, information sharing $(n = 3)$, entertain $(n = 9)$, and other $(n = 21)$. Using a lenient alpha criterion of .10, there were no effects of disclosure goal on egocentricity, temporal distance, certainty, or emotional language. However, disclosure goal was associated with causal and insight language, $F(6, 68) = 2.6$, $p < .03$, $\eta^2 = .19$. Univariate tests suggested that this was primarily due to insight language, $F(3, 34) = 2.4$, $p < .10$. Post-hoc contrasts showed that memories of events shared for information-sharing, M $(SD) = 3.0$ (1.8), and meaning-seeking goals, M $(SD) = 3.4$ (2.6), had significantly more insight language than did those shared for entertainment purposes, M $(SD) = 1.3$ (1.3), $p < .03$. Participants endorsing miscellaneous other goals had intermediate levels of insight language, M $(SD) = 1.5$ (1.6).

GENERAL DISCUSSION

Across two different studies involving different populations and research designs, the language used for autobiographical narratives differed significantly based on the disclosure history of the remembered events. Previously disclosed events were recalled with greater use of past tense, and emphasis on other-related pronouns rather than self-related pronouns. These effects were independent of the salience, positivity, or thematic content of the experiences. Further, disclosure for the purpose of finding or sharing meaning was associated with indicators of cognitive elaboration and emotion. These findings support the idea that the remembered self differs depending on whether that remembered self has been previously disclosed or not.

What do differences within the remembered self mean?

The present findings suggest that disclosure in general will reduce the use of highly self-focused and present-oriented language in remembering experiences. These differences suggest that disclosed memories are more integrated into a person's sense of history, and less bound up with current self-views. As such, disclosed parts of the remembered self are less likely to form the basis for intrusive and unwanted thoughts (Conway & Pleydell-Pearce, 2000). Further, the use of highly egocentric and present tense language is linked to neuroticism and suicidality (Pennebaker & King, 1999; Stirman & Pennebaker, 2001), and present tense constructions also relate to more intense affective experience during remembering (Pennebaker & King, 1999; Pillemer, Desrochers, & Ebanks, 1998). Thus, the differences observed here may also relate to well-being.

Disclosure is of real interest in clinical settings, as the majority of therapy clients withhold at least some information in those settings (Farber, 2003; Kelly, 2000). Non-disclosure of personal experiences in therapy involves the unimportant, as well as events that provoke shame and anxiety. Some clinicians have argued that it may be adaptive and beneficial for clients to fail to disclose shameful and anxiety-provoking events (Kelly, 2000), but there is good evidence that clients benefit more when they discuss important events with reasonable thoroughness (Farber, 2003). The present findings can be interpreted to suggest that the disclosure of important and problematic events in therapy benefits patients by rendering those events less intrusive and better integrated into the person's remembered self. It would be interesting to employ longitudinal work to examine changes in language for such memories over the course of their disclosure in the clinical context.

When events were disclosed in the service of seeking meaning, later memory for the events was higher in insight content. Thus, sharing per se did not change the insight content of subsequent memories—rather, sharing for particular reasons did so. Disclosure in the service of sharing information was associated with less negative emotion and increased causal language. This pattern makes sense in light of the "generative" or "transmissive" idea of this motive—when participants seek to share information about an event, they may focus on causal chains to "teach" others, and de-emphasise negative emotion for the same reasons. Because causal and insight language and positive emotion have very clearly established links to health and well-being (Pennebaker, 1997; Pennebaker et al., 1997; Pennebaker & Seagal, 1999; Smyth, 1998), further understanding of contexts that promote or constrain these elements in narrative memories is important. Also, earlier findings by Rimé and Finkenauer (Rimé et al., 1998) suggested that non-disclosed experiences were associated with a greater search for meaning—the present findings suggest that disclosure can help to establish meanings and reduce the intrusiveness of our experiences.

Unpacking prior disclosure to explain disclosure-based differences

Disclosing events entails at least three different features that independently or together may explain the findings. First, there are likely differences in disclosed and undisclosed events. Some of these differences emerged in the present data and did not explain the observed findings, but the data are far from a conclusive account of what kinds of events are, and are not, disclosed (Fivush, 2000). Importantly, all the events in the present studies became disclosed events by virtue of being recalled for the study. Thus, the "sampling" of participants' previously undisclosed experiences was biased in favour of those previously undisclosed experiences that were "tellable". In short, these data are limited in the extent to which they speak to differences in what people tell and do not tell more broadly. This latter issue remains an important one for understanding the remembered self (Fivush, 2000).

The process of disclosing, too, involves at least three different features that are worth further exploration. First, disclosing involves encoding into language, and that alone may result in greater distancing. Writing about events may produce similar effects (Pennebaker & Seagal, 1999) as might imagined telling (Liu & Pasupathi, 2004). Second, disclosure requires people to "relive" the event, which may result in desensitisation. From this view, conversational recall might be very egocentric and involve present tense, but subsequent memories would involve greater distance. This explanation could account for the distance findings, but does not explain the impact of meaning-seeking motives on subsequent insight language. The third possibility is that disclosure to a listener requires particular ways of recalling and serves as a "rehearsal", thus impacting subsequent memories.

The special case of disclosure to a listener

Remembering to others is a fundamental aspect of autobiographical memory (Fivush, 1991; Manier et al., 1996; Nelson, 1992; Norrick, 2000; Pasupathi, 2001). Such remembering is governed by two major principles (Pasupathi, 2001). First, a *principle of co-construction* dictates that recollections in conversation are collaborations between speakers and listeners, including the goals of speakers and the needs of listeners. Second, a *principle of consistency* means that recollections on one occasion influence subsequent recollections through a variety of mechanisms, including rehearsal. Listeners' needs require rememberers to take a less egocentric and more temporally ordered stance on their experiences. The consistency principle then suggests that subsequent recollections of the experiences will be less egocentric and immediate. Similarly, if people are seeking or sharing meaning in talking about their experiences, they are likely to focus on what they have learned or on what the experience meant for them. This focus is again reflected in subsequent recollections in terms of insight language.

Previous findings examining other aspects of memory have shown that storytelling has lasting consequences for the remembered self (Bavelas, Coates, & Johnson, 2000; Dudukovic et al., 2004; Manier et al., 1996; McGregor & Holmes, 1999; Pasupathi, 2002; Pasupathi et al., 1998; Tversky & Marsh, 2000). The current findings extend these results to linguistic features of narrative, in keeping with work on memories of bilingual individuals (Marian & Neisser, 2000; Schrauf & Rubin, 1998, 2000).

Importantly, the present data do not provide an unequivocal test of whether disclosure influences language causally. Relatedly, the assessments of motives for retelling, initial emotions elicited by the event, and other concepts were all retrospective; thus, the observed relationships could arise from concurrent associations. For example, people might use their narrative to infer their responses to the other questions. Prospective and experimental approaches could address many of these limitations in future work, and experimental approaches that contrast different features of the disclosure process (i.e., linguistic encoding, listener-oriented construction) would be especially useful.

In sum, the present findings suggest that the remembered self has different linguistic features depending on whether that remembered self has been previously disclosed to others or not. We may remember our lives to some extent as they happened, but we also remember them differently depending on whether or not we have told others.

REFERENCES

Bartlett, F. C. (1932/1995). *Remembering: A study in experimental and social psychology*. Cambridge, UK: Cambridge University Press.
Baumeister, R. F., & Newman, L. S. (1994). How stories make sense of personal experiences: Motives that shape autobiographical narratives. *Personality and Social Psychology Bulletin, 20*(6), 676–690.
Baumeister, R. F., Stilman, A., & Wotman, S. R. (1990). Victim and perpetrator accounts of interpersonal conflict: Autobiographical narratives about anger. *Journal of Personality and Social Psychology, 59*, 994–1005.
Bavelas, J. B., Coates, L., & Johnson, T. (2000). Listeners as co-narrators. *Journal of Personality and Social Psychology, 79*, 941–952.
Bluck, S., Levine, L. J., & Laulhere, T. M. (1999). Autobiographical remembering and hypermnesia: A

comparison of older and younger adults. *Psychology and Aging*, *14*, 671–682.

Clark, H. H. (1996). *Using language*. Cambridge, MA: Cambridge University Press.

Conway, M. A., & Pleydell-Pearce, C. W. (2000). The construction of autobiographical memories in the self-memory system. *Psychological Review*, *107*(2), 261–288.

Dickinson, C., & Givon, T. (1995). Memory and conversation: Toward an experimental paradigm. In T. Givon (Ed.), *Conversation: Cognitive, communicative, and social perspectives* (pp. 91–132). Amsterdam: John Benjamins.

Dudukovic, N. M., Marsh, E. J., & Tversky, B. (2004). Telling a story or telling it straight: The effects of entertaining versus accurate retellings on memory. *Journal of Applied Cognitive Psychology*, *18*, 125–143.

Edwards, D., & Middleton, D. (1986). Joint remembering: Constructing an account of shared experience through conversational discourse. *Discourse Processes*, *9*, 423–459.

Edwards, D., & Middleton, D. (1988). Conversational remembering and family relationships: How children learn to remember. *Journal of Social and Personal Relationships*, *5*, 3–25.

Farber, B. A. (2003). Patient self-disclosure: A review of the research. *Journal of Clinical Psychology*, *59*, 589–600.

Finkenauer, C., & Rimé, B. (1998). Socially shared emotional experiences vs. emotional experiences kept secret: Differential characteristics and consequences. *Journal of Social & Clinical Psychology*, *17*(3), 295–318.

Fivush, R. (1991). The social construction of personal narratives. *Merrill-Palmer Quarterly*, *37*, 59–82.

Fivush, R. (2000). Accuracy, authority, and voice: Feminist perspectives on autobiographical memory. In P. H. Miller & E. Kofsky Scholnick (Eds.), *Toward a feminist developmental psychology* (pp. 85–105). Florence, KY: Taylor & Francis/Routledge.

Gould, O. N., & Dixon, R. A. (1993). How we spent our vacation: Collaborative storytelling by young and old adults. *Psychology and Aging*, *8*, 10–17.

Greenwald, A. G. (1980). The totalitarian ego: Fabrication and revision of personal history. *American Psychologist*, *35*, 603–618.

Grice, H. P. (1957). Meaning. *Philosophical Review*, *66*, 377–388.

Hirst, W., Manier, D., & Apetroaia, I. (1997). The social construction of the remembered self: Family recounting. In J. G. Snodgrass & R. C. Thompson (Eds.), *The self across psychology* (pp. 163–188). New York: New York Academy of Sciences.

Hooker, K., & McAdams, D. P. (2003). Personality reconsidered: A new agenda for aging research. *Journals of Gerontology: Psychological Sciences*, *58*B, P296–P304.

Hyman, I. E. (1994). Conversational remembering: Story recall with a peer versus for an experimenter. *Applied Cognitive Psychology*, *8*, 49–66.

Hyman, I. E., & Faries, J. M. (1992). The functions of autobiographical memory. In M. A. Conway, D. C.

Rubin, H. Spinnler, & W. A. Wagenaar (Eds.), *Theoretical perspectives on autobiographical memory* (pp. 207–221). Dordrecht, The Netherlands: Kluwer Academic Publishers.

Kelly, A. E. (2000). Helping construct desirable identities: A self-presentational view of psychotherapy. *Psychological Bulletin*, *126*(4), 475–494.

Liu, T., & Pasupathi, M. (2004). *Imagined conversations: Introducing a phenomenon*. Salt Lake City, UT: University of Utah.

Manier, D., Pinner, E., & Hirst, W. (1996). Conversational remembering. In D. Hermann, C. McEvoy, C. Hertzog, A. Hertel, & M. K. Johnson (Eds.), *Basic and applied memory research* (Vol. 2, pp. 269–286). Mahwah, NJ: Lawrence Erlbaum Associates, Inc.

Marian, V., & Neisser, U. (2000). Language-dependent recall of autobiographical memories. *Journal of Experimental Psychology: General*, *129*(3), 361–368.

Marsh, E. J., & Tversky, B. (2004). Spinning the stories of our lives. *Journal of Applied Cognitive Psychology*, *18*, 491–505.

McAdams, D. P. (1996). Personality, modernity, and the storied self: A contemporary framework for studying persons. *Psychological Inquiry*, *7*, 295–321.

McAdams, D. P., Diamond, A., de St. Aubin, E., & Mansfield, E. (1997). Stories of commitment: The psychosocial construction of generative lives. *Journal of Personality and Social Psychology*, *72*, 678–694.

McAdams, D. P., Hoffman, B. J., Mansfield, E. D., & Day, R. (1996). Themes of agency and communion in significant autobiographical scenes. *Journal of Personality*, *64*, 339–377.

McGregor, I., & Holmes, J. G. (1999). How storytelling shapes memory and impressions of relationship events over time. *Journal of Personality and Social Psychology*, *76*, 403–419.

McLean, K. C. (2005). Late adolescent identity development: Narrative meaning-making and memory telling. *Developmental Psychology*, *41*, 683–691.

Moffitt, K. H., & Singer, J. A. (1994). Continuity in the life story: Self-defining memories, affect, and approach/avoidance personal strivings. *Journal of Personality*, *62*, 21–43.

Murray, E. J., Lamnin, A. D., & Carver, C. S. (1989). Emotional expression in written essays and psychotherapy. *Journal of Social and Clinical Psychology*, *8*, 414–427.

Murray, E. J., & Segal, D. L. (1994). Emotional processing in vocal and written expression of feelings about traumatic experiences. *Journal of Traumatic Stress*, *7*(3), 391–405.

Neisser, U. (1988). Five kinds of self-knowledge. *Philosophical Psychology*, *1*, 35–59.

Nelson, K. (1992). Emergence of autobiographical memory at age 4. *Human Development*, *35*, 172–177.

Norrick, N. R. (1997). Twice-told tales: Collaborative narration of familiar stories. *Language in Society*, *26*, 199–220.

Norrick, N. R. (2000). *Conversational narrative: Storytelling in everyday talk*. Amsterdam: John Benjamins BV.

Pasupathi, M. (2001). The social construction of the personal past and its implications for adult development. *Psychological Bulletin, 127*, 651–672.

Pasupathi, M. (2002). *Effects of prior disclosure on memory consistency over a 3-month period*. Unpublished manuscript, University of Utah, Salt Lake City, UT, USA.

Pasupathi, M. (2003). Social remembering for emotion regulation: Differences between emotions elicited during an event and emotions elicited when talking about it. *Memory, 11*, 151–163.

Pasupathi, M., & Carstensen, L. L. (2003). Age and emotion during mutual reminiscing. *Psychology and Aging, 18*, 430–442.

Pasupathi, M., Henry, R., & Carstensen, L. L. (2002). Age and ethnicity differences in storytelling to young children: Emotionality, relationality, and socialization. *Psychology and Aging, 17*, 610–621.

Pasupathi, M., Lucas, S., & Coombs, A. (2002). Functions of autobiographical memory in discourse: Long-married couples talk about conflicts and pleasant topics. *Discourse Processes, 34*, 163–192.

Pasupathi, M., Stallworth, L. M., & Murdoch, K. (1998). How what we tell becomes what we know: Listener effects on speakers' long-term memory for events. *Discourse Processes, 26*, 1–25.

Pennebaker, J. W. (1997). Writing about emotional experiences as a therapeutic process. *American Psychological Society, 8*(3), 162–166.

Pennebaker, J. W., & Francis, M. E. (1999). *Linguistic inquiry and word count* [computer software]. Mahwah, NJ: Lawrence Erlbaum Associates, Inc.

Pennebaker, J. W., & Graybeal, A. (2001). Patterns of natural language use: disclosure, personality, and social integration. *Current Directions in Psychological Science, 10*, 90–93.

Pennebaker, J. W., & Keough, K. (1999). Revealing, organizing, and reorganizing the self in response to stress and emotion. In R. J. Contrada & R. D. Ashmore (Eds.), *Self, social identity, and physical health: Interdisciplinary explorations* (Vol. 2, pp. 101–121). Oxford, UK: Oxford University Press.

Pennebaker, J. W., & King, L. A. (1999). Linguistic styles: Language use as an individual difference. *Journal of Personality and Social Psychology, 77*, 1296–1312.

Pennebaker, J. W., Mayne, T. J., & Francis, M. E. (1997). Linguistic predictors of adaptive bereavement. *Journal of Personality and Social Psychology, 72*, 863–871.

Pennebaker, J. W., & Seagal, J. (1999). Forming a story: The health benefits of narrative. *Journal of Clinical Psychology, 55*, 1243–1254.

Pillemer, D. B. (1998). *Momentous events, vivid memories: How unforgettable moments help us understand the meaning of our lives*. Cambridge, MA: Harvard University Press.

Pillemer, D. B., Desrochers, A. B., & Ebanks, C. M. (1998). Remembering the past in the present: Verb tense shifts in autobiographical memory narratives. In C. P. Thompson, D. J. Herrmann, D. Bruce, J. D. Read, D. G. Payne & M. P. Toglia (Eds.), *Autobiographical memory: Theoretical and applied perspectives*. Mahwah, NJ: Lawrence Erlbaum Associates, Inc.

Rimé, B., Finkenauer, C., Luminet, O., Zech, E., & Phillipot, P. (1998). Social sharing of emotion: New evidence and new questions. *European Review of Social Psychology, 9*, 145–189.

Rimé, B., Phillipot, P., Boca, S., & Mesquita, B. (1992). Long-lasting cognitive and social consequences of emotion: Social sharing and rumination. In W. Stroebe & M. Hewstone (Eds.), *European review of social psychology* (Vol. 3, pp. 225–258). New York: John Wiley & Sons.

Ross, M. (1997). Validating memories. In N. L. Stein, P. A. Ornstein, B. Tversky, & C. Brainerd (Eds.), *Memory for everyday and emotional events* (pp. 49–81). Mahwah, NJ: Lawrence Erlbaum Associates, Inc.

Ross, M., & Holmberg, D. (1990). Recounting the past: Gender differences in the recall of events in the history of a close relationship. In J. M. Olson & M. P. Zanna (Eds.), *Self-inference processes: The Ontario symposium* (Vol. 6, pp. 135–152). Hillsdale, NJ: Lawrence Erlbaum Associates, Inc.

Ross, M., & Wilson, A. E. (2002). It feels like yesterday: Self-esteem, valence of personal past experiences, and judgments of subjective distance. *Journal of Personality and Social Psychology, 82*(5), 792–803.

Schank, R. C., & Abelson, R. P. (1995). Knowledge and memory: The real story. *Advances in Social Cognition, 8*, 1–86.

Schrauf, R. W., & Rubin, D. C. (1998). Bilingual autobiographical memory in older adult immigrants: A test of cognitive explanations of the reminiscence bump and the linguistic encoding of memories. *Journal of Memory and Language, 39*, 437–457.

Schrauf, R. W., & Rubin, D. C. (2000). Internal languages of retrieval: The bilingual encoding of memories for the personal past. *Memory and Cognition, 28*, 616–623.

Singer, J. A. (2004). Narrative identity and meaning making across the adult lifespan: An introduction. *Journal of Personality, 72*, 437–459.

Skowronski, J. J., Gibbons, J. A., Vogl, R. J., & Walker, W. R. (2004). The effect of social disclosure on the intensity of affect provoked by autobiographical memories. *Self and Identity, 5*, 285–309.

Skowronski, J. J., & Walker, W. R. (2004). How describing autobiographical events can affect autobiographical memories. *Social Cognition, 22*, 555–590.

Smyth, J. M. (1998). Written emotional expression: Effect sizes, outcome types, and moderating variables. *Journal of Consulting and Clinical Psychology, 66*(1), 174–184.

Stirman, S. W., & Pennebaker, J. W. (2001). Word use in the poetry of suicidal and non-suicidal poets. *Psychosomatic Medicine, 63*, 517–522.

Thorne, A. (2000). Personal memory telling and personality development. *Personality and Social Psychology Review*, *4*(1), 45–56.

Thorne, A., McLean, K. C., & Lawrence, A. M. (2004). When remembering is not enough: Reflecting on self-defining memories in late adolescence. *Journal of Personality*, *72*, 513–541.

Tversky, B., & Marsh, E. J. (2000). Biased retellings of events yield biased memories. *Cognitive Psychology*, *40*(1), 1–38.

Webster, J. D., & McCall, M. E. (1999). Reminiscence functions across adulthood: A replication and extension. *Journal of Adult Development*, *6*, 73–85.

Weldon, M. S. (2000). Remembering as a social process. In D. L. Medin (Ed.), *Psychology of learning and motivation* (Vol. 40, pp. 67–120). San Diego, CA: Academic Press.

Weldon, M. S., & Bellinger, K. D. (1997). Collective memory: Collaborative and individual processes in remembering. *Journal of Experimental Psychology: Learning, Memory, and Cognition*, *23*, 1160–1175.

Wilson, A. E., & Ross, M. (2003). The identity function of autobiographical memory: Time is on our side. *Memory*, *11*(2), 137–149.

MEMORY, 2007, 15 (3), 271–279

Psychology Press
Taylor & Francis Group

The Trauma Memory Quality Questionnaire: Preliminary development and validation of a measure of trauma memory characteristics for children and adolescents

Richard Meiser-Stedman, Patrick Smith, and William Yule
Institute of Psychiatry, London, UK

Tim Dalgleish
MRC Cognition and Brain Sciences Unit, Cambridge, UK

It has been suggested that post-traumatic stress is related to the nature of an individual's trauma memories. While this hypothesis has received support in adults, few studies have examined this in children and adolescents. This article describes the development and validation of a measure of the nature of children's trauma memories, the Trauma Memory Quality Questionnaire (TMQQ), that might test this hypothesis and be of clinical use. The measure was standardised in two samples, a cross-sectional sample of non-clinic referred secondary school pupils ($n = 254$), and a sample participating in a prospective study of children and adolescents who had attended a hospital Accident and Emergency department following an assault or a road traffic accident ($n = 106$). The TMQQ was found to possess good internal consistency, criterion validity, and construct validity, but test–retest reliability has yet to be established.

Cognitive theories of post-traumatic stress disorder (Brewin, Dalgleish, & Joseph, 1996; Ehlers & Clark, 2000) propose that the phenomenological quality of an individual's autobiographical memories of a traumatic event plays a significant role in whether or not the individual goes on to develop the disorder. For example, Ehlers and Clark (2000) have argued that the characteristic re-experiencing symptoms of PTSD (e.g., nightmares, intrusive images, flashbacks, and so on; American Psychiatric Association, 1994) are attributable to the memories of a traumatic event: (a) being poorly elaborated and inadequately integrated into the autobiographical memory database; and (b) containing strong stimulus–stimulus and stimulus–response links that facilitate the elicitation of emotional responses redolent of those experienced at the time of the trauma (see also Foa, Steketee, & Rothbaum, 1989).

Brewin and colleagues (Brewin, 2001; Brewin et al., 1996) have taken a slightly different line in attributing importance to neuroscientific data indicating that memory for emotional events may be represented across separable brain regions. In line with this, they have drawn a distinction between situationally accessible memories (SAMs) and verbally accessible memories (VAMs). SAMs encode different sensory, physiological, and motor aspects of the traumatic

Address correspondence to: Richard Meiser-Stedman, Department of Psychology (P078), Institute of Psychiatry, De Crespigny Park, London, SE5 8AF, UK. E-mail: r.meiser-stedman@iop.kcl.ac.uk

The study was undertaken while RMS was supported by a research studentship awarded by the MRC. RMS is currently supported by a Peggy Pollak Fellowship, awarded by the Psychiatry Research Trust.

We would like to express our gratitude to all the young people who participated in these studies. We are grateful to Jen Rolfe and to two reviewers for their comments on earlier versions of this manuscript.

experience that, when elicited, lead to the characteristic re-experiencing symptoms of PTSD noted above. Crucially, it is proposed that SAM information is not readily accessible to conscious editing and amendment. In contrast, VAMs are representations of the narrative aspects of the trauma. VAMs, it is argued, can be readily interrogated via introspection, and drive the conscious discourse about the traumatic experience.

The emphasis placed by these two models on the role played by the phenomenological quality of autobiographical memories following trauma has received support from recent studies in adult trauma-exposed samples. Halligan, Michael, Clark, and Ehlers (2003) found that the presence of more disorganised and more perceptual memories predicted PTSD symptoms in a prospective study of adults who had been assaulted. In a subsequent analysis of this same dataset, Michael, Ehlers, Halligan, and Clark (2005) found that intrusive memory *characteristics* were a better predictor of later PTSD symptoms than the simple presence of intrusive memories. Convergent data come from a study examining the written narratives of adults with PTSD (Hellawell & Brewin, 2004), where participants noted which sections of their scripts were written while experiencing a flashback, and which sections were written during "normal" autobiographical memory recall. Flashback periods of the narratives were found to comprise more perceptual detail, to make more use of the present tense, and to contain more mentions of death, fear, helplessness, and horror, while non-flashback sections of the narratives made greater mention of secondary emotions such as guilt and anger. Analysis of the narratives given by women engaged in exposure therapy for PTSD following sexual assault showed that trauma narratives comprised less description of actions and dialogue and more thoughts and feelings (in particular attempts to organise the narrative) as treatment proceeded (Foa, Molnar, & Cashman, 1995).

Despite this intriguing initial research in adults, very little research has examined the phenomenology of trauma memories in children and adolescents and the relationship to PTSD. Studies of sexually abused children (Burgess, Hartman, & Baker, 1995) and of young children involved in an earthquake (Azarian, Lipsitt, Miller, & Skriptchenko-Gregorian, 1999) have suggested that there is some variability in the phenomenology of children's memories of trauma (with both verbal and non-verbal memories being reported). However, neither study has sought to examine whether memory quality is related to frequency of PTSD symptoms. Indeed, to our knowledge only one study (Stallard, 2003) has examined this issue. Stallard found that the presence of incomplete memories of the trauma did not differentiate between children with or without PTSD. However, the problems regarding the interpretation of null findings combined with an absence of well-validated measures of memory quality in this study suggest that these data cannot rule out the possibility that memory quality is significantly involved in the aetiology of child PTSD.

The present study therefore details the preliminary evaluation of a novel measure of trauma memory quality (the Trauma Memory Quality Questionnaire; TMQQ) suitable for use with children and adolescents, and, in the process, examines its relationship to PTSD and PTSD symptomatology. As well as allowing examination of cognitive theory in PTSD, it was anticipated that such a measure would be of clinical use in identifying which aspects of a child's memories merit therapeutic attention. The ability to measure session-by-session changes in the quality of a child's memories of a traumatic event would be helpful in assessing whether the memory-focused element of a psychological treatment (e.g., trauma-focused cognitive-behaviour therapy) was effective.

The initial development of the TMQQ utilised two child and adolescent samples. The first comprised a non-clinical sample recruited from secondary schools, while the second comprised youths exposed to assaults or road traffic accidents, who had attended a hospital Accident and Emergency (A&E) department. In addition to completing the TMQQ, participants in each sample completed a self-report measure of PTSD symptoms, while children and adolescents in the A&E sample also completed a structured interview assessing for Acute Stress Disorder (ASD) and PTSD. We predicted that scores on our memory questionnaire corresponding to more sensory-based and poorly verbalised memories would be related to greater PTSD symptoms. Furthermore, we predicted that greater scores on our measure would be correlated with stronger emotion experienced at the time of the trauma or frightening event.

METHOD

Participants

Participants were drawn from two sources. Sample 1 comprised children and adolescents recruited from two secondary schools in England, who were taking part in a study examining different aspects of children's responses to the most frightening event they had recently experienced. Of 433 children invited to participate in the study, 254 (58.7%) agreed. The sample contained 146 (57.5%) females, and had an age range of 11–18 years (mean = 14.5, standard deviation = 2.2). Participants in this sample reported experiencing a wide range of frightening events, including road traffic accidents, the illness or injury of a close friend or family member, bereavement, being attacked or pursued by a stranger, and bullying, among others.

Sample 2 comprised children and adolescents who participated in a study of PTSD in youth, who had attended an Accident and Emergency department in London following an assault or road traffic accident. Of 343 consecutive attendees at the department, 106 (30.9%) consented to participate in the study at a 2–4 week assessment. The sample contained 39 (36.8%) females, and had an age range of 11–16 years (mean 14.0, standard deviation = 1.9). A total of 60 (56.6%) participants had been involved in an assault, while 46 (43.4%) participants had been involved in a road traffic accident. Only 50 (47.2%) participants completed a questionnaire battery at 3 months post-trauma, and only 68 (64.1%) completed an assessment at 6 months post-trauma.

Measures

Revised Impact of Event Scale, child version. The child version of the Revised Impact of Event Scale (RIES-C) is an amended form of an adult measure of post-traumatic stress symptoms (Horowitz, Wilner, & Alvarez, 1979). It comprises 13 items and has a three-factor structure (pertaining to re-experiencing, avoidance, and hyperarousal symptoms). Children can respond either "Not at all", "Rarely", "Sometimes", or "Often" to each item, scored 0, 1, 3, and 5 respectively. The RIES-C has good reliability (Smith, Perrin, Dyregrov, & Yule, 2003).

Anxiety Disorders Interview Schedule for DSM-IV: Child and Parent Versions. ASD and PTSD diagnosis was assessed using a structured clinical interview, the Anxiety Disorders Interview Schedule for DSM-IV: Child and Parent Versions (ADIS-C; Silverman & Albano, 1996). The ADIS-C is a structured interview schedule designed for the assessment of anxiety disorders in children and adolescents, where diagnoses are derived from both child and parent reports. The ADIS-C has excellent test–retest reliability (Silverman, Saavedra, & Pina, 2001). The relative maturity of the sample of children and adolescents who participated in the study meant that parent reports were not considered in deriving diagnoses. We added some questions assessing dissociation into the ADIS-C at the first assessment so that a diagnosis of ASD could be made.

Trauma Memory Quality Questionnaire. When first designing this study, no existing multi-item measures of trauma memory quality were available, for adults or children. In devising the Trauma Memory Quality Questionnaire (TMQQ), we created a pool of 14 items that could be easily comprehended by children and easily used in the clinic (i.e., it should not be excessively long). Participants were asked to complete the measure in relation to their memories of the pertinent frightening experience. Face validity for these items was established by following the descriptions of the types of trauma memory that were associated with PTSD given by Ehlers and Clark (2000) and Brewin et al. (1996). The items referred to visual quality, a variety of non-visual sensory qualities (e.g., auditory, olfactory, proprioceptive sensations), temporal context, and the extent to which the memory was in a verbally accessible format. As much as possible, these items were designed to reflect the quality of the memories for a traumatic event, rather than the frequency of such memories. The items did not refer to how trauma memories were elicited, a feature of the PTSD that both Brewin and colleagues and Ehlers and Clark consider. This was because trauma memory cues may relate in part to other aspects of a child's response to a trauma (e.g., the use of avoidant coping strategies) rather than the quality of the memories themselves, and possible difficulties that children may have in remembering when such memories were elicited.

Rather, the items focused on qualities of the memories as they are experienced, or differences between such memories and more "normal", non-trauma-related memories. A list of these items is presented in Table 1. Participants could respond to each item by indicating "Disagree a lot", "Disagree a bit", "Agree a bit", or "Agree a lot", scored 1, 2, 3, or 4 respectively. Some items were reverse scored so that higher scores represented the sorts of memories hypothesised to be associated with greater post-traumatic stress.

Fear. A single item was used to index how scared participants were at the time of the event experienced. This allowed us to investigate whether greater peri-traumatic emotion would be associated with more sensory-based memories, as suggested by cognitive theorists (Brewin et al., 1996; Ehlers & Clark, 2000). Due to other concerns when assessing each sample, slightly different Likert scales were used to rate the participants' fear; in sample 1, a 0–10 scale was provided, while for sample 2 only four responses were available ("Disagree a lot", "Disagree a bit", "Agree a bit", or "Agree a lot", rated 1–4 respectively).

Procedure

Permission to conduct each individual study was granted by the Research Ethics Committee of the lead author's home institution. In addition to the consent of the individual child or adolescent, the opt-in consent of the child's parent or guardian was also required. In sample 1, however, this requirement was amended such that only opt-out consent (i.e., parents had to return a form if they did *not* want their child to participate) was required in order to make it more convenient for children and adolescents to take part.

Participants in sample 1 completed a battery of self-report questionnaires in relation to the most frightening event they had experienced in the preceding 2 months (more detailed findings from this study will be presented elsewhere). The lead author was present in the classroom during the completion of the questionnaires, in addition to a teacher. Participants in sample 2 were assessed at

TABLE 1
Item-total correlations and Cronbach's alpha if item removed for the Trauma Memory Quality Questionnaire

Item	Sample 1 (n =225)		Sample 2 (n =83)	
	Item-total correlation	Cronbach's alpha if removed	Item-total correlation	Cronbach's alpha if removed
1. My memories of the frightening event are mostly pictures or images.	.406	.694	.619	.684
2. When I think about the frightening event it is just like thinking about anything else that has happened to me. (Reverse scored)	.219	.716	−.131	.767
3. I can't seem to put the frightening event into words.	.311	.705	.448	.706
4. When I have memories of what happened I sometimes hear things in my head that I heard during the frightening event.	.481	.682	.550	.691
5. When I remember the frightening event I feel like it is happening right now.	.508	.681	.655	.684
6. When I think about the frightening event I can sometimes smell things that I smelt when the frightening event happened.	.269	.709	.374	.715
7. I can talk about what happened very easily. (Reverse scored)	.305	.706	.312	.721
8. I remember the frightening event as a few moments, and each moment is a picture in my mind.	.427	.691	.540	.694
9. My memories of the frightening event are like a film that plays over and over.	.562	.673	.710	.674
10. My memories of the frightening event are very clear and detailed.	.280	.708	.021	.752
11. Remembering what happened during the frightening event is just like looking at photographs of it in my mind.	.416	.692	.395	.711
12. I can remember the order in which things happened during the frightening event. (Reverse scored)	−.128	.752	−.214	.776
13. When memories come to mind of what happened, I feel my body is in the same position as when the frightening event occurred.	.316	.704	.523	.696
14. My memories of the frightening event feel like memories of other things that have happened to me that aren't very scary. (Reverse scored)	.265	.711	.186	.734

2–4 weeks, 3 months, and 6 months post-trauma. The lead author met with participants, most often in their homes, and conducted a structured interview assessing for ASD (at 2–4 weeks) or PTSD (at 6 months) as well as other emotional disorders. Participants then completed a self-report questionnaire pertaining to the event they had experienced. Participants only completed a self-report questionnaire at the 3-month assessment. The TMQQ and the fear item were only completed at the 2–4 week assessment, while the RIES-C was completed at each assessment. In the event that a participant continued to have PTSD at the 6-month assessment, they were offered referred treatment at the Maudsley Hospital Child Traumatic Stress Clinic.

Data analysis

As the measure comprised relatively few items from the outset, we opted to use principal components analysis and Cronbach's alpha coefficients to remove redundant items, and then evaluate the measure's internal consistency. Criterion validity was assessed in sample 2 by comparing TMQQ scores for participants with and without ASD/PTSD using a t-test, while construct validity was assessed in each sample by calculating correlations with scores on the RIES-C and a single item measure of fear experienced at the time of the event.

RESULTS AND DISCUSSION

Item reduction and internal consistency

Preliminary principal components analyses were performed in order to identify redundant items. In both samples 1 and 2, it appeared that three items (2, 12, and 14) were not loading consistently with other items. However, a clear component structure was not identifiable across the two samples. It was therefore decided to retain a single-factor structure and consider the properties of the individual items and their contribution to the overall measure.

Cronbach's alpha coefficients for the measure if the item was removed and item-total correlations for the 14-item measure are displayed in Table 1. These data suggested that item 12 was a poor contributor to the overall measure in the sample 1 data, while items 2 and 12 appeared to contribute least to the overall measure in the sample 2 data. Table 2 displays the correlations between the individual items and RIES-C scores for each sample. Items 2 and 12 showed the weakest association with PTSD symptoms as assessed by the RIES-C in both sample 1 and sample 2 (at the initial assessment point). Items 2 and 12 were therefore dropped from the measure, as was item 14, which, together with its poor contribution to the principal component analyses, only demonstrated weak item-total correlations and detracted from internal consistency (i.e., the Cronbach's alpha coefficient would improve if this item was removed).

Cronbach's alpha was used to assess the internal consistency for the 11-item TMQQ (see the Appendix for the final version of the measure). For sample 1 this coefficient was .76, while for sample 2 it was .82. These values suggest that the measure possesses satisfactory internal consistency (Cohen, 1960).

Criterion validity

T-tests were used to examine criterion validity for the TMQQ in sample 2. A total of 83 participants completed the ASD assessment and the TMQQ at 2–4 weeks post-trauma, of whom 17 (20.5%) had a diagnosis of ASD. Participants with ASD ($M = 32.00$, $SD = 5.61$) scored significantly higher on the TMQQ than participants without ASD ($M = 23.29$, $SD = 6.99$); $t(81) = 4.75$, $p < .0001$. Of the 55 participants who completed both the TMQQ at 2–4 weeks post-trauma and the 6-month PTSD interview, eight (14.5%) were found to have a diagnosis of PTSD. Participants with PTSD ($M = 30.19$, $SD = 9.64$) were found to score significantly higher on the TMQQ than participants without PTSD ($M = 24.18$, $SD = 7.26$); $t(53) = 2.06$, $p < .05$. While the numbers for the PTSD analysis were quite small, the data for ASD suggest that this measure does possess criterion validity.

Construct validity

In Table 3, correlations between the TMQQ and the RIES-C (and its sub-scales) and trauma-related fear are presented. The TMQQ was significantly and positively correlated with post-traumatic stress symptoms (as assessed by the RIES-C) and the fear items in each sample. This

TABLE 2
Correlations between TMQQ items and RIES-C

TMQQ item	Sample 1 (n = 225)				Sample 2 (2–4 week assessment; n = 83)			
	RIES-C total	RIES-C intrusion	RIES-C avoidance	RIES-C arousal	RIES-C total	RIES-C intrusion	RIES-C avoidance	RIES-C arousal
1.	0.21**	0.27***	0.15*	0.10	0.58***	0.58***	0.38***	0.55***
2.	0.13*	0.15*	0.10	0.08	−0.01	−0.06	0.07	−0.05
3.	0.27***	0.26***	0.18**	0.25***	0.53***	0.48***	0.46***	0.53***
4.	0.40***	0.44***	0.27***	0.30***	0.52***	0.54***	0.36***	0.49***
5.	0.51***	0.47***	0.40***	0.41***	0.66***	0.57***	0.55***	0.61***
6.	0.22***	0.19**	0.12	0.24***	0.33**	0.31**	0.20	0.32**
7.	0.29***	0.23	0.28***	0.18**	0.44***	0.38***	0.47***	0.32***
8.	0.31***	0.32***	0.25***	0.24***	0.53***	0.56***	0.36***	0.46***
9.	0.44***	0.47***	0.29***	0.37***	0.64***	0.64***	0.51***	0.59***
10.	0.22***	0.24***	0.15*	0.17*	0.13	0.16	0.02	0.10
11.	0.26***	0.25***	0.18**	0.22***	0.42***	0.50***	0.31**	0.32**
12.	0.02	−0.02	0.05	0.00	−0.06	−0.11	0.04	−0.05
13.	0.36***	0.31***	0.24***	0.36***	0.51***	0.54***	0.35**	0.42***
14.	0.28***	0.20**	0.25***	0.23***	0.18	0.23*	0.22	0.10

$*p < .05$; $**p < .01$; $***p < .001$.

TABLE 3
Correlations of the TMQQ with RIES-C sub-scales and event-related fear

Sample	Variable	Correlation with TMQQ
Sample 1	Fear rating	.41*** (n =233)
	RIES-C – total score	.59*** (n =224)
	RIES-C – intrusion	.58*** (n =225)
	RIES-C – avoidance	.43*** (n =225)
	RIES-C – arousal	.48*** (n =221)
Sample 2:	Fear rating	.37*** (n =86)
2–4 week	RIES-C – total score	.78*** (n =88)
measures	RIES-C – intrusion	.77*** (n =88)
	RIES-C – avoidance	.59*** (n =88)
	RIES-C – arousal	.69*** (n =84)
Sample 2:	RIES-C – total score	.50** (n =43)
3-month	RIES-C – intrusion	.51*** (n =41)
measures	RIES-C – avoidance	.41** (n =43)
	RIES-C – arousal	.52*** (n =41)
Sample 2:	RIES-C – total score	.54*** (n =57)
6-month	RIES-C – intrusion	.50*** (n =57)
measures	RIES-C – avoidance	.42** (n =57)
	RIES-C – arousal	.54*** (n =57)

RIES-C = Revised Impact of Event Scale, child version; TMQQ = Trauma Memory Quality Questionnaire.
**$p < .01$; ***$p < .001$.

supports the suggestion that the TMQQ possesses construct validity, i.e., the measure was related to PTSD symptomatology and peri-traumatic fear as proposed by cognitive models of PTSD.

Does the TMQQ account for unique variance in post-traumatic stress symptoms over and above that of the re-experiencing symptoms?

One criticism of this measure might be that it is simply assessing the re-experiencing symptoms of ASD/PTSD, as indicated by the strong correlations between the RIES-C intrusion sub-scale and the TMQQ. We assessed this possibility by investigating whether the TMQQ would account for any unique variance in post-traumatic stress as assessed by the RIES-C total score, over and above that of the re-experiencing sub-scale of the RIES-C. We chose this method as it is the most conservative; in other words, we were examining whether the TMQQ accounted for unique variance in a dependent variable over and above a sub-scale of that same dependent variable

In sample 1, both the TMQQ ($\beta = .15$, $t = 3.49$, $p < .002$) and the re-experiencing sub-scale of the RIES-C ($\beta = .76$, $t = 17.78$, $p < .0001$) did indeed account for unique variance in a linear regression model of the RIES-C total score, producing a significant model ($F = 303.93$, $df = 2$, 221, $p < .0001$) that accounted for 73% of variance in the dependent measure. The TMQQ accounted for 1.4% of the total variance that was not associated with the RIES-C intrusion sub-scale. Similarly, the RIES-C intrusion sub-scale accounted for 38.1% of the variance that was not associated with the TMQQ. In sample 2, both the TMQQ ($\beta = .25$, $t = 3.19$, $p < .003$) and the re-experiencing sub-scale ($\beta = .69$, $t = 8.92$, $p < .0001$) again accounted for unique variance in a linear regression model of concurrent RIES-C total scores, producing a significant model ($F = 166.65$, $df = 2$, 83, $p < .0001$) that accounted for 80% of variance in the dependent measure. The TMQQ accounted for 2.4% of the variance not associated with the RIES-C intrusion sub-scale, and the RIES-C intrusion sub-scale accounted for 19.1% of the variance not associated with the TMQQ. As an even more thorough test of whether the TMQQ was measuring the quality of trauma memories rather than just the frequency of such memories, we examined whether the TMQQ explained any unique variance in 6-month RIES-C scores, over and above 2–4 week scores on the RIES-C intrusion sub-scale. The TMQQ failed to account for any unique variance over and above the 2–4 week RIES-C intrusion sub-scale when the 6-month RIES-C total score was used as the dependent variable in a regression model (where R^2 for the overall model was .37, while RIES-C intrusion accounted for 8.2% of unique variance, and the TMQQ accounted for 1.4% of unique variance in the overall model). As a result of the poor response rate at the 3-month assessment point, there were not enough data to perform a similar analysis with RIES-C scores at this assessment as the dependent variable.

Aside from the non-significant model for RIES-C at 6 months (which may be the result of low power), these data suggest that the TMQQ is not simply an index of re-experiencing symptoms, in that along with the considerable shared variance with the RIES-C intrusion sub-scale, it also accounts for unique variance in RIES-C total scores. Furthermore, additional data from sample 1 (Meiser-Stedman, Dalgleish, Yule, & Smith, 2007) has indicated that memory quality accounts for variance in PTSD symptoms over and above intrusive memory frequency, suggesting that this measure is indexing memory *quality* rather than memory *frequency*.

Limitations

While the TMQQ was validated in moderately large samples, sample 1 comprised many non-trauma-exposed children. An additional limitation of this measure is the lack of data concerning test–retest reliability. Further work on this measure is necessary to replicate the relationship with PTSD in other trauma-exposed youth samples, including younger children (i.e., under 10 years). Clearly there would be developmental constraints on which children would be able to complete this measure. This investigation was preliminary, focusing on 10–18-year-olds who would have passed most major cognitive developmental milestones. Younger children may lack the capacity to reflect on the nature of such memories.

CONCLUSIONS

To our knowledge, the measure presented here is the only measure currently available to assess the quality of trauma memories in children and adolescents. We have preliminarily evaluated a brief measure that is comprehensible for children and possesses good face validity, internal consistency, criterion validity, and construct validity. Regression models were used to suggest that the TMQQ is not simply a measure of re-experiencing symptoms.

Our main hypothesis, that responses on our measure reflecting more sensory-based memories would be associated with greater post-traumatic stress, was supported. This suggests that a principal element of recent cognitive models of PTSD in adults, i.e., that the nature of the memories laid down for a trauma is linked to the onset of PTSD symptoms (Brewin et al., 1996; Ehlers & Clark, 2000), can be applied to children and adolescents. An additional hypothesis (that TMQQ scores would be associated with greater peri-traumatic emotion) was also supported, suggesting that fear at the time of a trauma is at least partly responsible for giving rise to these sorts of memories. Given these findings, and despite the limitations noted above, the TMQQ has promise as an index of trauma memory quality that may be used to track clinical improvement and investigate mechanisms involved in the development of PTSD in children and adolescents.

REFERENCES

American Psychiatric Association. (1994). *Diagnostic and Statistical Manual of Mental Disorders (4th Edition)*. Washington DC: American Psychiatric Association.

Azarian, A. G., Lipsitt, L. P., Miller, T. W., & Skriptchenko-Gregorian, V. (1999). Toddlers remember quake trauma. In L. M. Williams & V. L. Banyard (Eds.), *Trauma and memory* (pp. 299–309). Thousand Oaks, CA: Sage.

Brewin, C. R. (2001). A cognitive neuroscience account of post-traumatic stress disorder and its treatment. *Behaviour Research and Therapy, 39*, 373–393.

Brewin, C. R., Dalgleish, T., & Joseph, S. (1996). A dual representation theory of post-traumatic stress disorder. *Psychological Review, 103*, 670–686.

Burgess, A. W., Hartman, C. R., & Baker, T. (1995). Memory presentations of childhood sexual abuse. *Journal of Psychosocial Nursing and Mental Health Services, 33*, 9–16.

Cohen, J. (1960). A coefficient of agreement for nominal scales. *Educational Psychology Measures, 20*, 37–46.

Ehlers, A., & Clark, D. M. (2000). A cognitive model of post-traumatic stress disorder. *Behaviour Research and Therapy, 38*, 319–345.

Foa, E. B., Molnar, C., & Cashman, L. (1995). Change in rape narratives during exposure therapy for post-traumatic stress disorder. *Journal of Traumatic Stress, 8*, 675–690.

Foa, E. B., Steketee, G., & Rothbaum, B. O. (1989). Behavioral/cognitive conceptualizations of post-traumatic stress disorder. *Behavior Therapy, 20*, 155–176.

Halligan, S. L., Michael, T., Clark, D. M., & Ehlers, A. (2003). Post-traumatic stress disorder following assault: The role of cognitive processing, trauma memory, and appraisals. *Journal of Consulting and Clinical Psychology, 71*, 419–431.

Hellawell, S. J., & Brewin, C. R. (2004). A comparison of flashbacks and ordinary autobiographical memories of trauma: Content and language. *Behaviour Research and Therapy, 42*, 1–12.

Horowitz, M., Wilner, N., & Alvarez, W. (1979). The Impact of Event Scale: A measure of subjective stress. *Psychosomatic Medicine, 41*, 209–218.

Meiser-Stedman, R., Dalgleish, T., Yule, W., & Smith, P. (2007). *Intrusive memories and post-traumatic stress in a non-clinical child and adolescent population*. Manuscript submitted for publication.

Michael, T., Ehlers, A., Halligan, S. L., & Clark, D. M. (2005). Unwanted memories of assault: what intrusion characteristics are associated with PTSD? *Behaviour Research and Therapy, 43*, 613–628.

Silverman, W. K., & Albano, A. M. (1996). *Anxiety Disorder Interview Schedule for DSM-IV: Child and Parent Interview Schedule*. San Antonio, TX: The Psychological Corporation.

Silverman, W. K., Saavedra, L. M., & Pina, A. A. (2001). Test–retest reliability of anxiety symptoms and diagnoses with the anxiety disorders interview schedule for DSM-IV: Child and parent versions. *Journal of the American Academy of Child and Adolescent Psychiatry, 40*, 937–944.

Smith, P., Perrin, S., Dyregrov, A., & Yule, W. (2003). Principal components analysis of the impact of event scale with children in war. *Personality and Individual Differences, 34*, 315–322.

Stallard, P. (2003). A retrospective analysis to explore the applicability of the Ehlers and Clark (2000) cognitive model to explain PTSD in children. *Behavioural and Cognitive Psychotherapy, 31*, 337–345.

APPENDIX

The Trauma Memory Quality Questionnaire (TMQQ)

Item

1. My memories of the frightening event are mostly pictures or images.
2. I can't seem to put the frightening event into words.
3. When I have memories of what happened I sometimes hear things in my head that I heard during the frightening event.
4. When I remember the frightening event I feel like it is happening right now.
5. When I think about the frightening event I can sometimes smell things that I smelt when the frightening event happened.
6. I can talk about what happened very easily. [Reverse scored]
7. I remember the frightening event as a few moments, and each moment is a picture in my mind.
8. My memories of the frightening event are like a film that plays over and over.
9. My memories of the frightening event are very clear and detailed.
10. Remembering what happened during the frightening event is just like looking at photographs of it in my mind.
11. When memories come to mind of what happened, I feel my body is in the same position as when the frightening event occurred.

Participants could respond to each item by indicating "Disagree a lot", "Disagree a bit", "Agree a bit", or "Agree a lot", scored 1, 2, 3, or 4 respectively.

MEMORY, 2007, 15 (3), 280–294

Psychology Press
Taylor & Francis Group

Betrayal trauma theory: A critical appraisal

Richard J. McNally

Harvard University, Cambridge, MA, USA

Freyd's (1996) betrayal trauma theory holds that children sexually abused by their caretakers are prone to develop amnesia for their abuse because awareness of abuse would imperil the survival of victims by disrupting their attachment to caretakers on whom they depend for food, shelter, and clothing. The purpose of this article is to provide an empirical and conceptual critique of betrayal trauma theory. Data from studies adduced as supporting the theory have usually been open to alternative interpretations, whereas other studies have failed to provide any support for the theory. Moreover, there is no convincing evidence that children are *incapable* of remembering their abuse—develop genuine *amnesia* for it—shortly after their molestation. Also, even if children abused by caretakers fear disruption of their attachment to the offender, there is no reason to assume that they must develop amnesia for their abuse; they can maintain the relationship merely by failing to disclose their abuse. Finally, a more parsimonious explanation for why some adults may fail to think about their abuse until many years later is provided.

Traditionally, a *traumatic stressor* referred to "a life threatening event" (Jones & Wessely, 2005, p. 213), canonically exemplified by exposure to combat or confinement to a concentration camp (American Psychiatric Association, 1980, p. 236). The authors of the third edition of the *Diagnostic and Statistical Manual of Mental Disorders* (DSM-III; American Psychiatric Association, 1980, p. 236) distinguished traumatic stressors from ordinary stressors, affirming the unique capability of the former to cause post-traumatic stress disorder (PTSD). Although the DSM-IV concept of traumatic stressor still emphasises events that involve threat of death (American Psychiatric Association, 1994, p. 427), the concept has been greatly expanded to include events such as "developmentally inappropriate sexual experiences without threatened or actual violence or injury" (American Psychiatric Association, 1994,

p. 424).[1] Hence, having been fondled by one's stepfather and having survived Auschwitz both now qualify as traumatic stressors, providing that one experienced horror, intense fear, or helplessness during the event. Accordingly, traumatologists now speak of survivors of childhood sexual abuse (CSA) just as they speak of survivors of the Holocaust (La Fontaine, 1998, p. 3).

As behavioural neuroscientists have shown, negative emotional arousal fosters the consolidation and heightens the subsequent accessibility of

---

[1] Given the conceptual bracket creep in the definition of trauma (McNally, 2003a), an increasing number of life events are now deemed to qualify as traumatic stressors (Breslau & Kessler, 2001). Indeed, nearly 90% of American adults now qualify as *trauma survivors* (Breslau, Davis, Andreski, & Peterson, 1991). We are all trauma survivors now, or so it seems.

Address correspondence to: Richard J. McNally, Department of Psychology, Harvard University, 33 Kirkland Street, Cambridge, MA 02138, USA. E-mail: rjm@wjh.harvard.edu

© 2007 Psychology Press, an imprint of the Taylor & Francis Group, an Informa business
http://www.psypress.com/memory   DOI:10.1080/09658210701256506

the emotion-inducing experience (e.g., McGaugh, 2003). Perhaps for this reason, documented traumatic stressors are seldom, if ever, forgotten (Pope, Oliva, & Hudson, 1999). Indeed, for individuals to qualify for PTSD, they must suffer from persistent re-experiencing of the trauma (e.g., intrusive, distressing recollections of the event).

Some theorists, however, argue that CSA differs from traumatic stressors that are remembered all too well. They argue that many CSA victims develop amnesia for their abuse. According to Terr (1991), some youngsters acquire cognitive skills enabling them to dissociate their attention from ongoing abuse. Unable to escape physically from their assailants, they learn to escape mentally, thereby attenuating the negative emotional impact of what is unfolding. Encoding abuse episodes in this manner may result in traumatic dissociative amnesia for their CSA, according to Terr.

Summarising this perspective, Spiegel (1997, p. 6) asserted that "the nature of traumatic dissociative amnesia is such that it is not subject to the same rules of ordinary forgetting: it is more, rather than less, common after repeated episodes; involves strong affect; and is resistant to retrieval through salient cues." That is, the more often one has been abused, and the more terrifying the abuse has been, the *less* likely one will be able to remember having been traumatised, even when one encounters potent reminders of one's victimisation later in life.[2]

Differing in key aspects from the perspective of Terr and Spiegel, Freyd's (1994, 1996) betrayal trauma theory represents another attempt to explain why amnesia is "a natural and inevitable reaction to childhood sexual abuse" (Freyd, 1996,

p. 4).[3] According to Freyd, traumatic experiences vary along two orthogonal dimensions: a life threat dimension, and a social betrayal dimension. Events high on life threat provoke terror, and are highly memorable. Those high on betrayal produce emotional numbing and amnesia for the event. Hence, an earthquake is high on the dimension of life threat, but low on the dimension of betrayal. Sexual abuse by a parent is (usually) low on the dimension of life threat, but high on betrayal. A brutal date rape would be high on both dimensions, whereas events low on both are seldom traumatic.

Most traumatic dissociative amnesia theorists argue that victims develop amnesia for abuse *because* it is so emotionally overpowering (e.g., Brown, Scheflin, & Hammond, 1998, p. 97; Spiegel, 1997) or because repeatedly abused victims have developed finely honed dissociative cognitive avoidance skills (Terr, 1991). While not denying that abuse is extremely emotionally upsetting for victims, Freyd proposes a distinct mechanism to explain why it might be forgotten. Freyd argues that abuse is forgotten when the

---

[2] Spiegel rightly observes that such a phenomenon would run counter to the ordinary rules of remembering and forgetting (e.g., Ebbinghaus, 1885; McGaugh, 2003; Schacter, 1996). First, ordinarily, repetition enhances memory for the class of repeated event. For example, the more often one flies in an aeroplane, the more likely one will remember having flown in aeroplanes. Even though memories of some flights might fade, or memories of some flights might get confused with other ones, one is very unlikely to completely forget that one has flown in aeroplanes. If the frequency of sexual abuse increases the likelihood that one will be unaware of having been abused, then this would, indeed, run counter to the ordinary effect of repetition on memory. Second, strong affect triggered by an event usually heightens its subsequent accessibility; it does not impair it.

[3] Freyd claims that "psychogenic amnesia has been documented for a variety of traumatic experiences" (1996, p. 40), not just those relevant to CSA-related betrayal. For example, she cites Archibald and Tuddenham's (1965) study as showing "veterans' amnesia for their combat experiences" (Freyd, 1996, p. 40). In reality, the "difficulty in memory" reported by 65% of Archibald and Tuddenham's battle-fatigue cases refers not to amnesia for combat, but rather to everyday forgetfulness. Indeed, as they emphasised, these patients "cannot blot out their painful memories" of World War II (Archibald & Tuddenham, 1965, p. 480). This mistake is not unique to Freyd; traumatic dissociative amnesia theorists often seemingly misread the very studies they cite in support of the phenomenon (e.g., Brown et al., 1998; van der Kolk & Fisler, 1995), typically confusing diverse memory impairments, such as everyday forgetfulness, with an inability to remember the trauma itself (for detailed critiques, see McNally, 2003b, pp. 186–228; McNally, 2004). Another common interpretive problem is the DSM-IV PTSD criterion of "inability to remember an important aspect of the trauma" (American Psychiatric Association, 1994, p. 428). As one of the dozen core members of the DSM-IV PTSD committee, I believe that we made a mistake here. This ambiguously worded criterion cannot distinguish between a failure to encode aspects of a traumatic experience and an inability to recall an encoded aspect (i.e., amnesia). Because the mind does not operate like a video recorder, faithfully encoding every aspect of one's life, there is no reason to expect "complete" memories of any event, traumatic or otherwise. Not only do individuals with PTSD rarely endorse this ambiguous symptom in the first place (Breslau, Reboussin, Anthony, & Storr, 2005), but also the criterion cannot distinguish between encoding failure and inaccessibility, and hence does not constitute unambiguous evidence for (partial) amnesia.

perpetrator is a caretaker on whom the child depends for food, shelter, and clothing. As Freyd, DePrince, and Zurbriggen (2001) emphasised, "victims of abuse may remain unaware of the abuse, not to reduce suffering, but rather to maintain an attachment with a figure vital to survival, development, and thriving" (p. 6). The child is trapped in an untenable situation because the very person who is molesting the child is the same person on whom the child must rely for meeting his or her survival needs. For example, consider an 11-year-old girl who is exposed to repeated sexual molestation by her father, unbeknown to her mother or siblings. By abusing her, her father betrays the fundamental caretaking relationship between parent and child. Yet if the child does not develop amnesia for her ongoing abuse, she is likely to engage in avoidance behaviour that may imperil her relationship with her father and thereby imperil her own survival. Her blocking out memories of the abusive episodes after they occur thereby enables her to behave normally within the family and to avoid rupturing her relationship with her abusive caretaker.

Now one might think that children would be exquisitely sensitive to the betrayal integral to parental sexual abuse. Indeed, the eminent evolutionary psychologist, Cosmides (1989) has provided evidence and arguments to support the claim that human beings have evolved a specialised cognitive module for detecting instances of interpersonal betrayal—a "cheater detector". While endorsing Cosmides' hypothesis, Freyd holds that the operation of the cheater detection module can be overridden by more pressing matters, namely, literal survival. That is, the need to survive by maintaining one's attachment to a vital caretaker, however abusive this caretaker may otherwise be, prevents the victim from being aware of the betrayal. Betrayal trauma theory implies that abuse by noncaretakers should not interfere with the operation of the cheater detection module because awareness of it would not imperil survival. That is, the module remains operative except when overridden by the need to block out abuse by a caretaker.

ORGANISATION OF THE PRESENT REVIEW

The purpose of this article is to provide an empirical and conceptual appraisal of betrayal trauma theory. First, I provide a summary and critique of Freyd's reanalyses of key studies in the field of CSA and memory. Because this field is vast (for a review, see McNally, 2003b), I concentrate on the studies discussed in detail by Freyd (1996). Hence, my review is synoptic, not exhaustive. Second, I turn to work directly inspired by betrayal trauma theory. This work comprises questionnaire studies and experiments, many done by Freyd's research group, and some by mine. Third, I address potential conceptual problems with betrayal trauma theory, and discuss an alternative explanation for why some individuals may fail to think about their abuse for a long period of time, only to recall it years later in adulthood.

EMPIRICAL FINDINGS

Reanalyses of previous studies

In her book on betrayal trauma theory, Freyd (1996) examines in detail three important studies on CSA. Although none was designed to test her theory, she argues that each provides support for it. Freyd reanalysed data from Feldman-Summers and Pope's (1994) questionnaire survey of psychologists' memories of their own childhood abuse. Freyd grouped respondents into those reporting sexual abuse by a relative ($n = 36$) and those reporting sexual abuse by a nonrelative ($n = 43$). Members of the former group were significantly more likely to report having previously forgotten their abuse than were members of the latter group (53% versus 30%; Freyd, 1996, p. 143). Probing the data further, Freyd (1996, p. 145) found that the proportion of respondents reporting having forgotten their abuse for a period of time was greater among the incest survivors (95%) than among those sexually abused by nonrelatives (75%) or among those exposed to physical abuse (58%). Freyd interpreted these results as consistent with betrayal trauma theory.

However, it is unclear whether these data do, in fact, support the theory. Although Freyd grouped perpetrators into relatives versus non-relatives, many incest offenders are unlikely to have been caretakers of the victims. For example, in her landmark community study on incest, Russell (1986/1999, p. 216) found that uncles, brothers, and male first cousins consti-tuted 54% of the perpetrators, whereas fathers (including stepfathers and foster fathers) consti-tuted 24% of the perpetrators.[4] It is impossible to tell whether the incest offenders in Feldman-Summers and Pope's study were caretakers of the victims or whether they were noncaretaker relatives—fathers versus cousins, for example. If Russell's data provide any clue, most of the incest offenders were not caretakers of the victims, and if so, then the data fail to provide evidence in support of betrayal trauma theory. (For a data set on incest offenders to support the theory, victims abused by incestuous caretakers would have to experience amnesia more often than those abused by incestuous noncaretakers.)

Another potential problem is that Feldman-Summers and Pope group "partial amnesia" cases with "total amnesia" cases. Individuals in the latter group reported having totally forgotten that they had been abused, whereas those in the former group reported always having remem-bered being abused, despite also having remem-bered some episodes they had previously forgotten. So, when Freyd revisited these data, the "amnesia group" actually included indivi-duals who had never forgotten having been abused. According to betrayal trauma theory, victims must remain unaware of their abuse, lest this knowledge affect their behaviour in ways that undermine their relationship to the perpetrator. But only *complete* amnesia would safeguard the attachment relationship; partial amnesia see-mingly would not suffice.

---

[4] Interestingly, Russell (1986/1999, p. xxxvi) also remarked that none of the incest survivors in her study ever mentioned having previously forgotten their abuse, despite the lengthy accounts they provided during the interviews. But as Russell also pointed out, her interviewers did not explicitly ask participants whether they had ever forgotten that they had been victims of incest. Russell launched her study in 1977, and the idea that women would actually forget having been victims of incest was seldom entertained back then. The received view, as exemplified by the title of Russell's book, *The Secret Trauma*, was that victims feared *disclosing* their abuse, not that they had forgotten it.

Freyd (1996) also interpreted the findings of Williams's (1994a, 1994b, 1995) classic study on memory for CSA as consistent with betrayal trauma theory. Williams's research team inter-viewed 129 women who had been medically assessed for CSA approximately 17 years earlier. When asked about childhood sexual experiences they might have had, 38% ($n = 49$) of the women did not mention the index CSA event noted in the medical records, but most (33 of 49) mentioned other sexually abusive incidents. However, 16 women denied *ever* having been sexually abused, and 12 who did mention the index event said there had been a time when they had forgotten it. (It is unclear whether these 12 individuals had forgotten all incidents of CSA that they might have experienced or only the index event.)

The 12 women with recovered memories of the index event were younger at the time of the abuse than those who had never forgotten (6.5 years old versus 9.5 years old; Williams, 1995), and they were less likely to have been exposed to force during the molestation. Among the recovered memory participants, 25% had been molested by a nuclear family member, in contrast to 11% of those who had never forgotten the index incident (Williams, 1995). If the offenders in the nuclear family were fathers or stepfathers, not brothers, then this would be consistent with betrayal trauma theory.

Freyd (1996, pp. 151–153) interpreted the work of the sociologist Catherine Cameron (1994, 1996) as supportive of betrayal trauma theory. Cameron recruited her participants by contacting therapists who treat women seeking help for CSA-related psychological problems. Freyd was able to classify perpetrators according to parental status, clearly an improvement over a relative versus nonrelative taxonomy. A total of 21 patients in the "total amnesia" group cited parental perpetrators, whereas 8 in the "nonam-nesic" group did so. In the "amnesic" group, 3 patients cited nonparental perpetrators, and 13 in the "nonamnesic" group did so. Freyd (1996) interpreted these data as support for betrayal trauma theory's prediction that "sexual abuse by a trusted caregiver is the most likely sort of abuse to lead to amnesia" (Freyd, 1996, p. 153).

However, there are several potential limita-tions of Cameron's study. First, 10% of her cases reported ritualistic abuse. Reports of ritualistic abuse (aka satanic ritual abuse, cult abuse) raise a red flag about the authenticity of the memories; despite extensive investigation, the FBI failed to uncover any convincing evidence of these crimes (for a review of this controversy, see McNally, 2003b, pp. 234–256).[5] Second, Cameron's "amnesic" patients reported repeated, violent abuse, often lasting from preschool through most of the elementary school years. Yet as Parker and Parker (1986) stated, "intrafamilial child sexual abuse is generally not accompanied by physical abuse" (p. 533). Accordingly, reports of violent incest, entirely forgotten for years, are especially surprising. Third, "amnesic" patients often implicated their mothers as abusers as well as their fathers. But fathers (especially stepfathers; Parker & Parker, 1986) are far more likely to abuse their children sexually than are mothers. Indeed, in her large community study of incest victims, Russell (1986/1999) uncovered only *one* case of a maternal perpetrator (p. 216). It is very difficult to verify abuse reports, especially those of psychotherapy patients who report having recovered many episodes of incest after having forgotten all of it for years. Nevertheless, our confidence in Cameron's data would be stronger if she were able to obtain such verification.

Freyd (1996) also examined a study of women enrolled in a substance abuse program who reported having been sexually abused as children (Loftus, Polonsky, & Fullilove, 1994). Of those answering the question about the perpetrator's identity ($n = 55$), 13 cited a parent or step-parent. In the entire study group, 10 women reported having totally forgotten their CSA before later recalling it. However, having totally forgotten the abuse was unrelated to whether the offender was a family member. Reclassifying Loftus et al.'s

data, Freyd grouped partial forgetting cases with total forgetting cases, and also distinguished offender types. She found that 40% of those reporting either partial or complete forgetting cited a parent as the perpetrator—a rate higher than other categories (e.g., sibling 25%; 28% stranger; 25% step-parent). Freyd interpreted these data as consistent with betrayal trauma theory. But as mentioned above, it is questionable whether grouping partial forgetters with total forgetters is the best way to test betrayal trauma theory. Partial forgetters have never forgotten they were abused, and this fact would seemingly imperil their relationship with the perpetrator.

In addition to reanalysing the data of others through the lens of betrayal trauma theory, Freyd and her research team have conducted their own studies designed to test hypotheses derived from the theory. Administering a questionnaire to 202 college students, Freyd et al. (2001) found that 77% of them reported having been exposed to physical abuse at least once, and 39% reported having been exposed to sexual abuse at least once. One question queried participants about "memory persistence for the event", and although few reported any memory impairment for their abuse, those who cited a caretaker as the perpetrator of either physical or sexual abuse reported more impairment than did those who cited noncaretakers as perpetrators. The effect held even after Freyd et al. controlled for age at abuse and duration of abuse. While interpreting the data as consistent with betrayal trauma theory, Freyd et al. also acknowledged the study's limitations (e.g., lack of corroboration of the abuse, retrospective assessments of extent of forgetting). An additional limitation is that Freyd et al. did not assess whether participants reporting memory impairment for their abuse had completely forgotten it. Maintenance of the attachment to the perpetrator seemingly would be imperilled, according to betrayal trauma theory, if participants remained aware of *any* of their abuse.

On the other hand, we recently found that adults reporting recovered memories of CSA were no more likely to cite parental perpetrators than were adults reporting that they had never forgotten their abuse (McNally, Perlman, Ristuccia, & Clancy, 2006). Parental perpetrators were cited by 8 of 38 recovered memory participants, and by 18 of 91 continuous memory participants. Parents and step-parents were not significantly more likely to be mentioned as the offenders in the recovered memory group than in

---

[5] Indeed, the FBI's primary investigator first took allegations of ritual abuse very seriously. But after the bureau failed to uncover any credible evidence of these crimes, he concluded that the real question is why certain individuals "are alleging things that don't seem to be true" (Lanning, 1992, p. 146). Ironically, therapists convinced of the reality of ritual abuse cults then began to accuse Lanning himself of being a satanist who had infiltrated the FBI (Lanning, 1992)! A similar investigation in the United Kingdom also failed to uncover convincing evidence of satanic ritual abuse cults (La Fontaine, 1998). Although some therapists continued to maintain that the alleged victims must have been exposed to *some* kind of trauma, even if not by transgenerational, international satanic cults, many of these reports came either from young children whose coerced testimony has long been discredited (Nathan & Snedeker, 1995) or from adult patients whose memories of trauma only began to surface during hypnotic memory retrieval sessions (Acocella, 1999). Some of these patients later retracted their memories of trauma, and successfully sued their therapists for malpractice.

the continuous memory group (21% versus 20%). Our study, too, was limited by retrospective appraisal of forgetting, and by limited independent corroboration of abuse reports. For example, only 19 continuous memory participants and only one recovered memory participant were either able or willing to provide us with the name of an informant who could verify the abuse reports. We interviewed the informants, and in each case the abuse was verified. One additional continuous memory participant furnished a copy of diary entries dating from the time of the abuse, which we regarded as corroboration. On the other hand, unlike Freyd et al. (2001), we conducted in-depth interviews with our participants rather than administering questionnaires to assess abuse.

It is unclear why Freyd et al. (2001) obtained data consistent with betrayal trauma theory, whereas McNally et al. (2006) did not. Freyd et al. studied college students who were not explicitly recruited for·abuse history. In contrast, we studied a very diverse (age, ethnicity, social class) group of adults who were explicitly recruited for research on sexual abuse. Another important difference is that our recovered memory participants reported having forgotten *all* of their abuse, not merely certain episodes. In contrast, Freyd et al. (2001) did not distinguish between students who had forgotten some episodes and those who had completely forgotten they had been abused.

Experimental studies

According to DSM-IV, dissociation denotes "A disruption in the usually integrated functions of consciousness, memory, identity, or perception of the environment" (American Psychiatric Association, 1994, p. 766). The tendency to dissociate is commonly measured by the Dissociative Experiences Scale (DES; Bernstein & Putnam, 1986), a questionnaire tapping a diversity of events ranging from "spacing out" during conversations to failing to recognise one's face in the mirror. Some trauma theorists argue that the tendency to dissociate is linked with a history of trauma, especially repeated abuse during childhood (e.g., Terr, 1991). For example, van der Kolk and Kadish (1987) asserted "except when related to brain injury, dissociation always seems to be a response to traumatic life events" (p. 185). If this were true, then therapists would be justified in inferring a history of

trauma among dissociative individuals who report remembering no such history.

As Kihlstrom (1997) has emphasised, van der Kolk and Kadish's assumption is unwarranted. Trauma theorists who have noted a correlation between dissociation symptoms and exposure to traumatic events have failed to examine all four cells in the 2×2 matrix (trauma-exposed vs not exposed to trauma × dissociative symptoms present vs absent). That is, we cannot make any strong inferences about the relation of trauma exposure to dissociation until we have determined the frequency of dissociative symptoms in the absence of trauma, and the frequency of trauma in the absence of dissociative symptoms. Moreover, as one distinguished hypnosis scholar remarked, "dissociation is a creaky and imprecise 19th century metaphor that is much in need of an overhaul. It means too many different things to different people" (Perry, 1999, p. 367). For example, some trauma theorists refer to "dissociative amnesia" and "dissociative flashbacks", yet it is unclear how inability to remember having been traumatised and remembering one's trauma so well that it seems to be occurring once again can both be manifestations of the same dissociative process. Likewise, Holmes et al. (2005) have argued that the term "dissociation" denotes diverse phenomena, and they have made a case for two qualitatively distinct forms of dissociation: detachment (e.g., derealisation) and compartmentalisation (e.g., hysterical or conversion paralysis).[6]

Freyd and her research group have conducted studies on university students who score either high or low on the DES. In principle, psychologists may be keen to know whether dissociation, as measured by the DES, affects attention and memory in various ways. Freyd's interest, though, is theory driven. She holds that the cognitive characteristics of university students scoring high on the DES may illuminate the cognitive characteristics of adults who were sexually abused as children. That is, betrayal trauma theorists regard this work as potentially relevant to their theory because they consider dissociation as a mechan-

---

[6] Ironically, the appearance of Holmes et al.'s thoughtful theoretical analysis notwithstanding, scientific interest in dissociative amnesia seems to have waned. The number of articles on the topic rocketed from 1984 to 1997, but has plummeted sharply since then (Pope, Barry, Bodkin, & Hudson, 2006).

ism that might mediate failure to remember one's abuse, especially abuse by a caretaker.

Investigating the attentional correlates of dissociative tendency, Freyd, Martorello, Alvarado, Hayes, and Christman (1998) had college students scoring either high ($M = 32.50$) or low ($M = 5.56$) on the DES perform a Stroop colour-naming task. Although they did not assess participants for a history of trauma, Freyd et al. (1998) assumed "that our participants with high DES scores were also more likely to have had a trauma history than our participants with low DES scores" (p. S100). In addition to naming the colours of standard Stroop stimuli (e.g., the word *blue* printed in red letters), participants named the colours of XXXXs, words related to space (e.g., *planet*), animals (e.g., *baboon*), kinship (e.g., *dad*), and to the household (e.g., *bedroom*). Freyd et al. included kinship and household categories, suspecting that these might provoke either heightened (i.e., delayed colour naming) or attenuated interference in high-DES participants who may have been exposed to intrafamilial abuse. The basis for these contrasting predictions was that trauma-exposed individuals, especially those suffering from PTSD, take longer to name the words related to their trauma than to name neutral words, positive emotional words, or negative words unrelated to their trauma (e.g., McNally, Kaspi, Riemann, & Zeitlin, 1990; Williams, Mathews, & MacLeod, 1996), or that elevated dissociative tendencies might produce the opposite effect.

The results revealed that high-DES participants, relative to low-DES participants, were significantly slower to name the colours of colour-incongruent words. That is, they exhibited a pronounced classic Stroop effect. Failing to confirm the prediction, kinship words and household words were not associated with differential interference as a function of DES group. Although the authors concluded that heightened dissociative tendencies are associated with diminished ability to control attention, it is unclear whether these data support betrayal trauma theory. Had the data come out in the opposite direction—*better* attentional control in high-DES than in low-DES students—one might argue that this pattern of results confirms the theory. That is, one could just as easily argue that people who score high on the DES might be *better* at controlling their attention than other people because of their putative skill at diverting attention from disturbing stimuli.

Diminished attentional control in high-DES participants, evinced by heightened Stroop interference, occurred in a *selective* attention task (Freyd et al., 1998).[7] That is, despite their efforts to attend selectively to word colour, high-DES participants were disproportionately distracted by word meaning. However, DePrince and Freyd (1999) conjectured that high-DES individuals, under certain conditions, might outperform low-DES individuals on cognitive tasks. Because high-DES individuals, according to DePrince and Freyd, are seasoned at "generalised dual-tasking when attending to information in the world" (1999, p. 449), they ought to exhibit less Stroop interference under divided attention conditions relative to selective attention conditions, and relative to low-DES individuals. Moreover, they also predicted that "high-DES participants would be better able than low-DES participants to dissociate recall of emotionally charged items" (p. 449)—trauma-relevant words on the Stroop task.

In their next experiment, DePrince and Freyd (1999) tested high- and low-DES college students in a Stroop task under either selective or divided attentional conditions. Stimuli appeared one at a time on a computer screen, and participants were told to name the colour of each stimulus while ignoring its meaning. The stimuli were strings of Xs (i.e., nonwords), neutral words (e.g., *brother*, *kitchen*), colour-incongruent words (e.g., *red* in blue ink), colour-congruent words (e.g., *red* in red ink), and "charged" words (e.g., *shame*, *incest*) adopted from previous research on survivors of sexual abuse (McNally, Metzger, Lasko, Clancy, & Pitman, 1998). DePrince and Freyd divided the stimuli into two lists, and participants colour-named one list under selective attention conditions, and another list under divided attention conditions. The selective attention condition involved the standard method: name the colour of each stimulus as quickly and as accurately as possible while ignoring the meaning of the stimulus. The divided attention condition was identical to the former condition except that participants also had to memorise the stimuli for a recall test that followed the Stroop tasks.

---

[7] The mechanism driving the emotional Stroop task remains a topic of lively debate. For example, does its mechanism differ from that underlying the traditional Stroop task (e.g., Algom, Chajut, & Lev, 2004; Chajut, Lev, & Algom, 2005; Dalgleish, 2005)?

The results indicated that participants recalled more words in the divided attention condition than in the selective attention condition, as expected. A significant main effect of word type resulted from participants recalling more charged than neutral words overall, and a significant Word Type × Group interaction resulted from the low-DES group recalling more charged words than did the high-DES group. On the Stroop task, DePrince and Freyd detected a cross-over interaction attributable to high-DES participants exhibiting significantly more interference than low-DES participants for colour-incongruent stimuli under selective attention conditions. Nonsignificant trends emerged for high-DES participants to exhibit less interference than low-DES participants under dual-task conditions, for high-DES participants to exhibit more interference under selective than under dual-task conditions, and for low-DES participants to exhibit more interference under dual-task than under selective attention conditions.

DePrince and Freyd interpreted the trend for high-DES participants to exhibit less Stroop interference than low-DES under divided attention conditions as consistent with their prediction, and they also noted that high-DES participants recalled fewer charged words relative to their low-DES participants. On the other hand, such findings do not provide such strong support for their theory: the first finding was nonsignificant, and relative memory impairment for charged words in the high-DES group was not more pronounced when these participants encoded words under divided relative to selective attention. Moreover, the high-DES participants tended to exhibit nonsignificantly *less* interference than low-DES participants for charged, trauma-relevant words. This runs counter to the emotional Stroop literature: children with documented histories of abuse and who suffer from PTSD exhibit heightened Stroop interference when naming the colours of trauma-related words (Dubner & Motta, 1999).

Studying preschool-age children, Becker-Blease, Freyd, and Pears (2004) tested the hypothesis that certain "traumatised people use divided attention to keep threatening information out of awareness" (p. 114). Parents completed a questionnaire tapping dissociative behaviour (e.g., does the child act like he or she is in a trance?). Each child was shown either neutral or "charged" pictures from a children's book (e.g., Mama Bear pushing a wheelbarrow versus Papa

Bear slamming his fist down on a table as the Brother and Sister Bears look frightened). Under focused attention conditions, the children were shown each picture at a rate of 10 seconds per picture. Under divided attention conditions, they also listened to an audiotape of spoken animal names, and were instructed to squeeze and squeak a toy sheep whenever the word "sheep" occurred. Each child received counterbalanced conditions prior to a recognition memory test for the pictures. The researchers divided the children into high- and low-dissociation groups for some analyses, and divided them into abused and nonabused based on parental report that the child had experienced physical, sexual, or emotional abuse, or had witnessed domestic violence. High dissociators were not more likely than low dissociators to have experienced abuse.

Contrary to Becker-Blease et al.'s (2004) prediction, high-dissociative children, relative to low-dissociative children, did not recall fewer charged than neutral pictures after encoding them under divided versus focused attention. Becker-Blease et al. next compared the memory performance of 30 low-dissociation/nonabused children with that of eight high-dissociation/abused children. Under focused condition, there were no significant effects in the Group × Picture Type analysis. However, under divided attention, the interaction was significant: abused high dissociators recalled more neutral than charged pictures, whereas nonabused low dissociators recalled more charged than neutral pictures—a finding that Becker-Blease et al. interpreted as "consistent with the view that children exposed to abuse develop an attention style that helps keep threatening information out of awareness" (2004, p. 127). But as Becker-Blease et al.'s figure illustrates (2004, p. 127), and the statistics show, the abused dissociators tended ($p < .07$) to recall more pictures overall, charged as well as neutral, than did the nonabused dissociators. Indeed, the abused children tended to recall slightly *more* charged pictures than did the nonabused group.

Extending this line of work, DePrince and Freyd (2001) tested the hypothesis that individuals scoring high on the DES will exhibit superior directed forgetting of trauma words after having encoded these words under divided attention conditions. Their experiment was partly a response to one of our directed forgetting experiments (McNally et al., 1998). In our study, we tested three groups: women who reported CSA and who met criteria for PTSD; women who reported CSA and who were free from psychiatric illness; and women who reported never having been sexually abused. In our experiment, each word appeared one at a time for 2 seconds, and each was followed by a direction either to remember or to forget the word. After this encoding phase, participants attempted to recall all words, regardless of encoding instructions. Contrary to prediction, the PTSD group did not exhibit poor recall for trauma words relative to the other groups, or to positive and neutral words. Indeed, they exhibited recall deficits, but only for positive and neutral words they had been instructed to remember. CSA survivors without psychiatric illness and nonabused control participants recalled words they had been directed to remember better than those they had been directed to forget, irrespective of emotional valence (i.e., either trauma related, positive, or neutral).

Our failure to find memory impairment for trauma words among the CSA groups, according to DePrince and Freyd (2001), might have been attributable to the encoding context. That is, had we had participants encode trauma words under divided attention, we might have observed the predicted effect. Testing this hypothesis, DePrince and Freyd predicted that high-DES college students ought to exhibit impaired recall of trauma words after having encoded them under divided attention. In accordance with prediction, high-DES students recalled fewer trauma words, but more neutral words, after having encoded them under divided attention, whereas low-DES students exhibited the opposite pattern. (For some reason, Freyd et al. did not analyse the data for positive words.) Assuming that heightened proneness to dissociate, as measured by the DES, is linked to a trauma history, Freyd et al. concluded that their findings are consistent with the hypothesis that elevated dissociation scores may signify enhanced ability to keep disturbing material out of awareness, at least when it is encoded under divided attention conditions. However, Freyd et al. did not determine whether their students had histories of trauma, especially abuse by a caretaker, that they had forgotten.

Most recently, DePrince and Freyd (2004) addressed this issue in another directed forgetting experiment. They had participants view blocks of either trauma words or neutral words presented one at a time. Participants received instructions either to remember or forget the block. Under selective encoding instructions, they simply saw black words against the white background of the computer screen. Under divided attention encoding instructions, participants had to press a key on the laptop computer whenever a word—presented for 6 seconds during encoding—changed colour (e.g., red to blue). DePrince and Freyd (2004) found that high-DES college students exhibited recall impairment for trauma (but not neutral) words encoded under divided, but not selective, attentional conditions, relative to low-DES students. Moreover, high-DES students reported more exposure to trauma, including betrayal trauma, than did low-DES students. DePrince and Freyd interpreted these data as consistent with betrayal trauma's claim that dissociation ability helps keep disturbing information out of awareness.

We replicated DePrince and Freyd's (2004) protocol, comparing the directed forgetting performance of participants reporting either recovered or continuous memories of CSA or no history of CSA (McNally, Ristuccia, & Perlman, 2005). Following DePrince and Freyd's method, but in striking contrast to their findings, our recovered memory group did not exhibit superior forgetting of trauma words after having encoded them under divided attention conditions. Indeed, all three groups remembered trauma words more often than neutral words, regardless of encoding conditions.

Although our recovered memory participants reported abuse by various individuals, not only caretakers, their failure to exhibit superior forgetting of trauma cues, especially in view of their history of not having thought about their abuse for many years, seems inconsistent with betrayal trauma theory. Yet our experiment is consistent with other studies: adults reporting having forgotten and then recovering memories of CSA have not exhibited superior forgetting skills for trauma cues in laboratory directed-forgetting paradigms (Geraerts, Smeets, Jelicic, Merckelbach, & van Heerden, 2006; McNally, Clancy, Barrett, & Parker, 2004; McNally, Clancy, & Schacter, 2001). Therefore, mechanisms other than heightened forgetting skill may explain why some people fail to think about their abuse for many years.

These experiments failed to confirm the hypothesis that people who forget and then remember their abuse are characterised by superior ability to block disturbing material out of awareness. However, these studies, too, have their potential limitations. First, betrayal trauma theory predicts that individuals abused by caretakers will be those most likely to forget their abuse, but many of our recovered memory participants were abused by noncaretakers. Second, like Terr (1991), we have conceptualised heightened forgetting capacity as a *skill* that can be applied in the laboratory. That is, if someone has managed to forget autobiographical memories of abuse, surely they ought to be able to forget in the laboratory mere words related to these memories. But this assumption may be incorrect. It is possible that once individuals recover long-lost memories of CSA, they lose this ability to inhibit recollection of abuse-related information. Such material may now be so highly primed that it becomes very difficult to keep at bay. Indeed, nearly one-third of our recovered memory participants now qualify for abuse-related PTSD, a syndrome partly characterised by intrusive memories of trauma (Clancy & McNally, 2006).

As Freyd et al. (2005) have suggested, novel paradigms that differ from traditional directed forgetting methods may reveal the postulated heightened forgetting skills in those who have managed to avoid thinking about their abuse for many years (Anderson & Green, 2001; Anderson et al., 2004; Conway, 2001). Referring to these paradigms, Freyd et al. (2005, p. 501) have said that this research has identified the "Cognitive and neurological mechanisms that may underlie the forgetting of abuse" (but see Kihlstrom, McNally, Loftus, & Pope, 2005). It remains to be seen whether this holds true. The research of Anderson and his colleagues has not involved attempts to forget negative emotional material, let alone in individuals reporting CSA, including recovered memories of CSA. Moreover, the forgetting of material has been far from complete in these studies; about 75% of the words targeted for "repression" are still recalled by participants (Anderson & Green, 2001).

In summary, studies adduced in support of betrayal trauma theory have provided, at best, equivocal support. For example, cases of "partial amnesia" have been grouped with "complete amnesia" even though failure to forget that one has been abused ("partial amnesia") would seemingly imperil the caretaker relationship (Feldman-Summers & Pope, 1995); cases of forgotten incestuous abuse were not confirmed as cases of caretaker abuse (Williams, 1995); or cases not involving these limitations had other problems, such as reported chronic violence by

maternal offenders or satanic cultists (Cameron, 1994, 1996).

Finally, analogue studies on high-DES participants have not yielded consistent support for betrayal trauma theory. And occasionally, it is unclear what the theory actually predicts. For example, in one study Freyd et al. (1998) predicted that words potentially related to intra-familial abuse would either provoke more Stroop interference or less Stroop interference relative to words unrelated to abuse in high-DES participants. As it turns out, neither prediction was upheld. In another study, high-DES participants tended to exhibit less Stroop interference than low-DES participants for trauma-relevant words (DePrince & Freyd, 1999). Yet psychiatrically ill children with confirmed abuse histories exhibit increased interference for trauma words—precisely the opposite pattern to that of DePrince and Freyd's high-DES students. Potentially consistent with the theory, high-DES students exhibit more classic Stroop interference than do low-DES students (Freyd et al., 1998), and they remember fewer trauma-relevant words as well (DePrince & Freyd, 1999), but not more so under divided attention conditions. Enhanced directed forgetting of trauma words encoded under divided attention in high-DES students is consistent with prediction (DePrince & Freyd, 2004), but the effect has not replicated in adults reporting either continuous or recovered memories of CSA (McNally et al., 2005). Most importantly, with one exception (McNally et al., 2005), these high-DES experiments have not involved individuals reporting recovered memories of CSA.

CONCEPTUAL ISSUES

Further empirical tests will be aided by conceptual clarification of apparent ambiguities of betrayal trauma theory. The core postulate states that children abused by caretakers develop "traumatic amnesia" (Freyd, 1996, p. 11) for their abuse, lest awareness of ongoing abuse affect their behaviour in ways that imperil their dependent relationship with their abusive caretaker, thereby endangering the victim's life. There are several problems with this idea. First, it would seemingly require that victims banish memories of abuse from awareness shortly after each molestation episode. Indeed, the longer the memory of the abuse remains accessible to awareness, the greater the likelihood that the victim will alter his or her behaviour, thereby endangering his or her vital relationship to the abuser. Yet negative emotion tends to heighten memory for the emotion-producing experience, and memory tends to be better for recent than for remote events. Accordingly, becoming incapable of remembering abuse that occurred minutes or hours earlier would run counter to the well-established effects of emotion and recency on accessibility of memories. To be sure, the child may endeavour not to think about it, but would the desire to forget translate into an inability to remember?

Nevertheless, Freyd (1996) has discussed a range of possible mechanisms that might figure in "amnesia and memory recovery for childhood sexual abuse and other betrayal traumas" (p. 115). She proposes that "A continuum of possible forms of dissociation underlies this overall phenomenology" (p. 115). The key point, she believes, is that information about the abuse "needs only to be blocked from entering mechanisms that control attachment behaviour" (p. 115). This blockage, in some instances, "may be achieved by dissociating affective information from declarative or episodic knowledge. However, as our control of social interactions often involves consciousness, it is often adaptive for the information to be blocked from consciousness as well" (p. 115). In other words, the child may either be fully aware of the fact of his or her abuse, but not experience negative affect, or the child may be unable to recall the abusive event at all. She also holds that over time a "sort of blockage could very likely produce amnesia for conscious episodic memories but intact sensory and affective memories" (p. 117). Yet interpreting various sensory and emotional phenomena (e.g., spontaneous panic attacks) as "implicit" or "procedural" memories of abuse that are blocked from the person's awareness is an immensely hazardous process, for legal and professional reasons as well as clinical and scientific ones. There is just no solid basis for making these kinds of inferences.

Although writings in betrayal trauma theory suggest that forgetting of abuse is key to survival, it is possible that this motive or mechanism fails to disable the cheater detection module completely. Accordingly, some episodes of abuse are blocked from awareness, whereas others are not. Yet if *any* episodes are available to awareness and not forgotten, then this should imperil

survival. Hence, the concept of a continuum of memory blockage, or dissociation, or unawareness seems inconsistent with the survival imperative that seemingly requires complete blockage of the trauma memories; that is, genuine amnesia.

Second, Freyd assumes that Cosmides' (1989) cheater detection module is overridden by more pressing survival issues. As Freyd (1996) hypothesised, "the ability to detect betrayal may need to be stifled for the greater goal of survival" (p. 10). Indeed, she emphasises, it would be "actually dangerous" (Freyd, 1996, p. 11) for the child not to stifle this ability. All of this implies that Freyd does mean literal survival; "nonphysical" (psychological) survival would be either an oxymoron or a hyperbolic metaphor. If one fails to survive, one dies. But it is unclear how the child would perish. Would the perpetrator murder the child? Would he expose the child to fatal neglect, such as refusing to feed her?[8] Would he evict her from the parental home? How, precisely, would it be "actually dangerous" (Freyd, 1996, p. 11) for the child to know that she is being sexually abused?

Third, there is no reason to suppose that a child must develop amnesia for her abuse in order to maintain her relationship with the caretaker. Indeed, the victim merely needs to keep quiet about the abuse, not forget it, to avoid imperilling her relationship to the abusive caretaker. Public disclosure of the abuse, not accessible memory of the abuse, is what would threaten the relationship. Although a child experiencing ongoing abuse might find it difficult to act normally when a caretaker is sexually exploiting the child, there is no reason to assume that the child must forget the abuse; the child merely needs to avoid disclosing it. And, of course, many children do disclose the abuse, and family reactions range from shocked and supportive to shocked and dismissive.

Fourth, according to betrayal trauma theory, perpetrators ensure that their victims are fed, clothed, and housed properly. Indeed, preservation of this nurturing relationship is precisely why victims are theoretically motivated to block out memories of the caretaker's incestuous beha-

---

[8] For two reasons, I use "he" and "she" to refer to the perpetrator and victim, respectively. First, most perpetrators of CSA are men, and most victims are girls. Second, phrases such as "he or she" or "s/he" to refer to both perpetrators and victims would make these sentences almost unreadably awkward.

viour. But *are* incestuous abusers actually such reliable providers? At least in one study of corroborated father–daughter incest, incestuous fathers provided far less nurturance and caretaking than did a control group of non-abusing fathers (Parker & Parker, 1986). This study raises the possibility that the caretaking relationship may already be imperilled in at least some incestuous families, thereby eliminating the motivation for forgetting of abuse.

Fifth, betrayal trauma theory is designed to explain why someone might develop amnesia for having been sexually abused by a caretaker. But it is unclear whether those who *fail* to think about their abuse for many years were actually *unable* to remember what had happened—yet it is *inability* to remember that counts as amnesia. By repeatedly using the term *amnesia* (e.g., Freyd, 1996, p. 11), Freyd implies a (pathological?) process distinct from ordinary forgetting, absence of retrieval cues, and so forth. *Amnesia* denotes an abnormal, pathological inability to remember, not everyday forgetfulness. Although Freyd also uses the phrases "not knowing" (p. 4) and "not remembering" (p. 4) as apparent synonyms for amnesia, neither phrase implies actual memory blockage. If recovered memory cases do not actually involve amnesia, then betrayal trauma theory would amount to an explanation in search of a (nonexistent?) phenomenon.

ANOTHER EXPLANATION?

There is another explanation for why someone who was sexually molested (including by a caretaker) might not think about the abuse for many years, only to recall it later in life. One need not invoke repression, dissociation, amnesia triggered by betrayal, or memory blockage to explain this phenomenon parsimoniously. First, if the abuse was nonviolent, the chance of it counting as trauma in the original sense of the word—a terror-inciting event—is diminished. Because intense emotion tends to strengthen memory, its absence would be a factor rendering the event less intrusive. As Veldhuis and Freyd (1999) have shown, sex offenders often "groom" victims for abuse rather than terrorise them, and the emotionally bewildering experiences that a young child has with the offender may counteract fear.

Second, if the child were especially young at the time, he or she may have failed to understand the betrayal or its sexual nature until after having recalled the abuse years later, as many of our recovered memory participants have told us (Clancy & McNally, 2006). Older children, however, are far more likely to know what is occurring, but they may be less likely to forget it, too, even though they may dread disclosing the abuse, not for fear of their lives (i.e., survival), but for fear of breaking up the family by causing the offending parent to go to prison. These children may actively try not to think about the abuse, to put it out of mind, and so forth—processes that do not require one to postulate a dissociative mechanism (see Clancy & McNally, 2006, and Williams, 1995, for case examples).

The assumption that an active inhibitory mechanism must be at work stems from the effort to explain why someone would not think about a trauma for so many years. But as Freyd herself has pointed out, sexual abuse often does not trigger terror, and it is intense emotion that makes an experience unlikely to be forgotten. Sexual abuse is always morally reprehensible, but it may not involve terror and life threat, and therefore not count as a trauma in the original, narrow sense of trauma. Sexual abuse by caretakers always involves betrayal, but betrayal per se may have nothing to do with why the abuse was forgotten.

How might one test this alternative explanation for recovered memories of CSA? Ideally, testing this alternative of betrayal trauma theory requires that researchers secure independent confirmation that the abuse actually happened and that memories of the abuse had not come to mind during the long period of time when the victim reportedly had forgotten the abuse. To be sure, these methodological desiderata are often difficult to achieve, especially the second one. At any event, the alternative theory would predict that such instances of abuse would have involved infrequent, nonviolent (e.g., fondling rather than rape) abuse that did not provoke terror in the victim when it occurred. Victims should report a failure to understand the experience as sexual abuse when it was occurring. For the period of forgetting, there should be evidence of absent retrieval cues (e.g., victim moves to another neighbourhood, the perpetrator dies). Conversely, if the offender remains a salient stimulus in the victim's life (e.g., a typical caretaker), then all other things being equal (e.g., frequency of abuse, severity of abuse, age of victim), caretaker abuse should be less likely to be forgotten than noncaretaker abuse—a prediction opposite to that of betrayal trauma theory. Previous research studies relevant to whether victims should be more likely to forget caretaker or noncaretaker abuse (e.g., McNally et al., 2006; Williams, 1994) have too many other variables uncontrolled (e.g., lack of corroboration of either abuse or the forgetting, variability in severity of the abuse). However, to the extent that these confounding variables can be controlled, direct tests of betrayal trauma theory and other theories designed to explain recovered memories of CSA will be possible.

REFERENCES

Acocella, J. (1999). *Creating hysteria: Women and multiple personality disorder*. San Francisco, CA: Jossey-Bass.

Algom, D., Chajut, E., & Lev, S. (2004). A rational look at the emotional Stroop phenomenon: A generic slowdown, not a Stroop effect. *Journal of Experimental Psychology: General, 133*, 323–338.

American Psychiatric Association. (1980). *Diagnostic and statistical manual of mental disorders* (3rd ed.). Washington, DC: APA.

American Psychiatric Association. (1994). *Diagnostic and statistical manual of mental disorders* (4th ed.). Washington, DC: APA.

Anderson, M. C., & Green, C. (2001). Suppressing unwanted memories by executive control. *Nature, 410*, 366–369.

Anderson, M. C., Ochsner, K. N., Kuhl, B., Cooper, J., Robertson, E., Gabrieli, S. W., et al. (2004). Neural systems underlying the suppression of unwanted memories. *Science, 303*, 232–235.

Archibald, H. C., & Tuddenham, R. D. (1965). Persistent stress reaction after combat: A 20-year follow-up. *Archives of General Psychiatry, 12*, 475–481.

Becker-Blease, K. A., Freyd, J. J., & Pears, K. C. (2004). Preschoolers' memory for threatening information depends on trauma history and attentional context: Implications for the development of dissociation. *Journal of Trauma and Dissociation, 5*, 113–131.

Bernstein, E. M., & Putnam, F. W. (1986). Development, reliability, and validity of a dissociation scale. *Journal of Nervous and Mental Disease, 174*, 727–735.

Breslau, N., Davis, G. C., Andreski, P., & Peterson, E. (1991). Traumatic events and post-traumatic stress disorder in an urban population of young adults. *Archives of General Psychiatry, 48*, 216–222.

Breslau, N., & Kessler, R. C. (2001). The stressor criterion in DSM-IV post-traumatic stress disorder: An empirical investigation. *Biological Psychiatry, 50*, 699–704.

Breslau, N., Reboussin, B. A., Anthony, J. C., & Storr, C. L. (2005). The structure of post-traumatic stress disorder: Latent class analysis in 2 community samples. *Archives of General Psychiatry, 62*, 1343–1351.

Brown, D., Scheflin, A. W., & Hammond, D. C. (1998). *Memory, trauma treatment, and the law*. New York: Norton.

Cameron., C. (1994). Women survivors confronting their abusers: Issues, decisions, and outcomes. *Journal of Child Sexual Abuse, 3*, 7–35.

Cameron, C. (1996). Comparing amnesic and nonamnesic survivors of childhood sexual abuse: A longitudinal study. In K. Pezdek & W. P. Banks (Eds.), *The recovered memory/false memory debate* (pp. 41–48). San Diego, CA: Academic Press.

Chajut, E., Lev, S., & Algom, D. (2005). Vicissitudes of a misnomer: Reply to Dalgleish (2005). *Journal of Experimental Psychology: General, 134*, 592–595.

Clancy, S. A., & McNally, R. J. (2006). Who needs repression? Normal memory processes can explain "forgetting" of childhood sexual abuse. *Scientific Review of Mental Health Practice, 4*, 66–73.

Conway, M. A. (2001). Repression revisited. *Nature, 410*, 319–320.

Cosmides, L. (1989). The logic of social exchange: Has natural selection shaped how humans reason? Studies with the Wason selection task. *Cognition, 31*, 187–276.

Dalgleish, T. (2005). Putting some feeling into it – The conceptual and empirical relationships between the classic and emotional Stroop tasks: Comment on Algom, Chajut, and Lev (2004). *Journal of Experimental Psychology: General, 134*, 585–591.

DePrince, A. P., & Freyd, J. J. (1999). Dissociative tendencies, attention, and memory. *Psychological Science, 10*, 449–452.

DePrince, A. P., & Freyd, J. J. (2001). Memory and dissociative tendencies: The roles of attentional context and word meaning in a directed forgetting task. *Journal of Trauma and Dissociation, 2*, 67–82.

DePrince, A. P., & Freyd, J. J. (2004). Forgetting trauma stimuli. *Psychological Science, 15*, 488–492.

Dubner, A. E., & Motta, R. W. (1999). Sexually and physically abused foster care children and post-traumatic stress disorder. *Journal of Consulting and Clinical Psychology, 67*, 367–373.

Ebbinghaus, H. (1913). *Memory: A contribution to experimental psychology* (H. A. Ruger & C. E. Bussenius, trans.). New York: Teachers College, Columbia University. (Original work published 1885.)

Feldman-Summers, S., & Pope, K. S. (1994). The experience of "forgetting" childhood abuse: A national survey of psychologists. *Journal of Consulting and Clinical Psychology, 62*, 636–639.

Freyd, J. J. (1994). Betrayal trauma: Traumatic amnesia as an adaptive response to childhood abuse. *Ethics and Behaviour, 4*, 307–329.

Freyd, J. J. (1996). *Betrayal trauma: The logic of forgetting childhood abuse*. Cambridge, MA: Harvard University Press.

Freyd, J. J., DePrince, A. P., & Zurbriggen, E. L. (2001). Self-reported memory for abuse depends upon victim–perpetrator relationship. *Journal of Trauma and Dissociation, 2*, 5–16.

Freyd, J. J., Martorello, S. R., Alvarado, J. S., Hayes, A. E., & Christman, J. C. (1998). Cognitive environments and dissociative tendencies: Performance on the standard Stroop task for high versus low dissociators. *Applied Cognitive Psychology*, *12*, S91–S103.

Freyd, J. J., Putnam, F. W., Lyon, T. D., Becker-Blease, K. A., Cheit, R. E., Siegel, N. B., et al. (2005). The science of child sexual abuse. *Science*, *308*, 501.

Geraerts, E., Smeets, E., Jelicic, M., Merckelbach, H., & van Heerden, J. (2006). Retrieval inhibition of trauma-related words in women reporting repressed or recovered memories of childhood sexual abuse. *Behaviour Research and Therapy*, *44*, 1129–1136.

Holmes, E. A., Brown, R. J., Mansell, W., Fearon, R. P., Hunter, E. C. M., Frasquilho, F., et al. (2005). Are there two qualitatively distinct forms of dissociation? A review and some clinical implications. *Clinical Psychology Review*, *25*, 1–23.

Jones, E., & Wessely, S. (2005). *Shell shock to PTSD: Military psychiatry from 1900 to the Gulf War*. Hove, UK: Psychology Press.

Kihlstrom, J. F. (1997). Suffering from reminiscences: Exhumed memory, implicit memory, and the return of the repressed. In M. A. Conway (Ed.), *Recovered memories and false memories* (pp. 100–117). Oxford, UK: Oxford University Press.

Kihlstrom, J. F., McNally, R. J., Loftus, E. F., & Pope, H. G. Jr. (2005). The problem of child sex abuse [letter to the editor]. *Science*, *309*, 1182–1183.

La Fontaine, J. S. (1998). *Speak of the devil: Tales of satanic abuse in contemporary England*. Cambridge, UK: Cambridge University Press.

Lanning, K. V. (1992). A law-enforcement perspective on allegations of ritual abuse. In D. K. Sakheim & S. E. Devine (Eds.), *Out of darkness: Exploring satanism and ritual abuse* (pp. 109–146). New York: Lexington Books.

Loftus, E. F., Polonsky, S., & Fullilove, M. T. (1994). Memories of childhood sexual abuse: Remembering and repressing. *Psychology of Women Quarterly*, *18*, 67–84.

McGaugh, J. L. (2003). *Memory and emotion: The making of lasting memories*. New York: Columbia University Press.

McNally, R. J. (2003a). Progress and controversy in the study of post-traumatic stress disorder. *Annual Review of Psychology*, *54*, 229–252.

McNally, R. J. (2003b). *Remembering trauma*. Cambridge, MA: Belknap Press/Harvard University Press.

McNally, R. J. (2004). The science and folklore of traumatic amnesia. *Clinical Psychology: Science and Practice*, *11*, 29–33.

McNally, R. J., Clancy, S. A., Barrett, H. M., & Parker, H. A. (2004). Inhibiting retrieval of trauma cues in adults reporting histories of childhood sexual abuse. *Cognition and Emotion*, *18*, 479–493.

McNally, R. J., Clancy, S. A., & Schacter, D. L. (2001). Directed forgetting of trauma cues in adults reporting repressed or recovered memories of childhood sexual abuse. *Journal of Abnormal Psychology*, *110*, 151–156.

McNally, R. J., Kaspi, S. P., Riemann, B. C., & Zeitlin, S. B. (1990). Selective processing of threat cues in post-traumatic stress disorder. *Journal of Abnormal Psychology*, *99*, 398–402.

McNally, R. J., Metzger, L. J., Lasko, N. B., Clancy, S. A., & Pitman, R. K. (1998). Directed forgetting of trauma cues in adult survivors of childhood sexual abuse with and without post-traumatic stress disorder. *Journal of Abnormal Psychology*, *107*, 596–601.

McNally, R. J., Perlman, C. A., Ristuccia, C. S., & Clancy, S. A. (2006). Clinical characteristics of adults reporting repressed, recovered, or continuous memories of childhood sexual abuse. *Journal of Consulting and Clinical Psychology*, *74*, 237–242.

McNally, R. J., Ristuccia, C. S., & Perlman, C. A. (2005). Forgetting of trauma cues in adults reporting continuous or recovered memories of childhood sexual abuse. *Psychological Science*, *16*, 336–340.

Nathan, D., & Snedeker, M. (1995). *Satan's silence: Ritual abuse and the making of a modern American witch hunt*. New York: Basic Books.

Parker, H., & Parker, S. (1986). Father–daughter sexual abuse: An emerging perspective. *American Journal of Orthopsychiatry*, *56*, 531–549.

Perry, C. (1999). Review of the book *Memory, trauma treatment, and the law*]. *International Journal of Clinical and Experimental Hypnosis*, *47*, 366–374.

Pope, H. G. Jr., Barry, S., Bodkin, A., & Hudson, J. I. (2006). Tracking scientific interest in the dissociative disorders: A study of scientific publication output 1984–2003. *Psychotherapy and Psychosomatics*, *75*, 19–24.

Pope, H. G. Jr., Oliva, P. S., & Hudson, J. I. (1999). Repressed memories: The scientific status. In D. L. Faigman, D. H. Kaye, M. J. Saks, & J. Sanders (Eds.), *Modern scientific testimony: The law and science of expert testimony* (Vol. 1, Pocket part) (pp. 115–155). St. Paul, MN: West Publishing.

Russell, D. E. H. (1999). *The secret trauma: Incest in the lives of girls and women* (2nd ed.). New York: Basic Books. (Original work published in 1986.)

Schacter, D. L. (1996). *Searching for memory: The brain, the mind, and the past*. New York: Basic Books.

Spiegel, D. (1997). Foreword. In D. Spiegel (Ed.), *Repressed memories* (pp. 5–11). Washington, DC: American Psychiatric Press.

Terr, L. C. (1991). Childhood traumas: An outline and overview. *American Journal of Psychiatry*, *148*, 10–20.

van der Kolk, B. A., & Fisler, R. (1995). Dissociation and the fragmentary nature of traumatic memories: Overview and exploratory study. *Journal of Traumatic Stress*, *8*, 505–525.

van der Kolk, B. A., & Kadish, W. (1987). Amnesia, dissociation, and the return of the repressed. In B. A. van der Kolk (Ed.), *Psychological trauma* (pp. 173–190). Washington, DC: American Psychiatric Press.

Veldhuis, C. B., & Freyd, J. J. (1999). Groomed for silence, groomed for betrayal. In M. Rivera (Ed.), *Fragment by fragment: Feminist perspectives on memory and child sexual abuse* (pp. 253–282). Charlottetown, PEI, Canada: Gynergy Books.

Williams, J. M. G., Mathews, A., & MacLeod, C. (1996). The emotional Stroop task and psychopathology. *Psychological Bulletin*, *120*, 3–24.

Williams, L. M. (1994a). Recall of childhood trauma: A prospective study of women's memories of child sexual abuse. *Journal of Consulting and Clinical Psychology*, *62*, 1167–1176.

Williams, L. M. (1994b). What does it mean to forget child sexual abuse? A reply to Loftus, Garry, and Feldman (1994). *Journal of Consulting and Clinical Psychology*, *62*, 1182–1186.

Williams, L. M. (1995). Recovered memories of abuse in women with documented child sexual victimisation histories. *Journal of Traumatic Stress*, *8*, 649–673.

MEMORY, 2007, 15 (3), 295–311

The state of betrayal trauma theory: Reply to McNally—Conceptual issues and future directions

Jennifer J. Freyd
University of Oregon, Eugene, OR, USA

Anne P. DePrince
University of Denver, CO, USA

David H. Gleaves
University of Canterbury, Christchurch, New Zealand

Betrayal trauma theory (Freyd, 1994, 1996, 2001) is an approach to conceptualising trauma that points to the importance of social relationships in understanding post-traumatic outcomes, including reduced recall. We argue in this paper that child sexual abuse very often constitutes a severe betrayal trauma and that it is thus "genuinely traumatic". We will also argue that one reasonably common effect of child sexual abuse—particularly the more it involves betrayal trauma—is some degree of forgetting or "knowledge isolation" about the event. This last claim speaks to the heart of betrayal trauma theory that McNally has summarised and critiqued. In this paper we will respond to aspects of McNally's critique as well as offer our own perspective on the state of betrayal trauma theory. We discuss (1) conceptual issues, (2) critiques of empirical studies, and (3) future directions. Although our interpretation of data diverges from McNally's in many places, we have all arrived at a surprisingly common endpoint. McNally suggests a child may not think about the abuse for several reasons, such as fears that disclosure may break up the family. In accord with betrayal trauma theory, we note that the failure to think about events will contribute to poorer memory for the event and that these processes are mediated by the unique demands placed on a child exposed to betrayal traumas.

The notion that individuals can develop amnesia for seemingly unforgettable traumatic events, followed by "recovery" of these memories months or years later, has been part of the folklore of psychiatry and clinical psychology for more than 100 years . . . Genuinely traumatic events—those experienced at the time as overwhelmingly terrifying and life-threatening—are seldom, if ever, truly forgotten.
(Kihlstrom, McNally, Loftus, & Pope, 2005, pp. 1182–1183)

What is a "genuinely traumatic event"? Is child sexual abuse genuinely traumatic? McNally (2007, this issue) opens his contribution by suggesting that all traumas are not created equal. We certainly agree with this claim (see Freyd, 2001, as traumas can differ along several dimensions (see Figure 1). However, when McNally refers to the "the conceptual bracket creep in the definition of trauma" (2007, this issue, footnote 1 p. 280) and comments "traumatologists now speak of survivors of childhood sexual abuse (CSA) just as they speak of survivors of the Holocaust" (p. 280)

Address correspondence to: Jennifer J. Freyd, Department of Psychology, 1227 University of Oregon, Eugene, OR 97403-1227, USA. E-mail: jjf@dynamic.uoregon.edu

© 2007 Psychology Press, an imprint of the Taylor & Francis Group, an Informa business
http://www.psypress.com/memory   DOI:10.1080/09658210701256514

this might suggest to some readers that child sexual abuse may not always "count" as traumatic (see McNally, 2007, this issue). We argue in this paper that child sexual abuse very often constitutes a severe betrayal trauma and that it is thus *genuinely traumatic*. We will also argue that one reasonably common effect of child sexual abuse—particularly when it involves betrayal trauma—is some degree of forgetting or "knowledge isolation" about the event. This last claim speaks to the heart of betrayal trauma theory (Freyd 1994, 1996, 2001), the theory that McNally (2007, this issue) summarises and critiques. In this paper we will respond to aspects of McNally's critique, as well as offer our own perspective on the state of betrayal trauma theory. Our paper is organised into three main sections: (1) conceptual issues, (2) critiques of empirical studies, and (3) future directions.

CONCEPTUAL ISSUES

Terminology: Memory

McNally and others are correct when they note that the terminology in this area is fraught with inconsistency and ambiguity. He is also correct that there is a fundamentally fascinating and important question regarding the nature of not-knowing: Is it really traumatic amnesia or some more everyday sort of forgetting? We assume that the answer is "yes"—sometimes trauma survivors cannot recall an event due to a profound amnesia, and sometimes the underlying processes are better characterised as ordinary forgetting. We

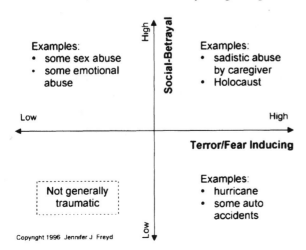

Figure 1. Freyd's two-dimensional model for traumatic events.

also assume that sometimes trauma survivors do not encode the event in a memorable way in the first place, and that, at other times, trauma survivors who have encoded an event well initially may later experience retrieval inhibition (Freyd, 1996).

Freyd (1996) addressed the confusion of terminology in this area. She wrote: "Whatever we call it—repression, dissociation, psychological defense, denial, amnesia, unawareness, or betrayal blindness—the failure to know some significant and negative aspect of reality is an aspect of human experience that remains at once elusive and of central importance" (1996, p. 16). She also noted (p. 15):

All of these concepts can be subsumed under the general term "knowledge isolation", though there are distinct types of knowledge isolation. For example, a distinction can be made between a lack of awareness of the past (which may be called memory repression or traumatic amnesia) and a lack of awareness of the current situation (which may be called repression of affect or dissociative state of consciousness).

Betrayal trauma theory was designed to address knowledge isolation, although at various times Freyd has used terms such as *amnesia* when she really should have used *knowledge isolation*. We often do not have sufficient information to know the cognitive or mechanistic details of the knowledge isolation. In such cases, it may be misleading to use a term such as *amnesia* (although *apparent amnesia*, e.g., Peters, Uyterlinde, Consemulder, & van der Hart, 1998, may describe the phenomenon). We are grateful that McNally reminds contributors to this field to be careful about terminology. For the purposes of this paper, we use the term *knowledge isolation* to encompass the range of ways in which information may be hidden from awareness, unless we are discussing more specific mechanisms of unawareness. We use the term *unawareness* to refer to the phenomenon of information inaccessibility; we use this term so that we do not imply a particular way by which information becomes inaccessible (e.g., dissociation, everyday forgetting, encoding failures). We use the terms *amnesia* or *apparent amnesia* if they were the terms used in the primary research. One more clarification is perhaps warranted. McNally defines amnesia as "an abnormal, pathological inability to remember"

(2007, this issue, p. 291). A more generic defini- tion is simply a lack of memory, and we would argue that in some situations it could be adaptive.

Terminology: Betrayal trauma theory

Before addressing specific comments by McNally, we provide a brief overview of the original tenets of betrayal trauma theory. This overview provides an important framework for evaluating several of McNally's claims. Betrayal trauma theory (BTT; Freyd, 1994, 1996, 2001) is, at its core, an attempt to account for *why* victims of abuse may appear to remain largely unaware of their abuse. Freyd's 1996 book explored motivations (the why ques- tion and core of BBT), as well as speculated on possible mechanisms (the how question). The ideas proposed in the 1996 book were further developed in subsequent articles (Freyd, 1999, 2001), and will presumably continue to evolve. BTT is an approach to conceptualising trauma that points to the importance of social relation- ships in understanding post-traumatic outcomes, including reduced recall.

The phrase *betrayal trauma* thus refers to a social dimension of trauma, independent of the individual's reaction to the trauma (Freyd, 1991, 1994, 1996). Betrayal trauma occurs when the people or institutions on which a person depends for survival violate that person in a significant way. Childhood physical, emotional, or sexual abuse perpetrated by a caregiver is an example of betrayal trauma. The phrase BTT refers to a theory about psychological response to betrayal traumas. Specifically, the theory proposes that the way in which events are processed and remem- bered will be related to the degree to which a negative event represents a betrayal by a trusted, needed other (Sivers, Schooler, & Freyd, 2002). The initial focus of BTT was on the response of unawareness, but as the theory has been extended and developed, other responses such as alexithy- mia, depression, and anxiety have been consid- ered (e.g., Goldsmith & Freyd, 2005).

Freyd (1996, 1999) also introduced the term *betrayal blindness*, which denotes unawareness of betrayals. Notably, BTT does not argue that this blindness needs to be complete. Partial awareness may protect the victim from knowledge that leads to behaviours that alienate the needed offender. The theory argues that victims, perpetrators, and witnesses may display betrayal blindness in order to preserve relationships, institutions, and social

systems upon which they depend. Thus, betrayal trauma theory in no way requires that knowledge isolation be complete.

McNally's critiques

As McNally (2007, this issue) reviews, BTT draws on studies of social contracts (e.g., Cosmides, 1989) to acknowledge that humans are usually excellent at detecting betrayals. Usually, people respond to violations or betrayals by withdrawing from the relationship or confronting the offender. However, BTT argues that in cases where a victim is dependent on a caregiver, withdrawal or con- frontation are often not viable options. A child could certainly respond to awareness of abuse by withdrawing (e.g., emotionally or in terms of proximity) or confronting; however, attachment is a two-way street. To the extent that the child's withdrawal or confrontation has a negative im- pact on elicitation of care-giving behaviours or increases violent behaviours in the caregiver, withdrawal will actually be at odds with ultimate survival goals. In such cases, the child's well-being would be better ensured by isolating the know- ledge of the event, thus remaining as engaged as necessary with the caregiver to continue to be an active participant in the attachment relationship.

In contrast to McNally's claims (2007, this issue), the theory does not require that abusive caregivers be highly reliable caregivers to argue that unawareness of the betrayal may help children maintain the attachment relationship. Presumably, a dependent child who receives minimal care is at an advantage compared to a child who receives less than minimal care; thus, unawareness of the betrayal may help the child engage in attachment behaviours that ensure at least the minimal care offered by the abusive caregiver. Recent research by DePrince (2005) points to conditions under which the cheater- detection abilities proposed by Cosmides (1989) are actually impaired, supporting the BTT pro- position that some experiences may be associated with diminished ability to detect betrayals. DePrince found that young adults who reported interpersonal revictimisations made more errors on social contract problems than those who did not report revictimisations; the groups did not differ in number of errors made in response to abstract (non-social) problems. Further, revictimisation status was significantly related to reporting the presence of a betrayal trauma before age 18.

McNally (2007, this issue) argues that "the caretaking relationship may already be imperilled in at least some incestuous families, thereby eliminating the motivation for forgetting abuse" (p. 291). Although this suggestion has some merit and may explain why forgetting is not always observed in certain samples (such as the prosecution sample of Goodman et al., below), the matter is not all-or-none. If the relationship is imperilled but the abuser continues to engage in some care-giving behaviours, the child may be motivated to maintain the attachment relationship in order to encourage whatever care-giving behaviours do occur. If the relationship is so imperilled that care-giving behaviours do not occur (or do not occur frequently), then presumably the motivation to remain blind would be reduced or eliminated. Betrayal blindness may then be most likely to be seen in instances where the families are otherwise high functioning and where all involved (or knowledgeable) family members behave as if nothing improper was happening.

McNally (2007, this issue) also argues that there is no necessity for amnesia in order for a child to maintain a relationship with an abuser— that simply not talking about the abuse would suffice. However, BTT recognises that attachment is an active process, requiring inputs from both the child and the caregiver (Bowlby, 1988). Thus, a core component of BTT is that a child can endanger an attachment relationship by failing to engage in an active way with the caregiver (e.g., by withdrawing); thus, simple silence is not sufficient. McNally's proposal also apparently assumes that children have control over their attachment behaviours (including non-verbal behaviours and emotional reactions), even at a young age. Related to this, McNally questions what danger the child would be in without unawareness. The danger arises precisely from the damaged attachment bonds that serve to ensure care giving. We would expect a graded relationship—if the caregiver becomes less attached, one would expect less care giving; in turn, decreased care giving would increase the child's risk of harm from poor care (whether this be failure to provide or protect) or increased abuse.

McNally asks (2007, this issue, p. 290): "If one fails to survive, one dies. But it is unclear how the child would perish. Would the perpetrator murder the child? Would he expose the child to fatal neglect, such as refusing to feed her? Would he

evict her from the parental home?" McNally is correct that most cases of child abuse do not end in children actually perishing (although the reality of child abuse fatalities should not be minimised; see Sirotnak, 2006); however, failure to consider survival as a motivation for many behaviours in the face of abuse would be shortsighted. Risk of perishing is probabilistic. If one does not wear a seatbelt on a given trip, one probably won't actually perish. However, one has certainly increased the odds of perishing by failing to wear a seatbelt. Care giving from parents is graded, and the lower the degree of care giving the higher the risks of perishing become—whether that is because the child is not monitored, not fed sufficiently, or not encouraged in ways that foster thriving, etc. Thus, just as a passenger in a car is wise to wear a seatbelt, the child may indeed make a good investment in survival by increasing the odds of care giving and thus decreasing the odds of perishing, even if the odds of perishing are not enormously high. Perhaps more importantly, McNally (2007, this issue) seems to focus only on physical survival, and does not consider the effect of emotional neglect on child development (e.g., difficulties with attachment, self-esteem, depression, etc.) and the needs children have to maintain close emotional attachment. Betrayal blindness may be the only mechanism by which children may seek out and accept emotional closeness from the same individual that is abusing them.

McNally (2007, this issue) writes that "if *any* episodes of abuse are available to awareness and not forgotten, then this should imperil survival" (italics in original; p. 290) Although BTT predicts unawareness, the theory does *not* predict that such unawareness and forgetting is (or needs to be) perfectly implemented. Indeed, because under most circumstances, awareness and remembering are adaptive, achieving complete unawareness or forgetting would be difficult. Thus, one might expect to see a range of degrees of unawareness and forgetting when pressures to maintain the attachment relationship cause lack of awareness to have some utility (Becker-Blease, Freyd, & Pears, 2004). This is what we would expect as a consequence of two opposing processes. Indeed, partial awareness may be an adaptive compromise under some conditions, allowing both the maintenance of necessary relationships and sufficient awareness for self-protection. Forgetting and unawareness may be more likely for events (or aspects of events) that are more threatening to the dependency relationship, so that survivors who later recover memories may report things like "I always knew things were bad, just not how bad." How useful partial awareness versus no awareness is to children navigating attachment relationships in which abuse occurs remains a very important empirical question, the answer to which is likely context dependent. McNally also argues that BTT requires "that victims banish memories of abuse from awareness shortly after each molestation episode" (p. 289). The theory actually makes no temporal predictions. In fact, one might assume that awareness could vary by situation and in response to a feedback system in which awareness does or does not cause problems for the victim.

It is also very likely that, in addition to implicit motivations for not-knowing that the betrayed person may have in order to maintain a relationship, the victim may have other reasons for not-knowing and silence. At least one such reason is demands for silence from the perpetrator and others (e.g., family, society). Demands for silence (see Veldhuis & Freyd, 1999) may lead to a complete failure to even discuss an experience. Experiences that have never been shared with anyone else may have a different internal structure from shared experiences (Freyd, 1996).

EMPIRICAL RESEARCH

Evidence for knowledge isolation

McNally (2007, this issue) argues that "... documented traumatic stressors are seldom, if ever, forgotten" (p. 281). Supporting this claim, McNally notes that negative emotional arousal results in the consolidation and heightening of emotional memories, thus arguing that amnesia is actually not possible (or at least very unlikely) in the face of trauma. However, research from the affective science literature points to decreases in deficits in processing caused by negative stimuli. For example, Most, Scholl, Clifford, and Simons (2005) found that emotionally negative pictures (taken from the International Affective Picture Stimuli set that include trauma-related material; e.g., images of physical assault) actually caused deficits in processing target pictures that followed the negative pictures. Termed *emotional bottlenecking*, these data provide initial evidence that emotionally negative stimuli do not uniformly attract attention and heighten processing. Speci-

fically, the authors state "Thus, attentional biases to emotional information induced a temporary inability to process stimuli ..." (Most et al., p. 654). A follow-up study revealed that individual differences in harm avoidance moderated the emotional bottlenecking phenomenon. Specifically, individuals low in harm avoidance were able to reduce the effects of the negative stimuli on processing later stimuli; however, individuals high in harm avoidance were unable to temper the bottlenecking effects. This research points to conditions under which emotionally salient stimuli are associated with decreased—and not heightened—processing. While these data do not speak to memory for stimuli, they do point to provocative alterations in attentional processes. Given the strong relationship between attention and memory, future work on emotional bottlenecking and memory may inform issues related to decreases in memory for trauma-related information.

Two lines of research have documented knowledge isolation following trauma and bear directly on McNally's claim that traumas are rarely (if ever) forgotten. In the first, descriptive line of inquiry (including naturalistic observations and case studies), memory disruptions following trauma have been observed for more than a century. These disruptions have included both intrusive memories and apparent inability to remember (see Freyd et al., 2005b, 2005c). The issue of intrusive memories per se is not controversial and will not be reviewed here. However, in marked contrast with the claims of McNally (2007, this issue) and colleagues (e.g., Kihlstrom et al., 2005), PTSD is not simply a disorder of intrusions. These memory disruptions are reflected in the criteria for post-traumatic stress disorder (PTSD; American Psychiatric Association, 2000) and, as noted by Leskin, Kaloupek, and Keane (1998, p. 986): "The hallmark of PTSD adjustment is the reciprocal oscillation between re-experiencing and avoidance." Similarly, as Widiger and Sankis (2000) noted, "difficulty forgetting (or letting go of) a horrifying experience may simply be the opposite side of the same coin of difficulty remembering (accepting or acknowledging) a horrifying experience" (p. 391). Further, McNally focuses on PTSD; however, PTSD is not the only diagnosis associated with childhood victimisation and alterations in memory. The dissociative disorders (including dissociative amnesia) are clearly associated with a history of trauma and are defined largely in the basis of alterations in memory (American Psychiatric Association, 2000).

Numerous examples of apparent amnesia have been well documented in the literature on combat and war trauma (e.g., Grinker & Spiegel, 1945; Sargant & Slater, 1941; Thom & Fenton, 1920). Sargant and Slater (1941) described a sample of 1000 cases during World War II. Over 14% exhibited "loss of memory" (either fugue states or large amnesic gaps). These cases were not thought to be organically based. The frequency of reported amnesia was associated with the severity of the psychological trauma that the person had experienced. Of those who had experienced severe stress, 35% exhibited significant amnesia. The alterations in memory experienced by victims of wartime trauma have been reported to range from selective amnesia to generalised amnesia (amnesia for one's entire life). In describing many of these cases, Grinker and Spiegel (1945, p. 10) wrote:

> There may be total amnesia, including both events on the battlefield and the patient's previous life, or memory for part of the battle experience may be retained, with a gap involving the actual precipitating traumatic factors and the events which followed. The majority of patients make persistent attempts to recover their lost memories, and in many instances their efforts may be successful without an aid from the therapist.

Such recovery of memory was well documented and became accepted and effective treatment for such psychiatric causalities. Thus, the topic of amnesia for trauma and subsequent memory recovery was never controversial when it was contained within the wartime trauma literature. The topics only became controversial when the same phenomenon was observed in the context of CSA.

The second line of research/evidence relies largely on correlational and non-experimental prospective and retrospective methods to examine the relationship between variables that moderate risk for reduced recall and to evaluate individuals' perceptions and reports of their memories. This research focuses on memory for trauma in the real world to address "what, who, why?" questions that help to define the phenomenon of apparent amnesia. For example, this line of inquiry asks what percentage of people report

amnesia, who is likely to report it, and what contextual factors predict its occurrence.

From this correlational approach, a significant body of research has now demonstrated a relationship between apparent amnesia and victimisation. Brown, Scheflin, and Whitfield (1999) reviewed the literature, concluding: "in just this past decade alone, 68 research studies have been conducted on naturally occurring dissociative or traumatic amnesia for childhood sexual abuse. Not a single one of the 68 data-based studies failed to find it" (p. 126). This body of work includes prospective (e.g., Williams, 1994, 1995) and retrospective (Elliot, 1997; Feldman-Summers & Pope, 1994; Freyd, DePrince, & Zurbriggen, 2001; Schultz, Passmore, & Yoder, 2003; Sheiman, 1999; Stoler, 2000) methods. Cases of amnesia have also been documented for corroborated cases of abuse (Cheit, 2005). Although most studies of this nature do not (and cannot) address McNally's question of whether actual forgetting, failure to think about the event, or failure to report the event have occurred, Williams (1992, 1994, 1995) provides converging data from a prospective sample that suggest a significant minority of women did not remember sexual abuse that was documented in an emergency room 17 years earlier.

Studies from this correlational line of research also indicate reduced recall in the case of abuse by caregivers or close others (e.g., Edwards, Fivush, Anda, Felitti, & Nordenberg, 2001; Freyd et al., 2001; Schultz et al., 2003; Sheiman, 1999; Stoler, 2000). In writing her book more than a decade ago, Freyd (1996) reported finding, from re-analyses of a number of relevant data sets, that incestuous abuse was more likely to be forgotten than non-incestuous abuse. These re-analysed data sets included the prospective sample assessed by Williams (1994, 1995), and retrospective samples assessed by Cameron (1993) and Feldman-Summers and Pope (1994).

Using data collected from a sample of undergraduate students, Freyd et al. (2001) found that physical and sexual abuse perpetrated by a caregiver was related to higher levels of self-reported less-persistent memories of abuse compared to non-caregiver abuse. Research by Schultz et al. (2003) and a doctoral dissertation by Stoler (2000; also see Stoler, 2001) have revealed similar results. For instance, Schultz et al. (2003, p. 67) noted that "Participants reporting memory disturbances also reported significantly higher numbers of perpetrators, chemical abuse in their families, and closer relationships with the perpetrator(s) than participants reporting no memory disturbances." Sheiman (1999) reported that, in a sample of 174 students, those participants who reported memory loss for child sexual abuse were more likely to experience abuse by people who were well known to them, compared to those who did not have memory loss. Similarly Stoler (2000, p. ii) noted: "Quantitative comparisons revealed that women with delayed memories were younger at the time of their abuse and more closely related to their abusers." Interestingly, Edwards et al. (2001) reported that general autobiographical memory loss measured in a large epidemiological study was strongly associated with a history of childhood abuse. Women and men with histories of sexual and/or physical abuse had twice and 1.5 times (respectively) the prevalence of autobiographical memory loss compared to those without abuse histories. One of the specific factors associated with this increased memory loss was sexual abuse by a relative.

Although there is much for future research to clarify about the nature of memory for traumatic experiences, the relationship between betrayal and reported reduced recall has been observed in at least seven data sets (see above). Some researchers have presumably failed to find a statistically significant relationship between betrayal trauma and recall. When a relationship is not found, the question then is whether it does not exist or simply cannot be detected due to sampling, measurement, or power limitations. For instance, Goodman et al. (2003) reported that "relationship betrayal" was not a statistically significant predictor for forgetting in their sample of adults who had been involved in child abuse prosecution cases during childhood. It is not clear whether the relationship truly does not exist in this population (which is very possible given the unusual sample in which children presumably did not need to remain dependent on perpetrators who were being charged with a crime) or whether there was simply insufficient statistical power to detect the relationship (see commentaries by Freyd, 2003, and Zurbriggen & Becker-Blease, 2003).

Several methodological issues can cloud interpretation of findings. For example, betrayal trauma theory identifies dependence as a crucial factor in the victim–perpetrator relationship. That is, the victim may have cause to remain unaware of the abuse to some extent in order to protect a necessary relationship when the perpetrator is a caregiver. Thus, to test betrayal trauma theory, one ideally measures dependence or care giving of the perpetrator (for such a study see Freyd et al., 2001). Betrayal and dependence cannot be equated with parents only; non-parental abuse may also include dependency in the victim–perpetrator relationship (priests and ministers, coaches, superior officers, babysitters, possibly extended family). This sentiment has been expressed by numerous survivors of abuse by trusted non-family members. For example, Frank Fitzpatrick, who recovered memories of sexual abuse and then initiated the investigation of James R. Porter, which led to a successful prosecution in part because dozens of victims came forward, described the feelings of betrayal he had during his memory recovery process: "I felt an immense, monstrous betrayal by someone that I loved" (Fitzpatrick, 1994, p. 5).

Operationalisation of memory phenomena in studies remains a critical issue. For example, McNally, Ristuccia, and Perlman (2005) stated that they "do not assume that memories were inaccessible (dissociated or repressed) at any time" (p. 9) in a group classified as "recovered memory", but that the participants did not think about the memory for a while. Using such operationalisations, some (or all) of the people in the "recovered" group might not have ever experienced any memory loss. In addition, memory loss is not simply an all-or-nothing categorisation (which is why we have frequently used the term *reduced recall*). Researchers must struggle with how to categorise people who report partial memory loss, such as remembering some but not all details of the event. If partial memory loss were to be categorised as continuous memory (because some aspect of the event was always remembered), the net effect would be to make it unlikely to see any differences between discontinuous and continuous memory groups.

Many researchers note the risk of false positives in sexual abuse research, but fail to consider the risk of false negatives. The literature on false negatives for abuse (e.g., Fergusson, Horwood, & Woodward, 2000) requires that researchers entertain and discuss the possibility that people reporting they were not abused, when actually they were (false negatives), end up in control (no-abuse) groups. False negatives may occur when people remember the abuse but decline to report it for myriad reasons, or when they do not remember the event. Given that little is known about what motivates people to self-select into research studies on sexual abuse, the possibility remains that both false positives *and* negatives influence findings.

Future research will also have to grapple with the populations in which memory or lack of it is expected. For example, betrayal trauma theory does not predict that there is a difference in awareness and memory for abuse in victim groups already selected on the basis of willingness to respond to a newspaper advertisement about child sexual abuse. Such identification will likely trump anything else going on regarding forgetting or unawareness—these are the victims who for whatever reason apparently embrace a social status and label that most victims avoid.

Experimental studies

McNally questions, broadly, whether evidence from experimental studies conducted by Freyd and colleagues supports BTT. Although the experimental studies reviewed by McNally were certainly guided by BTT, they notably do not contribute to the core "why" questions addressed by the theory. As a group, these studies represent tests of one of the "how" mechanisms proposed by the theory. Specifically, the studies examine the relationship between dissociation and memory in the lab. Because dissociation is associated with family violence and reduced recall, it was quite logical a decade ago to predict that dissociation would be associated with information-processing changes in the lab. Addressing McNally's concern that the experimental research provides "at best, equivocal support" (2007, this issue, p. 289) for BTT, it is notable that the studies were not designed to test the theory per se, but to test one factor predicted to be associated with both family violence and dissociation. To the extent that the core goal of BTT was to elucidate why unawareness of betrayal traumas may occur, using the experimental tests as evidence for or against the theory as a whole is problematic. If research fails to uphold a relationship between dissociation and memory, this does not negate the core premises of BTT; rather, such research would merely point to the need to evaluate other mechanisms to explain how unawareness occurs.

McNally's (2007, this issue) curiosity about whether experimental studies that he reviewed support BTT raises critical issues about the role

and implications of experimental research in understanding memory for trauma. The research motivation for lab-based studies and the interpretations that can be made to the more general issue of memory for victimisation must be carefully specified. Although research using both experimental and non-experimental methods contributes to a general understanding of memory for trauma, these approaches contribute in very different ways. Researchers must be clear about the logical inferences that can (or cannot) be made from each of the two approaches. Specifically, research in the cognitive psychology experimental lab (*how* questions) typically cannot be used to establish validity of forgetting outside the lab (*what*, *who*, and *why* questions). As noted by Mook (1983, p. 384), laboratory research may best illuminate "what *can* happen [in the real world], rather than what typically *does*."

Experimental and cognitive psychology laboratory-based research on mechanisms of forgetting has been completed using both trauma and non-trauma stimuli. There is a great deal more research on forgetting of non-trauma stimuli than trauma stimuli. Perhaps the latter are most directly generalisable to forgetting of trauma; however, the former research constitutes an enormous body of empirical evidence for potential mechanisms of forgetting that may operate in some cases of amnesia for trauma stimuli (see Anderson et al., 2004; Gleaves, Smith, Butler, & Spiegel, 2004; Sivers et al., 2001). Existing experimental research on the forgetting of trauma stimuli points to three conditions under which reduced recall for specifically trauma-related information is likely to occur in the laboratory. These conditions involve: (1) attentional context, (2) dissociation, and (3) intimate abuse.

McNally (2007, this issue) reports that his group has failed to replicate memory findings from Freyd and colleagues as they relate to dissociation. Given the "synoptic, not exhaustive" (p. 282) scope of McNally's review, it is important to note at the outset that researchers outside Freyd's group have found relationships between trauma-related distress and reduced recall in the lab (see DePrince, Freyd, & Malle, 2007). For example, Moulds and Bryant (2002) compared participants diagnosed with Acute Stress Disorder (ASD, a disorder partially characterised by dissociative symptoms; see Spiegel & Cardeña, 1991) and non-traumatised controls on a directed forgetting task, where participants were directed to remember some words and forget others. At the end of the task, participants were tested on their recall of all words, regardless of the instruction to remember or forget. All ASD participants had been exposed to some form of physical threat. The ASD group showed poorer recall of to-be-forgotten trauma-related words than the non-traumatised group. In a replication and extension, Moulds and Bryant (2005) found that membership in a trauma-exposed ASD group was associated with reduced recall compared to trauma-exposed-no-ASD and no-trauma groups.

McNally (2007, this issue) comments on findings from McNally et al. (2005), who claimed to replicate the procedure of DePrince and Freyd with a different participant population and obtained different results: participants recruited through newspaper advertisements who reported no, continuous, or recovered memories of child sexual abuse showed greater memory for trauma words under both selective and divided attention. However, the descriptive statistics suggest problems with their method. Curiously, the pattern of results points to better recall of some words under divided than selective attention conditions. When participants are trying to do something in addition to remembering the to-be-remembered words, they should be less able to commit the words to memory. In contrast, the descriptive statistics reported in McNally et al. suggest that the trauma words were remembered *more* in divided attention conditions by *all* groups whereas neutral words were remembered more in selective attention conditions as expected. This curious pattern makes it difficult to interpret much about other data discrepancies with De-Prince and Freyd.

Researchers outside McNally's group have also failed to find reduced recall in the lab. For example, Elzinga, de Beurs, Sergeant, van Dyck, and Phaf (2000) examined directed forgetting performance for neutral and sex words among undergraduate volunteers and dissociative-disordered patients. Under the standard selective attention instructions, directed forgetting of sex words decreased with higher levels of dissociation. Further, dissociative patients and highly dissociative students remembered more overall compared to the low-dissociative group. Elzinga and colleagues (2000) argued that the highly dissociative participants may demonstrate special learning abilities. In particular, drawing on activation/elaboration theory, the authors argued that highly dissociative participants may be skilled at elaboration and constructing conscious

experiences. Further, elaboration can be used to detect discrepancies. In the case of the directed forgetting paradigm, Elzinga and colleagues argued that forgetting threatening information, such as sex words, may actually be discrepant to dissociative participants. Thus, the dissociative participants exhibited better recall of sex words relative to the low-dissociative group. Elzinga and colleagues (2000) argued that highly dissociative individuals may use their capacity to construct separate conscious experiences to keep threatening or painful memories from current awareness.

Although there is ample evidence for apparent amnesia outside the lab, the phenomenon is not demonstrated uniformly in lab tasks. Of course, there is no reason to expect that it should necessarily be observed in the lab; rather, specific conditions under which forgetting occurs must be identified and tested. Reduced recall seems much less likely to occur in the lab under several conditions: presence of an anxiety (i.e., PTSD; McNally, Metzger, Lasko, Clancy, & Pitman, 1998) or personality disorder (e.g., Cloitre, Cancienne, Brodsky, Dulit, & Perry, 1996), and selective attention conditions (McNally et al., 1998). Several studies point to dissociative processes as candidate mechanisms for apparent amnesia in the lab (e.g., Moulds & Bryant, 2005), while also suggesting that high levels of anxiety are not likely to be associated with the phenomenon.

However, in general, failure to find apparent amnesia in the lab does not question the reality of the real-world phenomenon or theories seeking to account for it or similar phenomena. McNally (2007, this issue, p. 288) states that the failure of the recovered memory group to demonstrate "superior forgetting trauma cues, especially in view of their history of not having thought about their abuse for many years, seems inconsistent with betrayal trauma theory". The finding (and the entire study) actually seems completely irrelevant to BTT. Why should people who have been identified as sexual abuse survivors with recovered memories of abuse have poorer recall for trauma-related stimuli in the lab relative to people who have had continuous access to memories? If they are now able to remember their past, whatever factors led to the initial inability to remember are apparently no longer present. More critically, BTT predicts that individuals will not know or remember information that may threaten attachment relationships—thus, in grouping participants based on their history, the most important factor for BTT predictions will be the victim–perpetrator relationship.

McNally (2007, this issue) seems to be arguing that such individuals must have some special ability to block out unwanted information. If they could block out information in the past, they should be able to block out word lists. Again, above and beyond the fact that they have no real motivation to block out word lists, the argument is simply illogical if the inability to remember is viewed as *an effect* of the traumatic experience. The argument would basically be that if amnesia is not observed for minor stressors (e.g., reading stressful words), then it would not be observed for severe stressors (e.g., child sexual abuse). Using a physical trauma analogy and the same logic, one could argue that since a mild head trauma (e.g., an apple dropped on one's head) causes no significant brain damage, then there is no reason to believe that a more severe injury (e.g., from a shotgun blast) would have any effect. Failure to find the phenomenon in the lab suggests the appropriate conditions for forgetting are not present.

Identifying the conditions under which forgetting occurs in the lab is important to modelling how such phenomena in the real world may occur. However, researchers do not yet understand the scope and specificity of conditions for forgetting. For example, how idiosyncratic to the original trauma must stimuli be? Must participants be naive to show reduced recall? For example, differences in samples stand out in McNally et al.'s directed forgetting research (1998; McNally et al., 2005) compared to DePrince and Freyd (2001, 2004). McNally's group recruited participants who were apparently tested numerous times (although the number of times they were tested and whether they were previously exposed to the directed forgetting—or similar—task was not reported). DePrince and Freyd's (1999, 2001, 2004) studies involved college students selected on the basis of pre-screening for dissociation. Participants did not self-select for a study on trauma or memory, or have prior experience of participating in such research.

Is social betrayal really trauma? Research on betrayal, distress, and health

As noted earlier, McNally (2007, this issue) opens his paper by raising questions about what counts as a trauma. A wide range of events, such as child abuse, sexual assault, medical traumas, and natural disasters, meet the PTSD Criterion A1 for a traumatic event. Some of these events (such as some child abuse, sexual assault) involve social betrayals. A growing body of research now demonstrates that events high in betrayal are associated with significant distress, as would be expected if these events were traumatic by the more common use of the term. Freyd, Klest, and Allard (2005a) found that a history of betrayal trauma was strongly associated with physical and mental health symptoms in a sample of ill individuals. Goldsmith, Freyd, and DePrince (2004) reported similar results in a sample of college students.

Edwards, Freyd, Dube, Anda, and Felitti (2006) used data from the second wave collected as part of the Adverse Childhood Experiences (ACE) Study (Felitti et al, 1998) to examine the hypothesis that social betrayal is harmful in relation to a variety of adult health outcomes. Edwards et al. tested whether adults whose abuser was a family member or non-relative living in the home would report substantially poorer health than those whose abuser was a family friend, relative living outside the home, or a stranger. Participants in the second wave included slightly less than 7000 of the 17,337 full participant pool in the ACE study. All participants were HMO members undergoing a complete physical examination. A total of 3100 (17.4%) reported one form of childhood sexual abuse (fondling, attempted intercourse, or intercourse) and also identified their abuser. Of sexual abuse survivors, 32% reported exposure to events high in betrayal, defined as an abuser who was a family or non-family member living in the home. High-betrayal abuse was related to depression, anxiety, suicidality, panic, and anger. High-betrayal participants had poorer health functioning on the SF-36 role-physical, role-emotional, and social functioning scales than low-betrayal victims.

The Edwards et al. study is in line with other research that suggests abuse perpetrated by caregivers is associated with worse outcomes than non-caregiver abuse. For example, Atlas and Ingram (1998) reported that, in a sample of 34 hospitalised adolescents (aged 14 to 17.10 years), sexual distress was associated with histories of abuse by family members as compared to no abuse or abuse by a non-family member, whereas post-traumatic stress was not. Turell and Armsworth (2003) compared sexual abuse survivors who self-mutilate with those who do not. The authors reported that self-mutilators were more likely to have been abused in their family of origin than abused only by a non-family member.

Betrayal and dissociation

Betrayal trauma theory posits that knowledge isolation is predicted by the threat that the information poses to the individual's system of attachment (Freyd, 1994, 1996). Thus, it follows that high-betrayal traumas, as compared with low-betrayal traumas, should be associated with higher levels of dissociation. Consistent with this, Chu and Dill (1990) reported that childhood abuse by family members (both physical and sexual) was significantly related to increased dissociation scores (as measured by the Dissociative Experiences Scale) in psychiatric inpatients, and abuse by non-family members was not. Similarly, Plattner et al. (2003) found significant correlations between symptoms of pathological dissociation and intrafamilial (but not extrafamilial) trauma in a sample of delinquent juveniles. These correlations held up even when accounting for age and duration of abuse. DePrince (2005) found that the presence of betrayal trauma before the age of 18 was associated with membership in a pathological dissociation taxon group and with revictimisation after age 18. Further, individuals who reported being revictimised in young adulthood following an interpersonal assault in childhood performed worse on reasoning problems that involved social and safety information compared to individuals who did not report revictimisation. Goodman et al. (2003) found that higher levels of dissociation were associated with decreased likelihood of disclosing childhood sexual abuse in a sample of young adults who had participated in criminal proceedings related to sexual abuse allegations approximately 10 years earlier.

DISCUSSION

Implications for recovered memories

Betrayal trauma theory actually says little about the conditions under which people may later access memories that were previously inaccessible. Of course, the very fact that the knowledge is theoretically isolated, rather than banished or non-encoded, suggests that recovery is clearly possible. Although conscious appraisals of betrayal may be inhibited at the time of trauma and for as long as the trauma victim is dependent on the perpetrator, eventually the trauma survivor may become conscious of strong feelings of betrayal or other emotions (e.g., rage; DePrince & Freyd, 2002b). This would be most likely to occur after the individual is no longer dependent on the perpetrator. Future research is needed to uncover the motivations for and mechanisms of memory recovery.

Implications for "how" questions

Betrayal trauma theory implicates dissociative processes as a potential mechanism in apparent amnesia. By implicating dissociative processes, the theory does not require that there be special dissociative mechanisms for forgetting. Indeed, betrayal trauma theory does not ever argue that special cognitive processes are necessary. Rather, the theory builds on the observation that dissociative processes are associated with a range of cognitive alterations, including memory disruption. The theory makes no particular argument that dissociative processes are required for reduced recall to occur; nor does the theory argue that the same phenomenon cannot occur along various other routes, such as via inhibitory mechanisms. As reviewed above, several studies have examined dissociative tendencies and memory performance in the lab; however, these studies are not tests of betrayal trauma theory per se. Failure to detect associations between dissociation and reduced recall in the lab does not falsify betrayal trauma theory; such failures simply add to the available literature on whether dissociation contributes to the conditions under which the phenomenon occurs in the lab.

Failure to report traumas may occur for a variety of reasons, ranging from amnesia to simple nondisclosure in the context of intact memory. Interestingly, Foynes, Freyd, and DePrince (2006) reported that whether or not young adults report having previously disclosed childhood abuse (yes/no) was predicted by the closeness of the perpetrator, above and beyond participant gender, age at the time of the event, and severity of injuries in physical abuse. Thus, disclosure does appear to be an important factor to consider in the mix of recall and reporting of previous traumas. Lack of disclosure may influence recall to the extent that the abuse memories are not rehearsed. Future research will be necessary to evaluate the relationship between lack of disclosure and memory failure.

Although betrayal trauma theory did not originally focus on active inhibition processes in unawareness of betrayals (Freyd, 1996), recent work by Anderson and colleagues (Anderson, 2001; Anderson & Green, 2001; Anderson et al., 2004) converges nicely with betrayal trauma theory. Active inhibition induces forgetting when a representation (Representation A) is associated with two or more other representations (B and C) and links to one of those representations (B) is rehearsed more frequently than the other (C). Under those conditions, Anderson and others have observed reduced recall for C. That is, the act of rehearsing A–B seems to actively inhibit C. Anderson (2001) has proposed that a parallel learning context exists for children in the untenable position of rehearsing very different associations regarding caretakers—e.g., parent–abuse (A–C) and parent–care(A–B). To the extent that many socio-cultural forces encourage practising the association parent–care and/or the child victim is motivated to rehearse the parent–care association, active inhibitory processes may decrease recall for parent–abuse information. Active inhibition provides a parsimonious explanation for how children exposed to repeated abuse could forget the event. Although some have argued that repeated abuse must be all-too-well remembered because basic memory principles dictate that repetition is associated with strengthened memory traces, the active inhibition literature provides a tenable explanation for reduced recall in the context of repeated events (Anderson, 2001). Using the think/no-think paradigm, Anderson and Green (2001) extended this work by demonstrating that active inhibition (suppression) leads to reduced ability to recall previously formed memories. Anderson et al. (2004) identified neural systems involved in keeping such unwanted memories out of awareness. Research on active inhibitory processes in the context of trauma-related memory is needed.

Gender and betrayal trauma

Controversy about the reliability of abuse allegations, particularly those involving recovered memory, has often included explicit or implicit attributions of gender or gender politics. For instance, it is common to see the female pronoun used as the generic victim, or even to read of "radical feminists" (e.g., Van Til, 1997) who are presumably guilty of causing "hysteria" (e.g., Ofshe, 1994) and planting inaccurate memories. Is there in fact a relationship between these issues and those of gender? Various authors have analysed aspects of the gender politics involved in debates about the credibility of abuse allegations (see McFarlane & van der Kolk, 1996; Stoler, Quina, DePrince, & Freyd, 2001). McFarlane and van der Kolk (1996, p. 566) suggest that gender politics are in fact a factor in societal reaction to recovered memories:

It appears that as long as men were found to suffer from delayed recall of atrocities committed either by a clearly identifiable enemy or themselves, the issue was not controversial. However when similar memory problems started to be documented in girls and women in the context of domestic abuse, the news was unbearable; when female victims started to seek justice against their alleged perpetrators, the issue moved from science into politics.

Although gender assumptions are often made about memory and abuse, we are aware of no evidence that females are more likely to forget or remember a particular event as compared with males. However, to the extent that some abuse events are more likely to be remembered than others, as predicted by betrayal trauma theory, then gender effects on frequency of exposure for betrayal traumas may make it more likely that one gender or the other reports recovered memories. In fact Freyd and Goldberg (2004) discovered a strong relationship between gender and betrayal trauma exposure in an adult community sample. The Brief Betrayal Trauma Survey (BBTS; Goldberg & Freyd, 2006) was administered to a large community sample on two occasions separated by a 3-year interval. In contrast to previous surveys, the BBTS included separate items for events that involved mistreatment by someone close, mistreatment by someone not so close, and non-interpersonal events. For both kinds of interpersonal events, separate items focused on physical, sexual, and emotional types of potential abuse. For each event, respondents indicated separately the extent of their exposure prior to and after age 18. Substantial differences between men and women were found for many of the reported events on both occasions (see Table 1).

These large gender differences relate to the amount of betrayal inherent in the event: men report more traumas with lower betrayal (e.g., assault by someone not close to the boy or man) and women report more trauma with higher betrayal (e.g., assault by someone close to the girl or woman). We were able to rule out at least one response bias explanation for our results (that men and women interpreted the word "close" differently).

Closer inspection of the data from Freyd and Goldberg (2004) reveals patterns that are critical to thinking about the intersection of gender and trauma exposure. For example, men in this sample were more likely to report exposure to accidents, particularly in adulthood. Women report more sexual abuse in both childhood and adulthood. Rates of exposure to physical abuse appear comparable between men and women overall, although women report more physical abuse in adulthood and men in childhood. However, women report more physical abuse by someone with whom they were close in both childhood and adulthood (see Figure 2). These data reveal that even for an event, such as physical assault, that appears to affect men and women at a comparable rate, women experience assault by close others more often than men.

Freyd and Goldberg (2004) also examined rates of women and men reporting at least one event high in betrayal (e.g., abuse by a close other) or low in betrayal (e.g., motor vehicle accident). This analysis revealed a significant interaction of gender by trauma type (see Figure 3). Men and women did not differ in overall rates

of trauma; however, they differed in the types of events to which they were exposed. Women were more likely to report events perpetrated by a close other than males, who were more likely to report events that were perpetrated by someone with whom they were not close.

To the extent that betrayal traumas are potent for some sorts of psychological impact and non-betrayals potent for other impacts (e.g., Freyd, 1999), these gender differences would imply some very non-subtle socialisation factors operating as a function of gender (DePrince & Freyd, 2002b). These results may also help to account for the apparent gender asymmetry in reports of forgetting trauma. If we assume men and women have similar reactions to a given trauma but that frequency of some traumas that lead to forgetting is higher in women, we would expect to see higher rates of reports of forgetting trauma among women than men in the population.

Another explanation?

McNally (2007, this issue) asks if there is another explanation for why people may appear to recover memories of abuse after several years, then goes on to offer several possibilities. He notes many areas of overlap between his explanation for abuse-related memory phenomena and BTT. For example, Freyd (1996) noted that there are likely to be many routes to unawareness. Concurring with this, McNally notes (2007, this issue, p. 291): "One need not invoke repression, dissociation, amnesia triggered by betrayal, and so forth to explain this phenomenon parsimoniously." BTT also acknowledges important

TABLE 1
Gender differences: Freyd and Goldberg (2004)

	High Betrayal Items	Medium Betrayal Items	Low Betrayal Items (6 items)
Women report more of these events than men:	Emotional Abuse Adult Emotional Abuse Adult Close Sex Abuse Child Emotional Abuse Child Close Sex Abuse Adult	Not-close Sex Abuse Child Not-close Sex Abuse Adult Witness someone close attack family member Adult	
Men report more of these events than women:		Not-close Attack Child Not-close Attack Adult	Witnessed Not-close Death Adult Accident Adult Witness Not-close Attack Child

Observed gender differences in trauma exposure by betrayal level. From Freyd and Goldberg (2004). All differences are significant ($p < .001$).

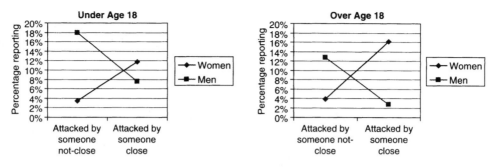

Figure 2. Physical abuse reported by gender and closeness to perpetrator before and after age 18 (Freyd & Goldberg, 2004).

developmental processes in children's cognitive development. As such, we agree with McNally's claim that "... if the child were especially young at the time, he or she may have failed to understand the betrayal or its sexual nature until after having recalled the abuse years later" (p. 291). Indeed, children may not think about the experience and years later may (appropriately) reinterpret experiences as abuse. Not thinking (and not talking) about events will of course decrease memory for the event because the event is not rehearsed (Freyd, 2003).

McNally (2007, this issue, p. 291) also argues:

Older children, however, are far more likely to know what is occurring, but they may be less likely to forget it, too, even though they may dread disclosing the abuse, not for fear of their lives (i.e., survival), but for fear of breaking up the family by causing the offending parent to go to prison. These children may actively try not to think about the abuse, to put it out of mind, and so forth—processes that do not require one to postulate a dissociative mechanism ...

We find this incredibly vague statement equally puzzling. Given that he is talking about

people who later recover memories of trauma, McNally is arguing that these children are somehow able to *successfully* "put out of mind" memories of incest for years. This statement is, of course, in complete contrast with the false-memory position that "Not only do victims of child incest not repress such painful memories ...; they try *unsuccessfully* [italics added] to forget them" (Gardner, 1993, p. 372). It is also inconsistent with what McNally has argued earlier in his own paper, that "documented traumatic stressors are seldom, if ever, forgotten" (2007, this issue, p. 281). Either he is saying that incest is not a documented traumatic stressor or he is simply wrong and there is some mechanism at work. If putting memories of incest "out of one's mind" does not involve "repression, dissociation, amnesia triggered by betrayal, or memory blockage" then it apparently involves some *other* mechanism that has the same properties but some other name. It seems to us that in trying to explain away the fact that many victims of incest report delayed recall, McNally has made a convincing argument that something special and worthy of study is going on in such individuals.

We also agree that children may fear breaking up the family. Where we diverge from McNally is in our appreciation that, from a developmental perspective, children's dependence on adults means that breaking up the family presents a potentially severe and threatening consequence of disclosure; such severe consequences may trigger appraisals related to the ability of the child (mother, family, siblings) to survive (literally or figuratively) in the face of that break up. Further, McNally's emphasis on literal death implies that attachment behaviours in children (which function to help the organism survive) would only emerge when survival is imminently threatened. An extensive attachment literature demonstrates that this is simply not the case;

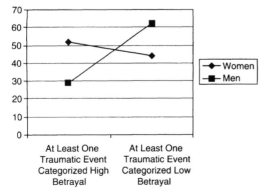

Figure 3. Betrayal trauma exposure by gender (Freyd & Goldberg, 2004).

children often respond to relatively minor threats by investing in the attachment relationship (Bowlby, 1988). As noted earlier in this article, children have reason to reduce the risk of survival threats even when the chance of actual death in the moment is relatively low, just as passengers have reason to wear seatbelts even when the chance of actual death in the moment is relatively low. As stated above, we agree that dissociative mechanisms are not required, as BTT (Freyd, 1996) clearly states that multiple routes to un-awareness likely exist.

Although our interpretation of data diverges from McNally's in many places, we have all arrived at a surprisingly common endpoint. McNally cites several central processes in the dynamics of familial violence. For example, a child may not think about the abuse for several reasons, such as fears that disclosure may break up the family, or a trusted other grooms the victim to believe non-violent abuse is OK. We diverge in that McNally stops here, arguing children may simply fail to think about events. While we agree that children may fail to think (and thus talk) about abuse events for many reasons, failure to think about events will contribute to poorer memory for the event. The processes proposed by McNally (e.g., failure to think about the event) are actually mediated by the unique demands placed on a child exposed to betrayal traumas, as children abused in contexts where there is no (or less) dependency do not face the pressures to avoid information about the abuse that children abused intrafamilially do.

CONCLUSION

This discussion provides a unique opportunity to revisit BTT more than a decade after its initial formulation. Good theories change over time in the face of new evidence and perspectives. BTT is no exception. We are delighted that a decade of research pushes thinking about this theory, as well as issues of memory and trauma more generally, forward. After a decade, we admit that we are not surprised that aspects of the original theory can be re-evaluated in light of new evidence. We look forward to additional research that will continue to contribute to the evolution of this and other theories related to how humans respond in the face of abuse and trauma.

REFERENCES

American Psychiatric Association. (2000). *Diagnostic and statistical manual of mental disorders IV-TR* (4th ed., text revision). Washington, DC: APA.

Anderson, M. C. (2001). Active forgetting: Evidence for functional inhibition as a source of memory failure. *Journal of Aggression, Maltreatment, Trauma*, *4*, 184–210.

Anderson, M. C., & Green, C. (2001). Suppressing unwanted memories by executive control. *Nature*, *410*, 131–134.

Anderson, M. C., Ochsner, K. N., Kuhl, B., Cooper, J., Robertson, E., Gabrieli, S. W., et al. (2004). Neural systems underlying the suppression of unwanted memories. *Science*, *303*, 232–235.

Atlas, J. A., & Ingram, D. M. (1998). Betrayal trauma in adolescent inpatients. *Psychological Reports*, *83*, 914.

Becker-Blease, K. A., Freyd, J. J., & Pears, K. C. (2004). Preschoolers' memory for threatening information depends on trauma history and attentional context: Implications for the development of dissociation. *Journal of Trauma & Dissociation*, *5*, 113–131.

Bowlby, J. (1988). *A secure base: Parent–child attachment and healthy human development*. New York: Basic Books.

Brown, D., Scheflin, A. W., & Whitfield, C. L. (1999). Recovered memories: The current weight of the evidence in science and in the courts. *Journal of Psychiatry & Law*, *27*, 5–156.

Cameron, C. (1993, April). *Recovering memories of childhood sexual abuse: A longitudinal report*. Paper presented at the Western Psychological Association Convention, Phoenix, Arizona.

Cheit, R. E. (2005). *The Recovered Memory Project*. www.brown.edu/PublicPolicy/Recovmem

Chu, J. A., & Dill, D. L. (1990). Dissociative symptoms in relation to childhood physical and sexual abuse. *American Journal of Psychiatry*, *147*, 887–892.

Cloitre, M., Cancienne, J., Brodsky, B., Dulit, R., & Perry, S. W. (1996). Memory performance among women with parental abuse histories: Enhanced directed forgetting or directed remembering? *Journal of Abnormal Psychology*, *105*, 204–211.

Cosmides, L. (1989). The logic of social exchange: Has natural selection shaped how humans reason? Studies with the Wason selection task. *Cognition*, *31*, 187–276.

DePrince, A. P. (2005). Social cognition and revictimisation risk. *Journal of Trauma and Dissociation*, *6*, 125–141.

DePrince, A. P., & Freyd, J. J. (1999). Dissociative tendencies, attention, and memory. *Psychological Science*, *10*, 449–452.

DePrince, A. P., & Freyd, J. J. (2001). Memory and dissociative tendencies: The roles of attentional context and word meaning in a directed forgetting task. *Journal of Trauma & Dissociation*, *2*(2), 67–82.

DePrince, A. P., & Freyd, J. J. (2002a). The harm of trauma: Pathological fear, shattered assumptions, or betrayal? In J. Kauffman (Ed.), *Loss of the assumptive world: A theory of traumatic loss* (pp. 71–82). New York: Brunner-Routledge.

DePrince, A. P., & Freyd, J. J. (2002b). The intersection of gender and betrayal in trauma. In R. Kimerling, P. C. Oumette, & J. Wolfe (Eds.), *Gender and PTSD* (pp. 98–113). New York: Guilford Press.

DePrince, A. P., & Freyd, J. J. (2004). Forgetting trauma stimuli. *Psychological Science*, *15*, 488–492.

DePrince, A. P., Freyd, J. J., & Malle, B. (2007). A replication by another name: A response to Devilly et al. (2007). *Psychological Science*, *18*, 218–219.

Edwards, V. J., Fivush, R., Anda, R. F., Felitti, V. J., & Nordenberg, D. F. (2001). Autobiographical memory disturbances in childhood abuse survivors. *Journal of Aggression, Maltreatment, Trauma*, *4*, 247–264.

Edwards, V. J., Freyd, J. J., Dube, S. R., Anda, R. F., & Felitti, V. J. (2006). *Health effects by closeness of sexual abuse perpetrator: A test of betrayal trauma theory*. Poster presented at the 22nd Annual Meeting of the International Society for Traumatic Stress Studies, Hollywood, CA, November 4–7.

Elliott, D. M. (1997). Traumatic events: Prevalence and delayed recall in the general population. *Journal of Consulting and Clinical Practice*, *65*, 811–820.

Elzinga, B. M., de Beurs, E., Sergeant, J. A., Van Dyck, R., & Phaf, R. H. (2000). Dissociative style and directed forgetting. *Cognitive Therapy and Research*, *24*, 279–295.

Feeny, N. C., Zoellner, L. A., & Foa, E. B. (2000). Anger, dissociation, and post-traumatic stress disorder among female assault victims. *Journal of Traumatic Stress*, *13*(1), 89–100.

Feldman-Summers, S., & Pope, K. S. (1994). The experience of "forgetting" childhood abuse: A national survey of psychologists. *Journal of Consulting and Clinical Psychology*, *62*, 636–639.

Felitti, V. J., Anda, R. F., Nordenberg, D., Williamson, D. F., Spitz, A. M., Edwards, V., et al. (1998). The relationship of adult health status to childhood abuse and household dysfunction. *American Journal of Preventive Medicine*, *14*, 245–258.

Fergusson, D. M., Horwood, L. J., & Woodward, L. J. (2000). The stability of child abuse reports: A longitudinal study of the reporting behaviour of young adults. *Psychological Medicine*, *30*, 529–544.

Fitzpatrick, F. L. (1994). Isolation and silence: A male survivor speaks out about clergy abuse. *Moving Forward*, *3*(1), 4–8.

Foynes, M. M., Freyd, J. J., & DePrince, A. P. (2006). *Child abuse, betrayal, and disclosure*. Poster presented at the 22nd Annual Meeting of the International Society for Traumatic Stress Studies, Hollywood, CA, November 4–7.

Freyd, J. J. (1991). *Memory repression, dissociative states, and other cognitive control processes involved in adult sequelae of childhood trauma*. Paper presented at the Second Annual Conference on A Psychodynamics – Cognitive Science Interface, Langley Porter Psychiatric Institute, University of California, San Francisco, August 21–22.

Freyd, J. J. (1994). Betrayal-trauma: Traumatic amnesia as an adaptive response to childhood abuse. *Ethics & Behaviour*, *4*, 307–329.

Freyd, J. J. (1996). *Betrayal trauma: The logic of forgetting childhood abuse*. Cambridge, MA: Harvard University Press.

Freyd, J. J. (1999). Blind to betrayal: New perspectives on memory for trauma. *The Harvard Mental Health Letter*, *15*(12), 4–6.

Freyd, J. J. (2001). Memory and dimensions of trauma: Terror may be "all-too-well remembered" and betrayal buried. In J. R. Conte (Ed.), *Critical issues in child sexual abuse: Historical, legal, and psychological perspectives* (pp. 139–173). Thousand Oaks, CA: Sage Publications.

Freyd, J. J. (2003). Memory for abuse: What can we learn from a prosecution sample? *Journal of Child Sexual Abuse*, *12*, 97–103.

Freyd, J. J., DePrince, A. P., & Zurbriggen, E. L. (2001). Self-reported memory for abuse depends upon victim–perpetrator relationship. *Journal of Trauma & Dissociation*, *2*, 5–17.

Freyd, J. J., & Goldberg, L. R. (2004). *Gender difference in exposure to betrayal trauma*. Spoken presentation at the 20th Annual Meeting of the International Society for Traumatic Stress Studies, New Orleans, LA, November 14–18.

Freyd, J. J., Klest, B., & Allard, C. B. (2005a). Betrayal trauma: Relationship to physical health, psychological distress, and a written disclosure intervention. *Journal of Trauma & Dissociation*, *6*(3), 83–104.

Freyd, J. J., Putnam, F. W., Lyon, T. D., Becker-Blease, K. A., Cheit, R. E., Siegel, N. B., et al. (2005b). The science of child sexual abuse. *Science*, *308*, 501.

Freyd, J. J., Putnam, F. W., Lyon, T. D., Becker-Blease, K. A., Cheit, R. E., Siegel, N. B., et al. (2005c). The problem of child sex abuse [Response to letters to the editor]. *Science*, *309*, 1183–1185.

Gardner, M. (1993). The false memory syndrome. *Skeptical Inquirer*, *17*, 370–375.

Gleaves, D. H., Smith, S.M., Butler, L.D., & Spiegel, D. (2004). False and recovered memories in the laboratory and clinic: A review of experimental and clinical evidence. *Clinical Psychology: Science and Practice*, *11*, 3–28.

Goldberg, L., & Freyd, J. J. (2006). The brief betrayal trauma survey: Personality correlates of potentially traumatic experiences in a community sample. *Journal of Trauma and Dissociation*, *7*(3), 39–63.

Goldsmith, R., & Freyd, J. J. (2005). Awareness for emotional abuse. *Journal of Emotional Abuse*, *5*(1), 95–123.

Goldsmith, R. E., Freyd, J. J., & DePrince, A. P. (2004). *Health correlates of exposure to betrayal trauma*. Poster presented at the Annual Meeting of the American Association for the Advancement of Science, Seattle, 12–16 February.

Goodman, G. S., Ghetti, S., Quas, J. A., Edelstein, R. S., Alexander, K. W., Redlich, A. D., et al. (2003). A prospective study of memory for child sexual abuse: New findings relevant to the repressed-memory debate. *Psychological Science*, *14*, 113–118.

Grinker, R. R., & Spiegel, J. P (1945). *War neuroses*. Philadelphia, PA: Blakiston.

Kihlstrom, J. F., McNally, R. J., Loftus, E. F., & Pope, H. G. Jr. (2005). The problem of child sex abuse [Letter to the editor]. *Science*, *309*, 1182–1183.

Leskin, G. A., Kaloupek, D. G., & Keane, T. M. (1998). Treatment for traumatic memories: Review and recommendations. *Clinical Psychology Review*, *18*, 983–1002.

McFarlane, A. C., & van der Kolk, B. A. (1996). Conclusions and future directions. In B. A. van der Kolk, A. McFarlane, & A. L. Weisaeth (Eds.), *Traumatic stress: The effects of overwhelming experience on mind, body, and society*. New York: Guilford Press.

McNally, R. J. (2007). Betrayal trauma theory: A critical appraisal. *Memory*, *15*, 280–294.

McNally, R. J., Metzger, L. J., Lasko, N. B., Clancy, S. A., & Pitman, R. K. (1998). Directed forgetting of trauma cues in adult survivors of childhood sexual abuse with and without post-traumatic stress disorder. *Journal of Abnormal Psychology*, *107*, 596–601.

McNally, R. J., Ristuccia, C. S., & Perlman, C. A. (2005). Forgetting of trauma cues in adults reporting continuous or recovered memories of childhood sexual abuse. *Psychological Science*, *16*, 336–340.

Mook, D. G. (1983). In defense of external invalidity. *American Psychologist*, *38*, 379–387.

Most, S. B., Scholl, B. J., Clifford, E. R., & Simons, D. J. (2005). What you see is what you set: Sustained inattentional blindness and the capture of awareness. *Psychological Review*, *112*(1), 217–242.

Moulds, M. L., & Bryant, R. A. (2002). Directed forgetting in acute stress disorder. *Journal of Abnormal Psychology*, *111*, 175–179.

Moulds, M. L., & Bryant, R. A. (2005). An investigation of retrieval inhibition in acute stress disorder. *Journal of Traumatic Stress*, *18*, 233–236.

Ofshe, R. (1994). *Making monsters: False memories, psychotherapy, and sexual hysteria works for hysteria*. New York: Charles Scribner.

Peters, M. L., Uyterlinde, S. A., Consemulder, J., & Van Der Hart, O. (1998). Apparent amnesia on experimental memory tests in dissociative identity disorder: An exploratory study. *Consciousness and Cognition*, *7*, 27–41.

Plattner, B., Silvermann, M. A., Redlich, A. D., Carrion, V. G., Feucht, M., Friedrich, M. H., et al. (2003). Pathways to dissociation: Intrafamilial versus extrafamilial trauma in juvenile delinquents. *The Journal of Nervous and Mental Disease*, *191*, 781–788.

Sargant, W., & Slater, E. (1941). Amnestic syndromes of war. *Proceedings of the Royal Society of Medicine*, *34*, 757–764.

Schultz, T. M., Passmore, J., & Yoder, C. Y. (2003). Emotional closeness with perpetrators and amnesia for child sexual abuse. *Journal of Child Sexual Abuse*, *12*, 67–88.

Sheiman, J. A. (1999). Sexual abuse history with and without self-report of memory loss: Differences in psychopathology, personality, and dissociation. In L. M. Williams & V. L. Banyard (Eds.), *Trauma & memory* (pp. 139–148). Thousand Oaks, CA: Sage.

Sirotnak, A. P. (2006). Child abuse fatalities. In C. R. Brittain (Ed.), *Understanding the medical diagnosis of child maltreatment: A guide for nonmedical professionals* (3rd ed., pp. 207–213). New York: Oxford University Press.

Sivers, H., Schooler, J., & Freyd, J. J. (2002). Recovered memories. In V. S. Ramachandran (Ed.), *Encyclopedia of the human brain, Volume 4* (pp. 169–184). San Diego, CA: Academic Press.

Spiegel, D., & Cardeña, E. (1991). Disintegrated experience: The dissociative disorders revisited. *Journal of Abnormal Psychology*, *100*, 366–378.

Stoler, L., Quina, K., DePrince, A. P., & Freyd, J. J. (2001). Recovered memories. In J. Worrell (Ed.), *Encyclopedia of women and gender, Volume 2* (pp. 905–917). San Diego, CA: Academic Press.

Stoler, L. R. (2000). *Recovered and continuous memories of childhood sexual abuse: A quantitative and qualitative analysis*. Doctoral Dissertation, University of Rhode Island. [Purchase as UMI Proquest Dissertation #9988236 – http://wwwlib.umi.com/dissertations]

Stoler, L.R. (2001). Recovered and continuous memories of childhood sexual abuse: A quantitative and qualitative analysis (Doctoral Dissertation, University of Rhode Island). *Dissertation Abstracts International*, *61*(10-B), 5582.

Thom, D. A., & Fenton, N. (1920). Amnesia in war cases. *American Journal of Insanity*, *76*, 437–448.

Turell, S. C., & Armsworth, M. W. (2003). A log-linear analysis of variables associated with self-mutilation behaviours of women with histories of child sexual abuse. *Violence Against Women*, *9*, 487–512.

Van Til, R. (1997). *Lost daughters: Recovered memory therapy and the people it hurts*. Grand Rapids, MI: Wm. B. Eerdmans Publishing Company.

Veldhuis, C. B., & Freyd, J. J. (1999). Groomed for silence, groomed for betrayal. In M. Rivera (Ed.), *Fragment by fragment: Feminist perspectives on memory and child sexual abuse* (pp. 253–282). Charlottetown, PEI, Canada: Gynergy Books.

Widiger, T., & Sankis, L. (2000). Adult psychopathology: Issues and controversies. *Annual Review of Psychology*, *51*, 377–404.

Williams, L. M. (1992). Adult memories of childhood abuse: Preliminary findings from a longitudinal study. *Advisor (American Professional Society on the Abuse of Children)*, *5*, 19–21.

Williams, L. M. (1994). Recall of childhood trauma: A prospective study of women's memories of child sexual abuse. *Journal of Consulting and Clinical Psychology*, *62*, 1167–1176.

Williams, L. M. (1995). Recovered memories of abuse in women with documented child sexual victimisation histories. *Journal of Traumatic Stress*, *8*, 649–674.

Zurbriggen, E. L., & Becker-Blease, K. (2003). Predicting memory for childhood sexual abuse: "Nonsignificant" findings with the potential for significant harm. *Journal of Child Sexual Abuse*, *12*, 113–121.

MEMORY, 2007, 15 (3), 312–323

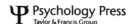

Cue self-relevance affects autobiographical memory specificity in individuals with a history of major depression

Catherine Crane, Thorsten Barnhofer, and J. Mark G. Williams
University of Oxford, UK

Previously depressed and never-depressed individuals identified personal characteristics (*self-guides*) defining their ideal, ought, and feared selves. One week later they completed the autobiographical memory test (AMT). For each participant the number of AMT cues that reflected self-guide content was determined to produce an index of AMT cue self-relevance. Individuals who had never been depressed showed no significant relationship between cue self-relevance and specificity. In contrast, in previously depressed participants there was a highly significant negative correlation between cue self-relevance and specificity—the greater the number of AMT cues that reflected self-guide content, the fewer specific memories participants recalled. It is suggested that in individuals with a history of depression, cues reflecting self-guide content are more likely to prompt a shift to processing of information within the long-term self (Conway, Singer, & Tagini, 2004), increasing the likelihood that self-related semantic information will be provided in response to cues on the autobiographical memory test.

Research has consistently demonstrated that the autobiographical memory of depressed individuals lacks specific detail. Most studies examining this phenomenon have used the Autobiographical Memory Test (AMT) in which participants are presented with a series of cue words (e.g., "Happy") and asked to come up with a memory of a specific event that each word reminds them of. When tested in this way, depressed individuals tend to retrieve generic summaries of past experience (e.g., "birthdays") rather than memories of specific events (e.g., "going swimming with my friends on my birthday last year"). This deficit has been demonstrated across a range of populations including individuals with major depression, suicidal patients, mothers with postnatal depression, and dysphoric students (see Williams et al., 2007). Over-general memory (OGM) is linked to the persistence of affective disturbance in depressed

populations (e.g., Brittlebank, Scott, Williams, & Ferrier, 1993; Dalgleish, Spinks, Yiend, & Kuyken, 2001; Peeters, Wessel, Merckelbach, & Boom-Vermeeren, 2002; cf. Brewin, Reynolds, & Tata, 1999) and is also observed in clinical groups following recovery from depression (e.g., Brittlebank, Scott, Williams, & Ferrier, 1993; Mackinger, Pachinger, Leibetseder, & Fartacek, 2000; Nadrino, Pezard, Poste, Reveillere, & Beaune, 2002; Spinhoven et al., 2006), suggesting that it may represent a relatively stable marker of vulnerability to depressive episodes.

In order to understand the mechanisms that contribute to OGM in depression, it is helpful to consider the phenomenon in the context of models of normative memory functioning and the relationship between autobiographical memory and the self. One contemporary model, shown in Figure 1, is the "Self Memory System" of

Address correspondence to: Catherine Crane, University Department of Psychiatry, Warneford Hospital, Oxford OX3 7JX, UK. E-mail: catherine.crane@psych.ox.ac.uk

The authors wish to thank everyone who gave their time to participate in this research. This research was supported by the Wellcome Trust GR067797.

DOI:10.1080/09658210701256530

Conway and Pleydell-Pearce (2000; see also Conway, Singer, & Tagini, 2004, for an elaboration). According to this model, autobiographical memories are the "transitory mental constructions" of a self memory system (SMS), comprising the working self, the episodic memory system, and the long-term self. The function of the *working self* is to initiate and monitor ongoing goal-directed activity, and to control the storage and retrieval of autobiographical memories. The *long-term self* represents self-related autobiographical knowledge in an abstract form, having two elements: the "conceptual self" (self-guides, schemata, attitudes and beliefs etc.) and the "autobiographical knowledge base" (representations of an individual's life story schema, distinct lifetime periods, e.g., "when I lived in London", and general events, e.g., "travelling to work by tube in the mornings"). Finally, the *episodic memory system* encodes sensory perceptual representations of discrete events (e.g., the sights, sounds, and smells of a particular subway journey), often in the form of visual imagery.

Within this model, *specific autobiographical memories* are conceptualised as the product of coordinated retrieval of sensory-perceptual information from the episodic memory system and contextualising information from the long-term self. *Over-general memories*, in contrast, appear to be dominated by information from the long-term self. Indeed, while general event memories (or "categoric memories" e.g., Williams & Dritschel, 1988) are the most common "error" seen on the autobiographical memory test, responses that may be better thought of as output of

life story schema information or information from the conceptual self are also observed.

Why might depressed individuals, and other clinical groups who display over-general memory, tend to respond with information from the long-term self? One possibility relates to the suggestion that autobiographical knowledge and autobiographical memories stored in the self memory system are of primary importance to an individual's ability to evaluate progress towards goals (e.g., Conway & Pleydell-Pearce, 2000). According to the Self Memory System model, information signalling challenges to goal progress (such as the awareness of discrepancies between one's current circumstances and desired goals) will prompt a shift of self memory system processing priorities from the encoding and retrieval of information in the episodic memory system ("adaptive correspondence") towards the long-term self, with an increased emphasis on the maintenance of self-coherence, such that "knowledge based in the long-term self is likely to dominate attention" (Conway et al., 2004, p. 495).

A considerable body of research has indicated that depressive states and other forms of negative affect are closely linked to the perception of discrepancy from approach goals (often referred to as "ideal or ought self-guides") and proximity to avoidance goals ("feared self-guides"; e.g., Carver, Lawrence, & Scheier, 1999; Carver & Scheier, 1998; Higgins, 1987; Higgins, Bond, Klein, & Strauman, 1986; Strauman, 1989). Rumination, which can also be regarded as a form of discrepancy-based processing in which an attempt is made to reduce the gap between a current state and desired state by mental analysis

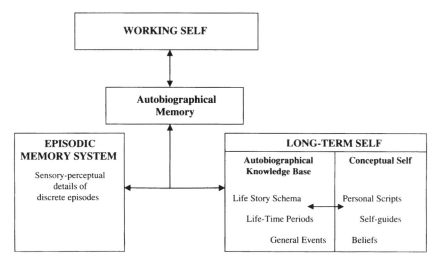

Figure 1. A summary of the self-memory system (SMS) as described by Conway et al. (2004).

(e.g., Martin & Tesser, 1989, 1996; Matthews & Wells, 2004; Watkins, Teasdale, & Williams, 2000), is also common during depressive episodes. If the Self Memory System model is correct then depressive episodes will be associated with the increased salience of abstract autobiographical information stored in the long-term self, more extensive processing and elaboration of this information, and an increased likelihood that individuals will respond with such information when asked to retrieve memories to cue words.

The observation that the induction of rumination (discrepancy-based processing) maintains over-general memory in depressed patients, whereas distraction reduces it (e.g., Watkins et al., 2000), is supportive of this suggestion, as are the findings of other studies demonstrating a link between rumination and over-general memory in clinical samples (Park, Goodyer, & Teasdale, 2004; Raes et al., 2005). Further, Dalgleish et al. (2003) hypothesised that over-general memory may be particularly likely to occur if cues forming the basis of a memory search actually map on to, and hence directly prime, concepts in the long-term self. These data suggest that over-general memory may be observed when an individual is prompted to shift to a mode of processing that favours self-coherence (and facilitation of information in the long-term self) over adaptive correspondence. This is most likely following exposure to salient self-relevant information, information related to important goals, or to stimuli that promote rumination.

In what circumstances might we expect to see the effects of priming of self-relevant concepts on autobiographical memory? The most obvious context is during episodes of depression. At such times, the predominance of rumination, negative self-referent thinking, and perceived discrepancies from goals or ideals are likely to ensure that the self memory system is focused on the processing of information within the long-term self, elaborating this content and producing high levels of over-general memory. However, a second context in which we might expect to see effects of self-relevant priming is in *previously* depressed individuals. The increased rehearsal of abstract autobiographical knowledge during prior periods of depressive rumination and the potential for self-referent cues to prime latent negative self-schemas are suggested to increase the likelihood that previously depressed individuals, relative to never-depressed controls, will experience a shift to processing information in the long-

term self when exposed to self-referent material. Given the relative absence in recovery of other factors (such as deficits in motivation and executive capacity) that may contribute to over-general memory during depressive episodes, over-general memory in previously depressed groups may be *particularly* related on the extent to which cues are salient and self-relevant, for example, relating to an individual's long-term goals or ideals.

The study reported here examines the effects of exposure to self-relevant material on autobiographical memory specificity in individuals with a history of depression and never-depressed controls. Participants were asked to complete a "self-guides" questionnaire (see Carver et al., 1999) in which they listed personal characteristics defining their ideal, ought, and feared selves (e.g., the characteristics they felt they ought to have, would ideally like to have, and most feared having). One week after completing the questionnaire, participants completed a standard version of the AMT. It was hypothesised that increased exposure to self-relevant material on the AMT would be associated with a general reduction in memory specificity in previously depressed individuals, but that this relationship would be attenuated or absent in never-depressed controls. It was unclear whether exposure to self-relevant information would act to influence retrieval on a cue-by-cue basis or would have a more pervasive impact on retrieval. Therefore the specificity of responses to self-relevant and non-self-relevant cues was compared, but no firm hypotheses were developed a priori.

METHOD

Recruitment

Advertisements in community buildings, in the local newspaper, and on a community internet site requested volunteers who had been depressed in the past but were currently well, and individuals who had never been depressed. Individuals who were interested in taking part were invited to attend two experimental sessions at the University Department of Psychiatry. Participants were paid £20 for participating in the study, which was approved by University of Oxford, Central Research Ethics Committee.

Participants

A total of 21 individuals without a history of major depression and 23 individuals with a history of major depression participated in the study. A further six individuals who reported significant past depressive symptoms but did not meet full criteria for past major depression (see later) were interviewed but excluded. Additionally, one individual was excluded due to current mania (which manifested itself in the week between psychiatric interview and cognitive testing) and two individuals were excluded as a result of equipment failure.

All previously depressed participants were recovered at the time of participation in the study, having had no or only minimal symptoms for at least 8 weeks (Frank et al., 1991; Keller, Shapiro, Lavori, & Wolfe, 1982). More detailed assessment of recovery as well as details of other psychiatric disorders were established when participants attended the Department of Psychiatry, using the Structured Clinical Interview for DSM-IV (SCID: First, Spitzer, Gibbon & Williams, 1996). All interviews were conducted by a post-doctoral clinical or research psychologist.

Other psychiatric diagnoses. The SCID interview identified current psychiatric diagnoses in two of the 21 individuals who had never been depressed, with one case of current alcohol dependence and one of current substance abuse. In contrast, current psychiatric diagnoses were identified in 12 of the 23 individuals with a history of major depression.[1] Two individuals had specific phobias and one individual had panic and specific phobia in partial remission. One individual had social phobia, one had agoraphobia, one panic disorder, one panic disorder with agoraphobia in partial remission, one alcohol abuse with PTSD, and two PTSD in partial remission. Finally, one individual had generalised anxiety disorder and

one individual had bulimia. These disorders were of mild to moderate severity in all cases.

Procedure

Session 1 began with a discussion of the study and the gathering of written informed consent. This was followed by the clinical interview and the completion of several questionnaires (those of relevance to the current study are described below). A second appointment was scheduled for approximately 1 week later. During this session, individuals completed the autobiographical memory test, followed by the Mill-Hill Vocabulary Test and Raven's Advanced Progressive Matrices, to assess current cognitive functioning. Following these tasks, participants were fully debriefed.

Questionnaires

Beck Depression Inventory. The Beck Depression Inventory (BDI-II; Beck, Steer, & Brown, 1996) is a well-established measure of depressive symptomatology that contains 21 groups of statements, referring to the presence of symptoms of depression over the preceding 2 weeks.

Self-Description Questionnaire (Carver et al., 1999). Participants completed a questionnaire in which they were asked to describe three different "self-concepts": their "ought self", "ideal self", and "feared self" (see Appendix for definition). Participants first identified and listed seven characteristics that described their "ought", "ideal", and "feared" self-concepts. They then copied each of the characteristics onto a second page and first rated their current similarity to each characteristic on a scale ranging from 1 ("presently I am the opposite of this characteristic") to 7 ("presently I am just like this characteristic"). In an addition to the questionnaire of Carver et al., they then rated the likelihood that they would possess each characteristic in the future, and the importance of each characteristic, again on scales ranging from 1 ("it is very unlikely that I will have this characteristic in the future"/ "this characteristic is not important to my xxxx self") to 7 ("it is very likely that I will have this characteristic in the future"/"this characteristic is very important to my xxxx self").

Autobiographical memory test (AMT)

Participants were presented one at a time with a series of cue words, which were read aloud by the

---

[1] Additional *past* psychiatric diagnoses were identified in 15 of the 23 individuals with a history of major depression. One individual had a past manic episode and a prior history of anorexia, three had a lifetime history of alcohol abuse, four had past dysthymia (one with a prior history of OCD), one had a prior history of bulimia, one non-alcohol substance abuse and dependence (cannabis), two alcohol dependence in sustained full remission (one with panic in full remission), two alcohol dependence in early full remission (one with lifetime alcohol dependence and non-alcohol substance dependence in full remission (cannabis, amphetamine), one non-alcohol substance abuse (cannabis) in early full remission.

experimenter and also presented on a computer screen. For each cue word, participants were asked to report an event that had happened to them of which the word reminded them—a *specific event*, defined as an event that had lasted less than a day and occurred at a particular time and place. Three practice words were given to participants, with practice continuing until specific memories had been recalled for at least two of these three words. In the test phase, participants were given 30 seconds to respond to each cue word. To ensure that all individuals received the same instructions, no prompts were given when a first response was not specific and participants were informed that they would not receive feedback on the specificity of their memories once the test phase had begun. After 18 cues had been presented (i.e., halfway through the task), the instructions were briefly reiterated to all participants. Participants' responses to each cue word were recorded verbatim by the experimenter and were also recorded on audio tape for later rating.

For the current study, 36 words were used as cues. Of these, 12 cue words related to interpersonal issues (affectionate, friendly, loved, sensitive, caring, loyal, lonely, needy, rejected, heartless, isolated, disliked), 12 related to achievement issues (efficient, thorough, successful, ambitious, able, determined, incompetent, unproductive, inept, inefficient, failure, useless), and 12 described emotional states (lively, happy, calm, excited, glorious, lucky, upset, tired, bad, awful, sad, bored), with 6 positive and 6 negative words in each category. These words were selected to increase the likelihood that cues would overlap to some extent with participants' self-guides. Words were identified from a larger pool, with positive and negative words matched for emotionality, frequency, and imageability on the basis of ratings made by 25 individuals blind to the research hypotheses. Words were presented in one of two pseudo-random orders, counterbalanced across participants.

Following previous studies, responses were rated by the experimenter as specific (events lasting less than a day), categoric (repeated events), extended (events lasting longer than one day), semantic associates of the cue word, and omissions (no response; details of scoring procedures for the AMT are available from the authors).

Other cognitive tasks

In order to ensure that general cognitive performance was matched between previously depressed and never-depressed controls, two cognitive tasks were administered.

Mill Hill Vocabulary Test. This test (Raven, Raven, & Court, 1998) assesses a participant's ability to reproduce previously acquired knowledge (crystallised intelligence), in this case word meanings. A total of 66 target words requiring definition were presented. For each target, participants were required to select from six alternative words one that was most similar in meaning to the target. The test was untimed, with the total number of target words correctly defined (out of a possible 66) recorded.

Ravens Advanced Progressive Matrices – Set 1. The progressive matrices (Raven, 1976) provide a culture-fair test of fluid intelligence—the ability to adapt reasoning skills to novel problems. Participants were presented with 12 problems to complete in 10 minutes. Each problem consisted of a visual pattern in which one "piece" was missing. Participants were required to select from eight options the piece that correctly completed the pattern. The total number of matrices correctly completed (out of 12) was recorded.

Deriving indices of AMT cue self-relevance

Two indices of AMT cue self-relevance were derived. First, we determined for each participant the *number of self-guides* that were represented by one or more AMT cue or AMT cue synonym. To do this, a document was created that contained each AMT cue (e.g., "affectionate") and each cue's synonyms (e.g., "loving", "demonstrative", "warm", "friendly", "kind"), based on the synonyms provided by the Thesaurus in Microsoft Office Word 2003. This document was searched electronically for each self-guide to identify exact matches, and the total number of matches was recorded. From time to time an individual reported the same attribute as both an "ideal" and an "ought" self-guide. Where these attributes matched an AMT cue, they were counted twice, as it was considered that the attribute was more important to the individual's sense of self.

Second, we identified the AMT cues that had represented matches to self-guides. Although some self-guides matched AMT cues exactly, others matched synonyms of the cues. If a self-guide had matched an AMT cue *synonym*, the "originating" cue was identified. The number of originating cues was counted for each individual to create an index of *the number of AMT cues* that were self-relevant. This index differs from the index corresponding to the *number of self-guides* whose content was represented in the AMT, because it was possible for two self-guides to be synonyms of a single AMT cue (e.g., "kind" and "loving" are both synonyms of the AMT cue "caring"). Identifying the originating cues also allowed for a comparison of specificity of responses to self-relevant cues and non-relevant cues on the AMT (see below).

RESULTS

Demographics

The mean age of the participants was 32.95 (SD = 12.66, range 18–62) years. Individuals with a past history of depression (M = 36.13, SD = 13.92) were somewhat older than those without such a history (M = 29.48, SD = 10.35). However, there was no significant difference between the groups in mean age (U = 186.00, Z = − 1.31, p = .19). There were nine male participants in each group.

Past depressive symptoms

Among those individuals with a history of depression, mean age of onset of depressive symptoms was 21.65 (SD = 8.79) years. The median number of past episodes of depression was 3 (M = 6.83, SD = 9.71, range 1–40). Of the 23 individuals, 14 had experienced thoughts of death or suicide during their worst episode of depression.

Current depression

Mean BDI score was 3.90 (SD = 4.01) in the never-depressed group and 6.26 (SD = 7.05) in the previously depressed group, with no significant difference between the groups in current depressive symptoms, $F(1, 42)$ = 1.81, MSE = 33.72, p > .18.

Cognitive tasks

Never-depressed and previously depressed participants did not differ in their performance on the Raven's Matrices (Never Depressed: M = 10.90, SD = 0.94; Previously Depressed: 10.81, SD = 1.22), $F(1, 41)$ = 0.07, MSE = 1.20, p > .70. Nor did they differ from one another on the Mill Hill Vocabulary Test (Never Depressed: M = 42.62, SD = 10.14; Previously Depressed: M = 43.26, SD = 11.39) $F(1, 42)$ = 0.04, MSE = 116.84, p > .80, indicating that the two groups were well matched in general cognitive abilities.

Self-description questionnaire

Similarity, likelihood, and importance ratings for ideal, ought, and feared self-guides were compared between groups. There was a trend towards previously depressed participants reporting less similarity to ought self-guides than never-depressed controls, $F(1, 39)$ = 3.62, MSE = 65.32, p = .06. There were no significant differences between groups in similarity ratings for ideal or feared self-guides (ps > .10), although mean differences were in the expected direction (i.e., less similarity to ideal self-guides and more similarity to feared self guides in the previously depressed group). Future likelihood ratings also did not differ between groups (all ps > .12), although again mean differences were in the expected direction. Previously depressed participants tended to rate ideal, ought, and feared self-guides as more important than never-depressed controls. However these differences did not reach statistical significance in any case (ps > .15). Descriptive statistics for the self-description questionnaire are shown in Table 1.

Autobiographical memory test (AMT)

Descriptive statistics for participants' performance on the AMT (number of responses that were specific, extended, categoric, associates, and omissions) are shown in Table 2. Visual inspection of the data indicates that specific memories were by far the most common response, but that in cases where participants failed to retrieve a specific memory, the most common response was an omission. Univariate analysis of variance revealed no significant difference between groups

TABLE 1
Descriptive statistics for self-discrepancy questionnaire

Self-guide	Never depressed		Previously depressed	
	M	SD	M	SD
Ideal				
Similarity	32.11	6.55	30.05	5.39
Likelihood	37.83	5.25	35.05	5.63
Importance	41.56	3.36	43.05	3.69
Ought				
Similarity	33.90	7.73	29.10	8.40
Likelihood	36.60	8.05	33.71	7.50
Importance	39.35	7.80	42.29	4.70
Feared				
Similarity	20.95	7.00	24.81	9.12
Likelihood	20.57	7.24	24.04	10.06
Importance	39.71	5.31	41.83	6.86

Scores on each variable could range from 0 (lowest similarity, importance, likelihood) to 49 (highest similarity, importance, likelihood). For feared self-guides higher ratings are more negative (i.e., more similarity to a feared self-concept).

in number of specific memories: $F(1, 42) = 1.07$, $MSE = 54.35$, $p > .30$; extended memories: $F(1, 42) = 0.00$, $MSE = 6.66$, $p > .99$; categoric memories: $F(1, 42) = 0.53$, $MSE = 7.45$, $p > .40$; semantic associates: $F(1, 42) = 1.53$, $MSE = 7.55$, $p > .20$; or omissions: $F(1, 42) = 0.23$, $MSE = 25.46$, $p > .60$. Given the relatively small number of responses that fell into each category of non-specific memory, number of specific memories was used as the primary outcome variable in subsequent analyses.[2]

Number of self-guides represented

The mean number of self-guides that were represented by an AMT cue or cue synonym was $M = 6.29$ $(SD = 3.16)$ for never-depressed individuals and $M = 6.09$ $(SD = 2.54)$ for pre-

---

[2] We examined number of specific memories rather than proportion of specific memories (number of specific memories controlling for omissions), because during debriefing most participants reported that when they had made an omission they actually had in mind non-specific content (for example, semantic associates, or self-related thoughts), which they withheld in order not to violate task instructions. It is possible that when in recovery, improvements in cognitive control reduce output of over-general memories—individuals are better able to retain task instructions and withhold incorrect responses. As such, omissions are likely to represent a mixture of different types of over-general response as well as true memory absences.

viously depressed individuals. ANOVA indicated no significant difference between groups in this index of self-relevance, $F(1, 42) = 0.05$, $MSE = 8.15$, $p > .80$. When this index was considered separately for ideal, ought, and feared self-guides, there were also no significant differences between groups (all $ps = .50$).

Number of self-relevant AMT cues

The mean number of AMT cues that matched a self-guide or had a synonym that matched a self-guide was $M = 5.57$ $(SD = 2.48)$ for never-depressed individuals and $M = 5.09$ $(SD = 1.98)$ for previously depressed individuals. ANOVA indicated no significant difference between the groups in the number of self-relevant cues presented on the AMT, $F(1, 42) = 0.52$, $MSE = 4.98$, $p > .40$.

Relationship between indices of cue self-relevance

As expected, the two indices of cue-self relevance, although distinct, were found to be highly correlated ($r = .84$, $p < .001$). For clarity, further analyses focus on the index corresponding to the number of AMT cues that were self-relevant, since this index is not influenced by repetition of attributes across two self-guide domains.

Cue self-relevance and memory specificity

A regression analysis was conducted to examine the impact of previous MDD, cue self-relevance (number of AMT cues that matched self-guides), and the interaction between cue self-relevance and previous MDD on the number of specific memories retrieved by participants. Depression status (never depressed, previously depressed) was entered at Step 1. The index of cue self-relevance was entered at Step 2 and the interaction at Step 3 (see Table 3 for summary of regression model). At Step 1, the regression model was non-significant. At Step 2, there was a significant improvement in the model, $\Delta F(1, 41) = 5.22$, $p = .03$, with the model becoming significant at trend level, $R^2 = .14$, $F(2, 41) = 3.20$, $p = .051$, and cue self-relevance entering as a significant predictor of number of specific

TABLE 2
Number of AMT responses falling into each category (36 items in total)

Type of response	Never depressed		Previously depressed	
	M (%)	SD	M (%)	SD
Specific	24.48 (68%)	6.05	22.17 (61.6%)	8.39
Extended	3.05 (8.5%)	2.82	3.04 (8.4%)	2.34
Categoric	2.10 (5.8%)	1.87	2.70 (7.5%)	3.32
Associate	1.19 (3.3%)	1.72	2.22 (6.2%)	3.42
Omission	5.14 (14.3%)	3.82	5.87 (16.3%)	5.94

memories ($p < .05$). With the addition of the interaction between past history of depression and AMT cue self-relevance at Step 3, there was a significant improvement in the model, $\Delta R^2 = .21$, $\Delta F(1, 40) = 12.69$, $p = .001$, and the overall regression model became highly significant, $R^2 = .34$, $F(3, 40) = 6.97$, $p = .001$. The interaction between cue self-relevance and past MDD entered as a significant predictor of specificity ($p = .001$), with the final model accounting for 34% of the variance in number of specific memories retrieved.

To examine the nature of the interaction between cue self-relevance and specificity, Pearson's correlation coefficients were calculated for the relationship between number of specific memories retrieved and number of self-relevant cues presented, separately for individuals with and without a history of major depression. These indicated that while there was no significant correlation between cue self-relevance and specificity in the never-depressed group ($r = .07$, $p > .70$), there was a highly significant correlation in the previously depressed group ($r = -.69$, $p < .001$). Thus, increased exposure to self-relevant cues was associated with reduced retrieval of specific memories, but only in individuals with a history of major depression. Scatter plots depicting these relationships are shown in Figure 2.

Specificity of responses to self-relevant and non-self-relevant cues

In order to examine whether the presence of self-relevant cues influenced only retrieval of specific memories to those cues, or had a broader impact on retrieval, the proportion of specific responses given to self-relevant cues and non self-relevant cues was calculated for each individual. Repeated measures analysis of variance was used to compare these two scores in individuals with and

without a history of major depression. This analysis revealed no significant effect of cue type, $F(1, 41) = 1.38$, $p = .25$ and no significant interaction between cue type and past MDD, $F(1, 41) = 1.08$, $p = .30$. Because the mean number of self-relevant cues was relatively low compared to the total number of cues presented, in some cases proportions were based on the very few responses to self-relevant cues. An alternative way of examining the pervasiveness of the effect of cue self-relevance is to examine the effect of number of self-relevant cues on specificity of responses to cues that were *not* matches to self-guides. Pearson's correlation coefficients revealed that in the previously depressed group, the greater the number of self-relevant cues presented, the less specific participants were in response to other, non-self-relevant cues, $r = -.76$, $p < .001$. In contrast, in the never-depressed group, the presence of self-relevant cues had no impact on specificity to non-self-relevant cues, $r = -.18$, $p > .40$.

DISCUSSION

The aim of this study was to examine whether the ability to retrieve specific autobiographical memories varies as a function of the self-relevance of memory cues. Results indicated that in never-depressed participants there was no systematic relationship between cue self-relevance and specificity. In contrast, previously depressed participants showed a highly significant negative correlation between the number of self-relevant cues presented on the AMT and the ability to retrieve specific autobiographical memories—the greater the number of self-relevant cues presented, the fewer specific memories participants recalled. Regression analysis confirmed that history of major depression moderated the association between cue self-relevance and specificity, with the

TABLE 3
Regression model examining the contribution of past history of MDD and cue self-relevance to the prediction of number of specific memories retrieved on the AMT

	Variable	B	SE B	β	t	p
Model 1	Past MDD	−2.30	2.23	.16	−1.03	.31
Model 2	Past MDD	−2.84	2.13	−.20	−1.33	.19
	Cue Self-Relevance	−1.11	.49	−.33	−2.28	.03
Model 3	Past MDD	13.57	4.98	.93	2.73	.009
	Cue Self-Relevance	.17	.56	.05	.30	.77
	Past MDD* Cue Self-Relevance	−3.11	.87	−1.23	−3.56	.001

Model 1: $R^2 = .03$, $F(1, 42) = 1.07$, $p = .31$.
Model 2: $R^2 = .14$, $F(2, 41) = 3.20$, $p = .051$, $\Delta R^2 = .11$, $\Delta F(1, 41) = 5.22$, Sig ΔF $p = .03$.
Model 3: $R^2 = .34$, $F(3, 40) = 6.97$, $p = .001$, $\Delta R^2 = .21$, $\Delta F(1, 40) = 12.69$, Sig ΔF $p = .001$.

variance in specificity explained by the regression model containing the interaction term rising to approximately 30%. Subsequent analyses indicated that the effect of exposure to self-relevant cues had a general deleterious effect in the previously depressed group, with specificity of retrieval to non-self relevant cues also being affected.

The current study examined the effects on retrieval specificity of AMT cues whose content reflected a participant's self-guides (desired or feared characteristics or attributes). The Self Memory System model suggests that when information that signals a challenge to goal progress is presented, the processing of information stored in the long-term self (e.g., general event memories, lifetime period, life story schema, and conceptual self-knowledge) will be prioritised, with an emphasis on the maintenance of self-coherence. Because, during depressive episodes, individuals report marked discrepancies from self-guides and spend significant amounts of time engaged in depressive rumination (a form of discrepancy-based processing), it was hypothesised that presentation of cues relating to an individual's self-guides would be more likely to produce a shift towards processing for self-coherence in the previously depressed group, reinstating a form of processing that has been over-rehearsed in the past. In addition, information relating to goals and self-guides stored within the long-term self may be more elaborated in individuals with a history of depression as a consequence of increased processing during prior episodes, making such a shift towards long-term self-processing more difficult to override. Although speculative at present, such a suggestion would be consistent with other studies showing that in recovered individuals with a history of depression, negative

cognitive biases remain latent and can be easily reactivated, for example when individuals process self-referent material in the context of mood challenge or cognitive load (e.g., Scher, Ingram, & Segal, 2005; Wenzlaff & Bates, 1998).

The fact that increased cue self-relevance influenced specificity of retrieval to all cues in previously depressed participants, not just those that were identified as matching self-guides, is interesting. One possibility is that because the cues on the AMT were selected to relate to interpersonal issues, achievement issues, and emotional states, the overlap in meaning between cues was too great for distinct effects to be observed for cues identified as matching or not matching self-guides. However, it is also possible that exposure to some self-relevant content may have been sufficient to have a more persistent effect on specificity. For example, previous research has indicated that brief rumination inductions maintain over-generality and brief distraction inductions reduce over-generality during subsequent AMT testing (e.g., Watkins et al., 2000), and it also appears that over-general memory increases across repeated trials in individuals with low self-esteem relative to those with high self-esteem (Roberts & Carlos, 2006). These findings may reflect the cumulative effects of activation of self-related content on retrieval in vulnerable groups. Further research incorporating distinct neutral cues would be required to clarify the scope of any effect of cue self-relevance on specificity.

A number of limitations should be borne in mind when interpreting the current results. First, although individuals with a history of depression did not differ significantly from never-depressed controls in ratings of self-discrepancy, in all cases mean differences were in the expected direction, suggesting that self-guide cues may have been more salient for those with a history of MDD.

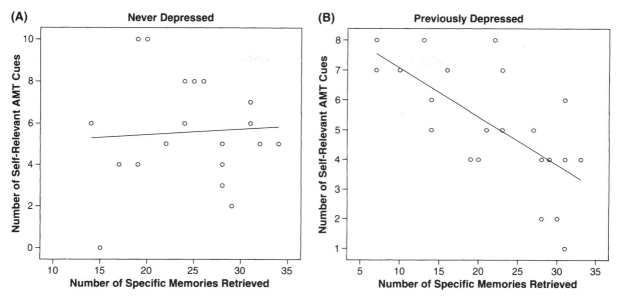

Figure 2. Relationship between the number of self-relevant AMT cues and number of specific memories recalled in never-depressed (A) and previously depressed (B) participants.

Additionally we measured self-guides 1 week before completion of the AMT, in order to reduce the likelihood that participants would see a link between the two tasks. However, it is possible that individuals with a history of depression show more stability in their ratings of self-guides (for example due to prolonged periods of rumination on these issues in the past). If this was the case, it is plausible that the measure of self-relevance of AMT cues would be more accurate for the previously depressed than the never-depressed group. Further research is required to address this possibility as well as to examine the extent to which the effect of self-relevance on specificity is restricted to discrepant self-relevant information.

Second, in the current study there was no significant effect of history of depression on memory specificity. While several studies have identified persisting over-generality in previously depressed patients (e.g., Brittlebank et al., 1993; Spinhoven et al., 2006), others have failed to find such an effect (e.g., Kuyken & Dalgleish, 1995; Wessel, Meeren, Peeters, Arntz, & Merckelbach, 2001; Williams, Barnhofer, Crane, & Beck, 2005). It is possible that differences between studies may relate to the extent to which different samples had residual symptoms, or had experienced past trauma, the proximity of the most recent depressive episode, or the number of depressive episodes an individual has experienced (e.g., Nandrino et al., 2002). Additionally, given the

current findings, it is possible that studies have differed by chance in the extent to which AMT cues primed previously depressed participants' core concerns.

Third, many of the previously depressed participants were experiencing other psychiatric symptoms at the time of testing. In most cases these were anxiety disorders, which do not usually appear to be associated with over-general memory (e.g., Burke & Matthews, 1992; Wenzel, Jackson, & Holt, 2002). However, the presence of these disorders may have acted to increase the likelihood that self-relevant cues would activate information stored in the long-term self, and it would therefore be premature to assume that the effect of self-relevance on memory specificity is a feature related specifically to a history of depression. Finally, while there was no difference between the groups in the extent to which AMT cues were self-relevant, it remains possible that some third factor may have contributed to the association between self-relevance and specificity seen in the previously depressed participants in this study.

There has been little previous research examining the impact of cue self-relevance on the ability to retrieve specific autobiographical memories (though see Spinhoven et al., 2007, this issue). Although preliminary, this study provides evidence to suggest that the presence of self-relevant memory cues may contribute to overgeneral retrieval in previously depressed individuals, as a result of the increased tendency of conceptual self-relevant information to capture attention. It has been demonstrated that both brief experimental manipulations (e.g., Watkins et al., 2000) and clinical interventions (e.g., Williams, Teasdale, Segal, & Soulsby, 2000) that facilitate disengagement from analytical self-focused thinking produce decreases in over-general autobiographical memory. The current findings further emphasise the importance of self-related processing in the manifestation of over-generality in depression and, although in need of replication, suggest that the integration of research examining self-related processing with research examining autobiographical memory retrieval (e.g., Conway et al., 2004; Williams et al., 2007) may provide valuable insights into how these aspects of cognitive functioning determine persisting vulnerability to depression.

REFERENCES

Beck, A. T., Steer, R. A., & Brown, G. K. (1996). *Manual for the BDI-II*. San Antonio, TX: Psychological Corporation.

Brewin, C., Reynolds, M., & Tata, P. (1999). Autobiographical memory processes and the course of depression. *Journal of Abnormal Psychology, 108*, 511–517.

Brittlebank, A. D., Scott, J., Williams, J. M. G., & Ferrier, I. N. (1993). Autobiographical memory in depression: State or trait marker. *British Journal of Psychiatry, 162*, 118–121.

Burke, M., & Mathews, A. (1992). Autobiographical memory and clinical anxiety. *Cognition & Emotion, 6*, 23–35.

Carver, C. S., Lawrence, J. W., & Scheier, M. F. (1999). Self-discrepancies and affect: incorporating the role of feared selves. *Personality and Social Psychology Bulletin, 25*, 783–792.

Carver, C. S., & Scheier, M. F. (1998). *On the self-regulation of behaviour*. Cambridge, UK: Cambridge University Press.

Conway, M. A., & Pleydell-Pearce, C. W. (2000). The construction of autobiographical memories in the self-memory system. *Psychological Review, 107*, 261–288.

Conway, M. A., Singer, J. A., & Tagini, A. (2004). The self and autobiographical memory: Correspondence and coherence. *Social Cognition, 22*, 491–529.

Dalgleish, T., Spinks, H., Yiend, J., & Kuyken, W. (2001). Autobiographical memory style in seasonal affective disorder and its relationship to future symptom remission. *Journal of Abnormal Psychology, 110*, 335–340.

Dalgleish, T., Tchanturia, K., Serpell, L., Herns, S., Yiend, J., de Silva, P., et al. (2003). Self-reported abuse relates to autobiographical memory in patients with eating disorders. *Emotion, 3*, 211–222.

First, M. B., Spitzer, R. L., Gibbon, M., & Williams, J. B. (1996). *User's guide for the Structured Clinical Interview for DSM-IV Axis I Disorders*. Washington, DC: American Psychiatric Press.

Frank, E., Prien, R. F., Jarrett, R. B., Keller, M. B., Kupfer, D. J., Lavor, P. W., et al. (1991). Conceptualisation and rational for consensus definitions of terms in major depressive disorder: response, remission, recovery, relapse, and recurrence. *Archives of General Psychiatry, 48*, 851–855.

Higgins, E. T., Bond, R. N., Klein, R., & Strauman, T. (1986). Self-discrepancies and emotional vulnerability: How magnitude, accessibility and type of discrepancy influence affect. *Journal of Personality and Social Psychology, 5*, 5–15.

Higgins, T. E. (1987). Self-discrepancy: A theory relating self and affect. *Psychological Review, 94*, 319–340.

Keller, M. B., Shapiro, R. W., Lavori, P. W., & Wolfe, N. (1982). Recovery in major depressive disorder: Analysis with Life Table and regression models. *Archives of General Psychiatry, 39*, 905–910.

Kuyken, W., & Dalgleish, T. (1995). Autobiographical memory and depression. *British Journal of Clinical Psychology, 34*, 89–92.

Mackinger, H. F., Pachinger, M. M., Leibetseder, M. M., & Fartacek, R. R. (2000). Autobiographical memories in women remitted from major depression. *Journal of Abnormal Psychology, 109*, 331–334.

Martin, L. M., & Tesser, A. (1989). Towards and motivational and structural model of ruminative thought. In J. S. Uleman & J. A. Baragh (Eds.), *Unintended thought: Limits of awareness, intention and control* (pp. 306–326). New York: Guilford Press.

Martin, L. M., & Tesser, A. (1996). Some ruminative thoughts. In R. S. Wyer Jr. (Ed.), *Advances in social cognition* (Vol. 9 pp. 1–47). Mahwah. NJ: Lawrence Erlbaum Associates, Inc.

Matthews, G., & Wells, A. (2004). Rumination, depression and metacognition: The S-REF model. In C. Papageorgiou & A. Wells (Eds.), *Depressive rumination: Nature, theory & treatment*. Chichester, UK: Wiley.

Nandrino, J., Pezard, L., Poste, A., Reveillere, C., & Beaune, D. (2002). Autobiographical memory in major depression: A comparison between first-episode and recurrent patients. *Psychopathology, 35*, 335–340.

Park, R. J., Goodyer, I. M., & Teasdale, J. D. (2004). Effects of induced rumination and distraction on mood and overgeneral memory in adolescent major depressive disorder and controls. *Journal of Child Psychology and Psychiatry, 45*, 996–1006.

Peeters, F., Wessel, I., Merckelbach, H., & Boom-Vermeeren, M. (2002). Autobiographical memory specificity and the course of major depressive disorder. *Comprehensive Psychiatry*, *43*, 344–350.

Raes, F., Hermans, D., Williams, J. M. G., Demyttenaere, K., Sabbe, B., Pieters, G., et al. (2005). Reduced specificity of autobiographical memory: A mediator between rumination and ineffective problem solving in major depression? *Journal of Affective Disorders*, *87*, 331–335.

Raven, J., Raven, J. C., & Court, J. H. (1998). *Manual for the Mill Hill Vocabulary Scale*. Oxford, UK: Oxford Psychologist Press.

Raven, J. C. (1976). *Manual for the Advanced Progressive Matrices: Set 1*. Oxford, UK: Oxford Psychologist Press.

Roberts, J. E., & Carlos, E. L. (2006). Impact of depressive symptoms, self-esteem and neuroticism on trajectories of overgeneral autobiographical memories over repeated trials. *Cognition and Emotion*, *20*, 383–401.

Scher, C. D., Ingram, R. E., & Segal., Z. V. (2005). Cognitive reactivity and vulnerability: Empirical evaluation of construct activation and cognitive diathesis in unipolar depression. *Clinical Psychology Review*, *25*, 487–510.

Spinhoven, P., Bockting, C. L. H., Kremers, I. P., Schene, A. H., & Williams, J. M. G. (2007). The endorsement of dysfunctional attitudes is associated with an impaired retrieval of specific autobiographical memories in response to matching cues. *Memory*, *15*, 324–338.

Spinhoven, P., Bockting, C. L. H., Schene, A. H., Koeter, M. W. J., Wekking, E. M., Williams, J. M. G., et al. (2006). Autobiographical memory in the euthymic phase of recurrent depression. *Journal of Abnormal Psychology*, *115*, 590–600.

Strauman, T. J. (1989). Self-discrepancies in clinical depression and social phobia: cognitive structures that underlie emotional disorders? *Journal of Abnormal Psychology*, *98*, 14–22.

Watkins, E., Teasdale, J. D., & Williams, R. M. (2000). Decentring and distraction reduce overgeneral autobiographical memory in depression. *Psychological Medicine*, *30*, 911–920.

Wenzel, A., Jackson, L. C., & Holt, C. S. (2002). Social phobia and the recall of autobiographical memories. *Depression and Anxiety*, *15*, 186–189.

Wenzlaff, R. M., & Bates, D. E. (1998). Unmasking a cognitive vulnerability to depression: How lapses in mental control reveal depressive thinking. *Journal of Personality and Social Psychology*, *75*, 1559–1571.

Wessel, I., Meeren, M., Peeters, F., Arntz, A., & Merckelbach, H. (2001). Correlates of autobiographical memory specificity: The role of depression, anxiety and childhood trauma. *Behaviour Research & Therapy*, *39*, 409–421.

Williams, J. M. G., Barnhofer, T., Crane, C., & Beck, A. T. (2005). Problem solving deteriorates following mood challenge in formerly depressed patients with a history of suicidal ideation. *Journal of Abnormal Psychology*, *114*, 421–431.

Williams, J. M. G., Barnhofer, T., Crane, C., Hermans, D., Raes, F., Watkins, E., et al. (2007). Autobiographical memory specificity and emotional disorder. *Psychological Bulletin*, *133*, 122–148.

Williams, J. M. G., Teasdale, J. D., Segal, Z. V., & Soulsby, J. (2000). Mindfulness-based cognitive therapy reduces over-general autobiographical memory in formerly depressed patients. *Journal of Abnormal Psychology*, *109*, 150–155.

APPENDIX

Definitions of ought, ideal, and feared selves

The "ought self" was described as "the kind of person you believe you have a duty or obligation to be, or that you believe people think you should be. It's defined by the personality characteristics you think you ought to possess, or feel obligated to possess. It's not necessary that you have these characteristics now, only that you believe you ought to have them."

The "ideal self" was described as "The kind of person you'd really like to be. It's defined by the personality characteristics you would ideally like to have. It's not necessary that you have these characteristics now, only that you believe you want to have them."

The "feared self" was described as "the kind of person that you fear being, worry about being, or dislike being. It's defined by the personality characteristics that you think you might have now or in the future, but that you would rather not have. It's not necessary that you have these characteristics now, only that you do not want to have them, or want to avoid having them.

MEMORY, 2007, 15 (3), 324–338

The endorsement of dysfunctional attitudes is associated with an impaired retrieval of specific autobiographical memories in response to matching cues

Philip Spinhoven
Leiden University, The Netherlands

Claudi L. H. Bockting
University of Amsterdam, The Netherlands

Ismay P. Kremers
Leiden University, The Netherlands

Aart H. Schene
University of Amsterdam, The Netherlands

J. Mark G. Williams
University of Oxford, UK

Two studies investigated a hypothesis of Dalgleish et al. (2003) that overgeneral memory may arise from matching between task cues and dysfunctional attitudes or schemas. In the first study, 111 euthymic patients with at least two previous major depressive episodes completed the Dysfunctional Attitude Scale: Form A (DAS-A) and the Autobiographical Memory Test (AMT). In the second study, 82 patients with a borderline personality disorder completed the Young Schema Questionnaire (YSQ) and the same version of the AMT. In both studies, patients retrieved less specific autobiographical memories in response to cue words that matched highly endorsed attitudes or schemas. These results suggest that an impaired retrieval of specific memories may be the result of certain cues activating generic, higher-order mental representations.

Implicit in most theoretical models of autobiographical memory is the assumption of a hierarchical architecture of human memory. In Conway's model (Conway & Pleydell-Pearce, 2000), knowledge stored at the level of a lifetime period (e.g., when I was at university) or knowledge at the level of general events (e.g., attending lectures) indexes event-specific knowledge

Address correspondence to: Philip Spinhoven PhD, Department of Psychology, Leiden University, Wassenaarseweg 52, 2333 AK Leiden, The Netherlands. E-mail: spinhoven@fsw.leidenuniv.nl

We are most grateful to the participants of our study. In addition we would like to express our appreciation to the participating psychiatric sites for their recruitment efforts, and to our interviewers and independent raters, Catherine Crane for her comments on an earlier version of this article, and Willem Heiser for his statistical advice. The first study was granted by the Health Research Development Counsel (ZON), Department Prevention Program and National Foundation for Mental Health (NFGV). The second study was supported by a grant from the fund for evaluative research in medicine of the Dutch Healthcare Insurance Board.

http://www.psypress.com/memory   DOI:10.1080/09658210701256555

(e.g., the lecture of professor x on topic y). If retrieval of specific episodes is to succeed, the intermediate categoric description at the level of general events has to be inhibited so that contextual (time and place) information can be introduced in the mnemonic search. In the last two decades, numerous studies have found that this memory search process can be disrupted in individuals with depressive disorder (e.g., Brittlebank, Scott, Williams, & Ferrier, 1993), post-traumatic stress disorder (McNally, Lasko, Macklin, & Pitman, 1995), or acute stress disorder (Harvey, Bryant, & Dang, 1998). These patient groups all show an enhanced tendency to retrieve overgeneral autobiographical memories when asked to retrieve specific memories of events in response to cue words.

It has been proposed that emotional factors such as abuse or chronic adversity in childhood or adolescence can affect the ability to learn to fully control the retrieval process (Williams, 1996), with failure to retrieve specific details of autobiographical events representing a form of learned passive avoidance of distressing material. In addition to this developmental perspective, it has also been suggested that the memory search process may be aborted at the categoric stage because various factors reduce the functioning of working memory, executive functioning, or the supervisory attentional system (Wheeler, Stuss, & Tulving, 1997). Biological factors (e.g., frontal lobe dysfunction) and cognitive intrusions, as observed in acute stress disorder (Harvey et al., 1998) or depression (Brewin, Reynolds, & Tata, 1999; Kuyken & Brewin, 1995) have been implicated because of their potential to drain processing resources necessary for generating specific memories. From this alternative perspective, the memory system may be developmentally normal, but individuals are not able to retrieve specific memories because the memory system is temporarily disrupted.

It is noteworthy that in these accounts of the retrieval of overgeneral memories, relatively little attention is paid to the meaning of the specific words used in the cue-word task. Up until now, more formal attributes of the cue words have been investigated, such as their frequency or imageability (e.g., Williams, Healy, & Ellis, 1999). Further, in studies where results on memory for positive and negative cue words are reported separately, overgenerality is found sometimes for positive cues only, sometimes for negative cues only, and sometimes for both (van

Vreeswijk & de Wilde, 2004). Explanations proposed to account for these inconsistent findings with respect to cue valence such as mood congruency (e.g., Maccallum, McConkey, Bryant, & Barnier, 2000) have not been completely satisfactory.

Dalgleish et al. (2003) have recently proposed an alternative theory. They state that one of the reasons an individual may "fail" to retrieve a specific memory in response to a particular cue word has less to do with whether it is positive or negative, than whether it maps closely onto the content of coherent, more generic, higher-order mental representations—e.g., dysfunctional attitudes (Clark, Beck, & Alford, 1999) or schematic models (Power & Dalgleish, 1997). Specifically, Dalgleish et al. (2003) suggest that responses to cue words amount to a propositional "read-off" of activated mental representations. Cue words that match dysfunctional attitudes or schemas will cause these attitudes or schemas to become (more) activated. When cue words map closely onto the content of highly endorsed dysfunctional attitudes, these attitudes may become more activated and may promote task-irrelevant processing of themes related to salient concerns and well-rehearsed generic self-knowledge. Consequently, fewer processing resources will be available for memorial search, and this potentially leads to the memory search being aborted prematurely, increasing the chance that categoric-level descriptors will be accepted as a suitable response.

We tested Dalgleish's hypothesis in two populations, both recruited for randomised controlled trials of cognitive treatment, one aimed at the prevention of relapse/recurrence of depression (Bockting et al., 2005), and the other at the long-term treatment of borderline personality disorder (Giesen-Bloo et al., 2006). The baseline assessments of these patient samples were judged to be very suitable to test our research question for the following reasons: (a) The previously depressed patients (Spinhoven et al., 2006), as well as those borderline patients who also had a comorbid depression (Kremers, Spinhoven, & Van der Does, 2004), displayed overgeneral memory; (b) It is widely assumed that in both patient groups, reactivation of dysfunctional attitudes or maladaptive schemas is associated with the onset or maintenance of these disorders (Clark et al., 1999; Lau, Segal, & Williams, 2004; Young, 1994). The primary aim of our study was to investigate whether the endorsement of dysfunctional attitudes is associated with the generation of more overgeneral and less specific memories when the words of a cue-word task map closely onto the content of such attitudes. First, the results of testing this hypothesis in a sample of recurrently depressed patients will be described (Study 1), followed by a description of the results found in a sample of patients with a borderline personality disorder (Study 2).

STUDY 1

Method

Participants

To be eligible, participants had to meet the following criteria: (a) at least two Major Depressive Episodes in the last 5 years, as defined according to DSM-IV (American Psychiatric Association, 1994) and assessed by the Structured Clinical Interview for DSM-IV (SCID: First, Spitzer, Gibbon, & Williams, 1997) by trained evaluators; (b) current remission status according to DSM-IV criteria, for longer than 10 weeks, and no longer than 2 years ago; (c) a current score on the Hamilton Rating Scale for Depression (Hamilton, 1960) of < 10. Exclusion criteria were: current mania or hypomania or a history of bipolar illness, any psychotic disorder (current and previous), organic brain damage, alcohol or drug misuse, predominant anxiety disorder, recent ECT, recent cognitive treatment, receiving CT at the start of the study or current psychotherapy with a frequency of more than twice a month.

Participants were recruited at psychiatric centres and through media announcements in The Netherlands. After a complete description of the study had been given to the participants, written informed consent was obtained prior to randomisation. The protocol was approved by the institutional ethics review committees. A total of 111 participants completed the DAS-A and AMT. The mean age of the patients was 44.4 ($SD = 9.4$), and 71.4% of the sample was female. Mean education level (theoretical range 0–6) was 3.4 ($SD = 1.6$; range 0–6). The mean HRSD score was 3.6 ($SD = 2.8$; range 0–9). A total of 20% of the participants reported two previous depressive episodes in the past, 23.8% reported three previous episodes, 29.5% reported four to six previous episodes, and 26.7% reported six or more previous episodes.

Materials and measures

Axis I diagnosis. Psychiatric diagnoses on Axis I were assessed with the Structured Clinical Interview for DSM-IV (SCID-I; First et al., 1997).

Severity of depressive symptoms. The 17-item Hamilton Rating Scale for Depression (HRSD; Hamilton, 1960) was used to assess patients' levels of depressive symptomatology.

Autobiographical Memory Test (AMT). McNally et al. (1995) modified the autobiographical memory paradigm, which was used by Williams and Broadbent (1986). In their modified version, respondents are asked to mention a specific moment at which they exhibited a personal trait that is written on a card. In this study, we used this modified version of the AMT. A specific memory is defined as a memory that refers to a particular event in the past that happened on one particular day, lasting no longer than 1 day. Words were read aloud and at the same time were shown on a card. Respondents were asked to retrieve a memory as quickly as possible, and were allowed 60 seconds to remember an event. The cue words were presented after three practice words.

Answers were recorded on audiotape. The following scoring categories were used: (a) specific: when the respondent's first memory referred to a particular event on one particular day; (b) categoric: when the memory referred to repeated events; (c) extended: when the remembered event lasted longer than 1 day; and (d) no memory/omission: when the respondent did not mention a memory or did not respond. One trained research assistant blind to the research question scored all the tapes. Inter-rater agreement on 50% of the retrieved memories ($n = 555$) indicated good reliability, 88.5% agreement, kappa = 0.79, comparable with previous studies. The following positive ($+$) and negative ($-$) words were used: friendly ($+$), guilty ($-$), impolite ($-$), honest ($+$), helpful ($+$), jealous ($-$), intelligent ($+$), selfish ($-$), humorous ($+$), and hostile ($-$). At face value it seemed that four of the 10 AMT cues referred to a common trait associated with helpfulness. Consequently, two positive (friendly and helpful) and two negative cue words (impolite and selfish) were selected and combined into a subscale reflecting personal traits involved in helping others: Helpfulness-Relevant (HR). The other six AMT items formed the second subscale of the AMT: Helpfulness-Irrelevant (HI).[1]

Dysfunctional attitudes. Dysfunctional attitudes were assessed with the Dutch translation of the Dysfunctional Attitude Scale, Form A (DAS-A; Douma, 1991; Weissmann, 1979). Four items were selected that directly pertained to attitudes related to a specific aspect of Need for Approval: helping others: "I should be able to please everybody"; "To be a good moral worthwhile person, I must help everyone who needs it"; "It is best to give up your own interests in order to please other people"; "If someone performs a selfish act, this means he is a selfish person". In order to compose a subscale that specifically relates to attitudes with respect to helping others and which could be activated by the matching helpfulness-relevant AMT cue words, a subscale comprising these four DAS-A items was formed and named Helpfulness-Relevant (HR). The other 36 items of the DAS-A were combined into a Helpfulness-Irrelevant (HI) subscale.

Procedure

After telephone screening on inclusion and exclusion criteria, patients were administered the SCID and HRDS by research assistants. Patients were tested with the DAS-A followed by the AMT in a fixed order before random assignment to treatment condition.

RESULTS

Preliminary analyses

In order to investigate the inter-rater reliability of categorising the 10 cue words of the AMT and the 40 items of the DAS-A as relevant or irrelevant with respect to helpfulness, 15 colleagues of the section of Clinical and Health Psychology at Leiden University, blind to the research question of the present study, independently rated these 50 items on a 6-point Likert scale ranging from 1 ("not at all relevant") to 6

---

[1] All remaining cue words of the AMT and also all remaining items of the DAS-A were included in a Helpfulness-Irrelevant (HI) scale, in order to counteract the risk of inadvertently maximising the difference between the Helpfulness-Relevant versus the Helpfulness-Irrelevant subscale by only selecting and including into the HI subscale those items that are clearly irrelevant with respect to helpfulness.

("extremely relevant"). The four AMT items of the Helpfulness-Relevant scale obtained the four highest mean ratings. The mean rating for these four items combined ($M = 4.7$; $SD = 1.0$) was significantly higher than the mean rating for the six other AMT items combined ($M = 2.7$; $SD = 0.90$) $t(14) = 6.484$, $p < .001$. The four DAS-A items of the Helpfulness-Relevant subscale also obtained the four highest mean ratings. The mean rating for these four items combined ($M = 4.1$; $SD = 1.5$) was significantly higher than the mean rating for the 36 other AMT items combined ($M = 2.5$; $SD = 0.93$) $t(14) = 3.982$, $p < .001$. The results of these analyses indicate a good inter-rater reliability in forming a priori subscales of the AMT and DAS-A reflecting personal traits or attitudes relevant versus irrelevant in helping others.

Number of specific responses

For the 10 items of the AMT, the participants produced a mean number of 5.4 ($SD = 2.7$) specific responses. The scores ranged from 0 to 10. A t-test for dependent samples revealed no significant differences between the percentage of specific answers retrieved on the HR subscale ($M = 52.1$; $SD = 29.9$) and on the HI subscale ($M = 56.2$; $SD = 29.3$), $t(110) = 1.763$, *ns*.

Number of categoric responses

For the 10 items of the AMT, the participants produced a mean number of 2.0 ($SD = 1.9$) categoric responses. A total of 25% of the participants gave no categoric answer in reaction to any of the 10 AMT cues words. A t-test for dependent samples revealed no significant differences between the proportion of categoric answers retrieved on the HR subscale ($M = 20.8$; $SD = 23.5$) and on the HI subscale ($M = 19.2$; $SD = 21.6$), $t(110) = 0.773$, *ns*.

Number of extended responses and no memories/omissions

For the 10 items of the AMT, the participants produced a mean number of 0.4 ($SD = 0.8$) extended responses and 2.2 ($SD = 2.2$) no memories/omissions. T-tests for dependent samples revealed no significant differences between the proportion of extended answers, $t(110) = 0.187$, *ns*, and the proportion of no memories/omissions, $t(110) = 1.479$, *ns*, in reaction to the HR subscale versus HI subscale of the AMT.

TABLE 1
First-order correlations of autobiographical memory, biographic, illness-related, and attitude variables

Variables	I.	II.	III.	IV.	V.	VI.	VII.	VIII.	IX.	X.	XI.	XII.
I. Number of specific memories (AMT)		.87***	.95***	−.61***	−.54***	−.53***	−.23*	.28***	.02	.11	.17	−.20*
II. Number of specific HR memories (AMT)			.67***	−.53***	−.63***	−.34***	−.24*	.27***	.03	.14	.11	−.28**
III. Number of specific HI memories (AMT)				−.58***	−.41***	−.58***	−.20*	.25*	.02	.07	.18	−.11
IV. Number of categoric memories (AMT)					.82***	.91***	.19*	−.15	−.03	−.04	−.06	.10
V. Number of categoric HR memories (AMT)						.51***	.22*	−.15	−.02	−.03	.08	.26**
VI. Number of categoric HI memories (AMT)							.13	−.12	−.03	−.03	−.16	−.04
VII. Age								−.11	−.08	.13	−.10	.25**
VIII. Education									−.01	−.11	.03	−.09
IX. HDRS										.16	.23*	.04
X. History of depression											.14	−.03
XI. Total DAS-A score												.28**
XII. Δ HR-HI DAS-A												

$n = 111$ previously depressed patients. AMT = Autobiographical Memory Test; HDRS = Hamilton Depression Rating Scale; DAS-A = Dysfunctional Attitude Scale: Form A; Δ HR-HI DAS-A = Helpfulness relevant minus helpfulness irrelevant DAS-A scores.
* $p < .05$; ** $p < .01$; *** $p < .001$.

Scores for dysfunctional attitudes

Our sample of patients with recurrent depression manifested moderately high scores for dysfunctional attitudes, as witnessed by a mean total score of 124.2 ($SD = 33.5$; range 52–226) on the DAS-A (Dozois, Covin, & Brinker, 2003). Using a t-test for dependent measures, a significant difference between the mean item score on the HR subscale ($M = 3.2$; $SD = 1.3$) in comparison to the mean score on the other 36 items of the DAS-A (HI subscale) ($M = 3.1$; $SD = 0.8$) was found, $t(110) = 2.01$, $p < .05$. However, the effect size of this difference is negligible (Cohen's $d < .15$).

Relationship of dysfunctional attitudes with specific memories

Table 1 gives an overview of the first-order correlations of the number of specific and categoric memories, biographic (age and level of education) and illness-related variables (depression severity and number of previous depressive episodes), and DAS-A scores. As can be derived from this table, the number of specific and categoric memories proved to be highly intercorrelated. Moreover, age and level of education are especially predictive of the number of specific memories.

The relationship of dysfunctional attitudes with specific memories was analysed with hierarchical multiple regression analyses. In all analyses, age, level of education—scored from 0 (primary school) to 6 (university education)—depression severity (HRDS), and number of previous depressive episodes were forced into the equation in the first step, and total DAS-A scores and the difference between scores on the HR and HI subscales of the DAS-A (Δ DAS-A scores) in the second step. In the multiple regression analyses, Δ DAS-A represents the unique effect of scoring differently with respect to helpfulness-relevant compared to helpfulness-irrelevant attitudes on autobiographical memory, independent of and above the effect of the general level of dysfunctional attitudes. In none of the analyses was evidence for multicolinearity found (all tolerance values > .826). In the first analysis, the number of specific memories on the total AMT was the criterion. Age, level of education, depression severity, and number of previous depressive episodes were forced into the equation in the first step and accounted for a significant proportion of 14% of the variance in AMT scores, F change $(4, 106) = 4.194$,

$p < .01$. Total DAS-A scores and Δ DAS-A scores forced into the equation in the second step did not improve upon the model, F change $(2, 104) = 2.702$, ns. So, after statistically correcting for differences in biographic and illness-related variables, the significant first-order correlation of the number of specific memories with Δ DAS-A scores ($r = -.20$, $p < .05$) was no longer statistically significant.

Next, the number of specific responses on the HR subscale of the AMT served as criterion. Age, level of education, severity of depression, and number of previous depressive episodes entered in the first step accounted for a significant proportion of 15% of the AMT HR scores, F change $(4, 106) = 4.574$, $p < .01$. Total DAS-A scores and Δ DAS-A scores were entered into the equation in the second step and significantly improved on the model, F change $(2, 104) = 3.971$, $p < .05$. In the final significant prediction model, F $(6, 104) = 4.544$, $p < .001$, level of education, $β = .237$, $t = 2.673$, $p < .01$, and Δ DAS-A scores, $β = -.261$, $t = -2.714$, $p < .01$, were the only significant predictor variables. These results imply that the significant first-order correlation of the number of specific HR memories with Δ DAS-A scores ($r = -.28$, $p < .01$) also remained significant after statistically correcting for differences in biographic and illness-related variables, and indicate that a higher endorsement of helpfulness-relevant than helpfulness-irrelevant dysfunctional attitudes predicts retrieval of fewer specific memories in response to cues referring to traits related to helpfulness, over and above the effect of the endorsement of dysfunctional attitudes on the

total DAS-A scale in general. Table 2 displays the standardised beta-coefficients, t and p values of each predictor variable, and the semi-partial correlation of each predictor with the criterion variable, as well as the amount of variance explained by each step in the final model.

Subsequently, the same analysis was repeated with retrieval of specific memories to helpfulness-irrelevant cues as the criterion variable. Total DAS-A and Δ DAS-A scores entered as predictors in the second step only accounted for 3% of additional variance in AMT HI scores, $F(2, 104) = 1.72$, ns.

Relationship of dysfunctional attitudes with categoric memories

The relationship of dysfunctional attitudes with categoric memories was analysed with similar hierarchical multiple regression analyses. In the first analysis, the number of categoric memories on the total AMT was the criterion. Age, level of education, depression severity, and number of previous depressive episodes did not account for a significant proportion of the variance in AMT scores in the first step, F change $(4, 106) = 1.622$, ns. The total DAS-A and Δ DAS-A scores forced into the equation in the second step did not improve on the model, F change $(2, 104) = 0.235$, ns.

Next, the number of categoric responses on the HR subscale of the AMT served as criterion. Age, level of education, severity of depression, and number of previous depressive episodes entered in the first step did not account for a significant proportion of the AMT HR scores, F change

TABLE 2
Hierarchical regression analyses: Specific memories on the HR subscale

Variable	B	t	R^2	ΔR^2 of step	Semipartial R
Step 1					
Age	−.146	−1.561	.147**	.147**	−.14
Education level	.237	2.673**			.23
HDRS	−.033	−.367			−.03
History of depression	.157	1.723			.15
Step 2			.208***	.061*	
Total DAS-A	.153	1.596			.14
Δ HR/HI DAS-A	−.261	−2.714**			−.24

Summary of hierarchical regression analyses with respect to number of specific memories on the Helpfulness-Relevant subscale of the AMT in the final model. $n = 111$ previously depressed patients. AMT = Autobiographical Memory Test; HDRS = Hamilton Depression Rating Scale; DAS-A = Dysfunctional Attitude Scale: Form A; Δ HR-HI DAS-A = Helpfulness relevant minus helpfulness irrelevant DAS-A scores.
* $p < .05$; ** $p < .01$; *** $p < .001$.

TABLE 3
Hierarchical regression analyses: Categoric memories on the HR subscale

Variable	B	t	R^2	ΔR^2 of step	Semipartial R
Step 1					
Age	.169	1.707	.069	.069	.16
Education level	−.126	−1.339			−.12
HDRS	−.022	−.226			−.02
History of depression	−.071	−.733			−.07
Step 2			.113*	.044	
Total DAS-A	.066	.653			.06
Δ HR/HI DAS-A	.187	1.835			.17

Summary of hierarchical regression analyses with respect to number of categoric memories on the Helpfulness-Relevant subscale of the AMT in the final model. $n = 111$ previously depressed patients. AMT = Autobiographical Memory Test; HDRS = Hamilton Depression Rating Scale; DAS-A = Dysfunctional Attitude Scale: Form A; Δ HR-HI DAS-A = Helpfulness relevant minus helpfulness irrelevant DAS-A scores.
$p < .05$.

$(4, 106) = 1.964$, *ns*. The total DAS-A and Δ DAS-A scores were entered into the equation in the second step, and the resulting improvement of the model was borderline significant, F change $(2, 104) = 2.552$, $p = .08$. In the final significant prediction model, $F(6, 104) = 2.198$, $p < .05$, none of the independent variables significantly contributed to the prediction of the number of categoric memories on the HR subscale of the AMT (see Table 3). These results indicate that the significant first-order correlation of the number of HR categoric memories with Δ DAS-A scores ($r = .26$, $p < .01$) was no longer significant after statistically correcting for differences in biographic and illness-related variables.

Subsequently, the same analysis was repeated with retrieval of categoric memories to helpfulness-irrelevant cues as the criterion variable. Total DAS-A and Δ DAS-A scores entered as predictors in the second step only accounted for 2% of additional variance in AMT HI scores, $F(2, 104) = 1.082$, *ns*, and the final prediction model was not significant, $F(6, 104) = .907$, *ns*.

Discussion

This study examined the extent to which overgeneral memory might arise from a synchrony between long-held dysfunctional attitudes and the trait words used to cue memory in previously depressed patients. The results showed that the retrieval of less specific memories in response to cue words of the Autobiographical Memory Test (AMT) denoting personal traits involved in helping others was, as predicted, associated with a higher endorsement of items of the Dysfunctional Attitude Scale (DAS-A) referring to dysfunctional attitudes with respect to helpfulness than of helpfulness-irrelevant items, also after statistically correcting for the influence of age, level of education, depression severity, and number of previous depressive episodes. However, the higher endorsement of dysfunctional attitudes related to helpfulness no longer resulted in a propensity to retrieve more categoric memories in response to matching cues after statistically correcting for the effect of biographical and illness-related variables. We suggest that, in patients for whom helpfulness is seen as critical in maintaining their self-esteem, the presence of cues that activate the helpfulness construct is sufficient to distract the person away from the task to retrieve a specific memory. Before speculating further, however, it is important to see if this effect applies only to the DAS-A and only to previously depressed patients. Study 2 used the opportunity provided by a parallel trial that had used the identical measure of autobiographical memory alongside another measure of long-held attitude/schema in a different group of patients, to examine Dalgleish's hypothesis further.

STUDY 2

Method

Participants

To be eligible, participants had to meet the following criteria: (a) a main diagnosis of Borderline Personality Disorder (BPD) as defined according to DSM-IV (American Psychiatric Association, 1994) and assessed by the Structured Clinical Interview for DSM-IV (SCID-II; First, Spitzer, Gibbon, & Williams, 1994) by independent trained research assistants; (b) age between 18 and 60 years; (c) a Personality Disorder Severity Index, fourth version (BPDSI-IV; Arntz et al., 2003; Giesen-Bloo, Wachters, Schouten, & Arntz, 2007) score above 20; (d) Dutch literacy. Exclusion criteria were: psychotic disorders (except short, reactive psychotic episodes); bipolar disorder; dissociative identity disorder; antisocial personality disorder; attention deficit hyperactivity disorder; addiction of such severity that clinical detoxification was indicated; psychiatric disorders secondary to medical conditions; and mental retardation.

Participants were referred by therapists in secondary and tertiary community mental health institutes in each centre's area. After a complete description of the study was given to the participants, written informed consent was obtained prior to randomisation. The protocol was approved by the medical ethical committees of the four participating centres. A total of 82 participants completed the YSQ and AMT. The mean age of the patients was 30.8 ($SD = 8.0$), and 92.7% of the sample was female. Mean education level (theoretical range $0-11$) was 7.6 ($SD = 2.4$; range $0-11$). The mean score on the BPDSI (theoretical range $0-90$) was 33.9 ($SD = 8.1$; range $20-63$). A total of 57.3% of the patients had a current depressive episode. Patients had a mean number of 2.7 ($SD = 2.1$) Axis I disorders (SCID-I) and 2.1 ($SD = 1.2$) Axis II disorders (SCID-II).

Materials and measures

Beck Depression Inventory (BDI). The BDI (Beck, Ward, Medelsohn, Mock, & Erbaugh, 1961) is a 21-item self-report questionnaire, which measures the severity of depressive symptoms during the past week.

Young Schema Questionnaire (YSQ). The YSQ is a 205-item self-report questionnaire developed to measure 16 core beliefs or early maladaptive schemas (Young, 1994; see also Lee, Taylor, & Dunn, 1999; Schmidt, Joiner, Young, & Telch, 1995). Core beliefs or early maladaptive schemas refer to stable and enduring themes that develop during childhood. The items are answered on a 6-point Likert-type scale ranging from 1 ("totally inapplicable to me") to 6 ("describes me per-

fectly"). The 16 core beliefs are grouped into five domains or higher-order factors (Lee et al., 1999):

a. *Disconnection*, comprising: (1) Abandonment/instability; (2) Defectiveness/shame; (3) Emotional deprivation; (4) Mistrust/abuse; (5) Social isolation/alienation
b. *Impaired autonomy*, comprising: (6) Dependence/ incompetence; (7) Vulnerability to danger; (8) Enmeshment; (9) Failure
c. *Impaired limits*, comprising: (10) Entitlement/domination; (11) Insufficient self-control/self-discipline
d. *Other-directedness*, comprising: (12) Self-sacrifice; (13) Subjugation
e. *Overvigilance and inhibition*, comprising: (14) Emotional inhibition; and (15) Unrelenting standards.

The sixteenth subscale for Social Undesirability failed to emerge as an independent factor (Lee et al., 1999) and was excluded from further analyses. The domain that directly pertained to attitudes related to helping others (i.e., Other-directedness) constituted the Helpfulness-Relevant (HR) subscale, while the domain that pertained to attitudes related to taking no responsibility for others, difficulty in respecting the rights of others, and problems in cooperating with others (i.e., Impaired limits), constituted the Helpfulness-Irrelevant (HI) subscale. Example items from the Helpfulness-Relevant subscale are: "I worry a lot about pleasing other people so they won't reject me" (Subjugation subscale) and "I put others' needs before my own or else I feel guilty" (Self-sacrifice subscale). Example items from the Helpfulness-Irrelevant subscale are: "I usually put my needs ahead of the needs of others" (Entitlement subscale) and "Often I allow myself to carry through on impulses and express emotions that get me into trouble or hurt other people" (Insufficient self-control/self-discipline subscale). By summation of the mean item scores for both subscales, a total score was computed for the YSQ. A higher score on a scale indicates a higher endorsement of early maladaptive schemas.

Autobiographical Memory Test (AMT). The same version of the AMT as in Study 1 was administered. One of the authors (IPK), blind for this post hoc research question, scored all the tapes. Inter-rater agreement on 20% of the retrieved memories $(n = 360)$ indicated good reliability, kappa $= 0.89$.

Procedure

Patients' first assessment was made after inclusion and before randomisation by independent trained research assistants. Patients who met inclusion criteria and no exclusion criteria were tested with the AMT followed by the YSQ in a fixed order before random assignment to treatment condition.

Results

Preliminary analyses

In order to investigate the inter-rater reliability of categorising the five domains of the YSQ as relevant or irrelevant with respect to helpfulness, 12 colleagues of the section of Clinical and Health Psychology at Leiden University, blind to the research question of the present study, independently rated these five domains on the same 6-point Likert scale as used in Study 1. The domain Other-directedness clearly obtained the highest mean rating, and the domain Impaired limits the lowest, while the scores for the other three domains were intermediate. The mean rating for Other-directedness $(M = 5.4; SD = 0.51)$ was significantly higher than the mean rating for Impaired limits $(M = 3.2; SD = 1.5)$ $t(11) = 6.413, p < .001$. The results of these analyses indicate a satisfactory inter-rater reliability in forming a priori subscales of the YSQ reflecting personal traits or attitudes relevant versus irrelevant in helping others.

Number of specific responses

For the 10 items of the AMT, the participants produced a mean number of 6.3 $(SD = 2.0)$ specific responses. All of the participants gave at least three specific answers. A t-test for dependent samples showed that the percentage of specific answers retrieved on the HR subscale $(M = 59.4; SD = 26.5)$ was significantly lower than on the HI subscale $(M = 65.6; SD = 22.3)$, $t(81) = 2.11, p < .05$. However, the effect size of this difference is small (Cohen's $d = .25$).

Number of categoric responses

For the 10 items of the AMT, the participants produced a mean number of 2.1 $(SD = 1.8)$ categoric responses. A total of 28% of the

participants gave no categoric answer in reaction to any of the 10 AMT cues words. A t-test for dependent samples revealed no significant differences between the proportion of categoric answers retrieved on the HR subscale $(M = 23.8; SD = 25.1)$ and on the HI subscale $(M = 19.7; SD = 18.7)$, $t(81) = 1.57, ns$.

Number of extended responses and no memories/omissions

For the 10 items of the AMT, the participants produced a mean number of 0.2 $(SD = 0.5)$ extended responses and 1.3 $(SD = 1.3)$ no memories/omissions. T-tests for dependent samples revealed a significant difference between the proportion of extended answers retrieved on the HR subscale $(M = 1.2; SD = 4.4)$ and the proportion retrieved on the HI subscale $(M = 7.3; SD = 2.6)$, $t(81) = 2.529, p < .05$. No significant differences in the proportion of no memories/omissions in reaction to the HR subscale versus HI subscale of the AMT were observed, $t(81) = 0.399, ns$.

Scores for early maladaptive schemas

Our sample of patients with BPD manifested relatively high scores for early maladaptive schemas, as witnessed by a mean total score of 704.5 $(SD = 150.8;$ range 337–995) on the YSQ (Young, 1994; see also Lee et al., 1999; Schmidt et al., 1995). Using a t-test for dependent measures, a significant difference between the mean item score on the HR subscale $(M = 3.3; SD = 0.7)$ in comparison to the mean score on the HI subscale $(M = 3.5; SD = 0.8)$ was found, $t(81) = 3.65, p < .001$. However, the effect size of this difference is small (Cohen's $d = .27$).

Relationship of early maladaptive schemas with specific memories

Table 4 gives an overview of the first-order correlations of the number of specific and categoric memories, biographic (age and level of education) and illness-related variables (severity of depression and presence of a depressive disorder), and YSQ scores. As can be derived from this table, the number of specific and categoric memories proved to be highly intercorrelated. Moreover, severity of depression and especially the presence of a comorbid depressive disorder predict the number of specific and categoric memories.

TABLE 4
First-order correlations of autobiographical memory, biographic, illness-related, and schema variables

Variables	I.	II.	III.	IV.	V.	VI.	VII.	VIII.	IX.	X.	XI.	XII.
I. Number of specific memories (AMT)												
II. Number of specific HR memories (AMT)	.80***											
III. Number of specific HI memories (AMT)	.88***	.42***										
IV. Number of categoric memories (AMT)	-.75***	-.57***	-.68***									
V. Number of categoric HR memories (AMT)	-.60***	-.66***	-.39***	.83***								
VI. Number of categoric HI memories (AMT)	-.67***	-.33***	-.76***	.87***	.46***							
VII. Age	-.06	-.13	.02	.09	.10	.05						
VIII. Education	.06	-.00	.09	-.20	-.14	-.20	.03					
IX. BDI	-.19	-.34***	-.02	.16	.30**	-.01	-.10	-.11				
X. History of depression	-.28*	-.30*	-.19	.27*	.35**	.12	-.14	.08	.34**			
XI. Total YSQ score	-.11	-.25*	.03	.09	.15	.02	-.07	-.09	.48***	.13		
XII. Δ HR-HI YSQ	-.20	-.26*	-.10	.08	.16	-.10	-.05	.10	.08	.07	.23*	

$n = 82$ patients with borderline personality disorder. AMT = Autobiographical Memory Test; BDI = Beck Depression Inventory; YSQ = Young Schema Questionnaire (HR and HI scores combined); Δ HR-HI YSQ = Helpfulness relevant minus helpfulness irrelevant YSQ scores.
* $p < .05$; ** $p < .01$; *** $p < .001$.

The relationship of early maladaptive schemas with specific memories was analysed with hierarchical multiple regression analyses. In all analyses, age, level of education—scored from 0 (no schooling) to 11 (university education)—depression severity (BDI), and comorbid depression (SCID-I) were forced into the equation in the first step, and the sum score of the means on the HR and HI YSQ subscales (total YSQ score) and the difference between scores on the HR and HI subscales of the YSQ (Δ YSQ) in the second step. In the multiple regression analyses, Δ YSQ represents the unique effect of scoring differently with respect to helpfulness-relevant compared to helpfulness-irrelevant attitudes, independent of and above the effect of the endorsement of early maladaptive schemas. In none of the analyses was evidence for multicolinearity found (all tolerance values > .702). In the first analysis, the number of specific memories on the total AMT was the criterion. Age, level of education, depression severity (BDI), and comorbid depression (SCID-I) were forced into the equation in the first step and accounted for 10% of the variance in AMT scores, F change $(4, 77) = 2.247$, $p = .07$. A comorbid depression, $\beta = -.267$, $t = -2.301$, $p < .05$, was the only significant predictor of the number of specific memories. The total YSQ and Δ YSQ scores forced into the equation in the second step did not improve on the model, F change $(2, 75) = 1.551$, ns.

Next, the number of specific responses on the HR subscale of the AMT served as criterion. Age, level of education, depression severity, and comorbid depression entered in the first step accounted for a significant proportion of 19% of the variance in AMT scores, F change $(4, 77) = 4.459$, $p < .01$. Total YSQ and Δ YSQ scores were entered into the equation in the second step and resulted in a borderline significant improvement of the prediction model, F change $(2, 75) = 2.949$, $p = .06$. In the final significant prediction model, $F (6,75) = 4.106$, $p < .01$, age, comorbid depression, and Δ YSQ scores, $\beta = -.223$, $t = -2.142$, $p < .05$, were the only significant predictor variables, indicating that a higher endorsement of helpfulness-relevant than helpfulness-irrelevant dysfunctional schemas predicted retrieval of fewer specific memories in response to cues referring to these traits. These results indicate that the significant first-order correlation of the number of specific HR memories and Δ YSQ scores ($r = -.26$, $p < .01$) also remained significant after statistically correcting for differences in biographic and illness-related variables. Table 5 displays the standardised beta-coefficients, t and p values of each predictor variable, and the semi-partial correlation of each predictor with the criterion variable, as well as the amount of variance explained by each step in the final model.

Subsequently, the same analysis was repeated with number of specific memories retrieved to helpfulness-irrelevant cues as the criterion variable. None of the steps was significant and no significant model emerged, $F(6, 75) = 0.850$, ns.

Relationship of early maladaptive schemas with categoric memories

The relationship of early maladaptive schemas with categoric memories was analysed with similar hierarchical multiple regression analyses. In the first analysis, the number of categoric memories on the total AMT was the criterion. Age, level of education, depression severity (BDI), and comorbid depression (SCID-I) were forced into the equation in the first step and accounted for 14% of the variance in AMT scores, F change $(4, 77) = 3.140$, $p < .05$. Level of education, $\beta = -.215$, $t = -2.008$, $p < .05$, and a comorbid depression, $\beta = .289$, $t = 2.540$, $p < .05$, were both significant predictors of the number of categoric memories. The total YSQ and Δ YSQ scores forced into the equation in the second step did not improve on the model, F change $(2, 75) = 0.340$, ns.

Next, the number of categoric responses on the HR subscale of the AMT served as criterion. After forced entry of age, level of education,

depression severity, and comorbid depression in the first step, total YSQ and Δ YSQ scores were entered into the equation in the second step and did not significantly improve on the model, F change $(2, 75) = 1.067$, ns (see Table 6). Repeating the same analysis with the number of categoric memories retrieved to helpfulness-irrelevant cues as the criterion variable, the total YSQ and Δ YSQ scores also did not improve on the model, F change $(2, 75) = 0.017$, ns.

Discussion

In the second study, we examined whether there was evidence for a matching of cue words to schema in patients with a borderline personality disorder. The results yielded additional evidence for Dalgleish's hypothesis, with a synchrony between the retrieval of specific memories to helpfulness-related cues and a relatively higher endorsement of schemas concerned with other-directedness than helpfulness-irrelevant schemas observed. This relation remained significant after correcting for the effects of age, education level, depression severity, and comorbid depression. However, no evidence was found for a synchrony between the retrieval of categoric memories to helpfulness-related cues and the endorsement of corresponding schemas. Also of note is that comorbid depression was and remained a strong and significant predictor of both indices of memory specificity in the final prediction models.

TABLE 5
Summary: Specific memories

Variable	B	t	R^2	ΔR^2 of step	Semipartial R
Step 1					
Age	−.204	−2.010*	.188**	.188**	−.20
Education level	.012	.115			.01
BDI	−.227	−1.902			−.19
Comorbid depression	−.228	−2.110*			−.21
Step 2			.247**	.059†	
Total YSQ	−.072	−.621			−.06
Δ HR/HI YSQ	−.223	−2.142*			−.22

Summary of hierarchical regression analyses with respect to number of specific memories on the Helpfulness-Relevant subscale of the AMT in the final model. $n = 82$ patients with borderline personality disorder. AMT = Autobiographical Memory Test; BDI = Beck Depression Inventory; Total YSQ = Young Schema Questionnaire (HR and HI YSQ scores combined); Δ HR-HI YSQ = Helpfulness relevant minus helpfulness irrelevant YSQ scores.
† $p < .10$; * $p < .05$; ** $p < .01$.

TABLE 6
Summary: Categoric memories

Variable	B	t	R^2	$\Delta\ R^2\ of\ step$	Semipartial R
Step 1					
Age	.180	1.757	.208**	.208**	.17
Education level	−.161	−1.552			−.16
BDI	.182	1.507			.15
Comorbid depression	.322	2.951**			.30
Step 2			.230**	.022	
Total YSQ	−.015	−.128			−.01
Δ HR/HI YSQ	.152	1.446			.15

Summary of hierarchical regression analyses with respect to number of categoric memories on the Helpfulness-Relevant subscale of the AMT in the final model. $n = 82$ patients with borderline personality disorder. AMT = Autobiographical Memory Test; BPDSI-IV = Borderline Personality Disorder Severity Index, Version IV; Total YSQ = Young Schema Questionnaire (HR and HI YSQ scores combined); Δ HR-HI YSQ = Helpfulness relevant minus helpfulness irrelevant YSQ scores.
** $p < .01$.

GENERAL DISCUSSION

The present study investigated whether the matching of memory cue words with highly endorsed schemas plays a role in contributing to the retrieval of less specific and more categoric autobiographical memories. The data from both studies provide preliminary evidence supporting the hypothesis that the activation of basic dysfunctional attitudes may result in impaired retrieval, with both previously depressed patients and patients with borderline personality disorder (BPD) responding with less specific memories to dysfunctional attitude-related cue words. The fact that these results were found in two groups of patients using two different assessments of attitudes, and after statistically correcting for differences in biographical and illness-related variables, may be considered to strengthen the evidence, although the fact that the pattern was not found with respect to the retrieval of categoric memories remains a puzzling feature of the results.

Studies that assessed autobiographical memory performance in remitted patients in comparison to depressed (Nandrino, Pezard, Poste, Reveillere, & Beaune, 2002; Park, Goodyer, & Teasdale, 2002) or normal controls (Mackinger, Pachinger, Leibetseder, & Fartacek, 2000; Park et al., 2002) suggest that autobiographical memory impairment persists after recovery and is also characteristic of remitted patients. In a previous study, in the present sample of recurrently depressed patients, we also found evidence for a tendency for overgenerality of memory compared to normal controls, with memory impairment being related to age and education level but not to the

number of previous depressive episodes (Spinhoven et al., 2006). It is therefore of note that in the present study, after controlling for age, education level, history of depression, and depression severity, the significant association of autobiographical memory impairment in response to matching cues remained.

Jones et al. (1999) compared autobiographical memory specificity of outpatients with a borderline personality disorder to that of normal controls and observed that BPD patients manifested more overgeneral memories. However, subsequent studies (Arntz, Meeren, & Wessel, 2002; Renneberg, Theobald, Nobs, & Weisbrod, 2005) did not find evidence for a lack of memory specificity in BPD. In a previous study, in the present sample of patients with borderline personality disorder, we found evidence for a tendency to retrieve less specific memories only in borderline patients with a comorbid depression (Kremers et al., 2004). Interestingly, the retrieval of less specific memories in response to matching cues in the present study was still observed after accounting for the significant effect of a comorbid depression on memory specificity.

Taken together, these results strongly suggest that the disruption to memory produced by matching of cue to schema cannot be easily explained by some specific property of the measure used to assess dysfunctional attitudes (since the same results were observed for the DAS-A and the Young Schema Questionnaire), by differences in demographic characteristics such as age or education level, or by the presence of depression or depression severity. Memory impairment might be associated with overarching factors common to various forms of psychopathology (e.g., severity of illness, motivational deficits, effortful processing deficits; Dalgleish & Watts, 1990). In particular, depressive disorders and post-traumatic stress disorders are associated with deficits in executive functioning and autobiographical memory impairments. Executive functioning refers to cognitive processes that control and integrate other cognitive activities such as semantic and autobiographical memory. As has already been noted by Williams (1996), executive dysfunction may be one of the pathways leading to overgeneral memory retrieval. Prospective studies experimentally manipulating executive control and schema activation while using a theory-driven and more extensive set of memory cue words would provide a more stringent test to study whether activation of dysfunctional schemas indeed constitutes one of the factors influencing executive control and memory retrieval.

A number of factors could be responsible for the disruption of the autobiographical memory system we observed. We suggest that the selected cue words of the AMT captured the attention of individuals who endorsed attitudes pertaining to these cue words. As has recently been proposed (Conway & Kane, 2001) individuals differ in the extent to which their attention is captured. Individuals with greater working memory capacity exhibit greater attentional control than individuals with lesser working memory capacity. Susceptibility to attentional capture depends on the ability to maintain goal-relevant information, especially in contexts providing sources of competition or interference with that goal. When cue words map closely onto the content of highly endorsed dysfunctional attitudes, these attitudes may become more activated, with processing pressure as a result. This impairment in executive functioning may distract the person away from the task of the AMT to the detriment of his/her ability to retrieve specific memories.

Dalgleish et al. (2003) proposed that following schema activation, fewer processing resources will be available for memorial search, and that this potentially leads to the memory search being aborted prematurely, increasing the chance that categoric-level descriptors will be accepted as a suitable response. This account is in agreement with the results of a recent experimental study, which suggest that the existence of less elaborate and differentiated schematic models including affective dimensions contributes to the retrieval of more categoric memories in contrast to more differentiated schematic models (Ramponi, Barnard, & Nimmo-Smith, 2004). However, because in the present study the primary effect of matching cue to schema on autobiographical memory seems to be to reduce the number of specific memories, rather than to specifically increase the number of categoric memories, this reduced capacity to retrieve specific memories could also result from other mechanisms.

A complementary explanation is that certain cue words disrupt controlled processing by promoting rumination. This more process-based hypothesis is consistent with the original idea of Williams and Dritschel (1988) that it is the ruminative aspect of depression rather than mood per se that contributes to the proneness to retrieve categoric memories. The results of some recent experimental studies are in support of this idea that more ruminative, verbal-analytical, and self-focused cognitive processes may result in the retrieval of less specific memories (Ramponi et al., 2004; Watkins & Teasdale, 2001; Watkins, Teasdale, & Williams, 2000).

A further alternative explanation of these results is that, for any such long-held attitudes, there are more actual instances of relevant situations in the past, and so these events are more likely to have been encoded in generic form. Although an encoding explanation remains possible, the fact that overgenerality in memory can be manipulated experimentally (e.g., Watkins & Teasdale, 2004) suggests a retrieval explanation. Nevertheless, future research might examine this possibility directly by using independent judges (e.g., a family member) to assess the frequency of certain types of event.

Given this uncertainty about which factors are responsible for the disruption of the autobiographical memory search, further studies that match cue words with schematic models are needed and may help to throw light on the cognitive processes involved in the generation of overgeneral autobiographical memories. Because the present study was an opportunistic post-hoc study to test Dalgleish's hypothesis in the context of recruiting and assessing patients for two randomised controlled trials, it suffers from all the limitations inherent in such a post-hoc analysis, notably the risk of obtaining spurious results. Of note is that post hoc only a small set of cue words on the AMT could be identified referring to a special schema (i.e., helpfulness). Because of this post-hoc classification, cue words may also have differed beyond the helpfulness dimension, e.g., in frequency, imageability, or emotionality. However, it seems rather unlikely that these possible differences in cue words critically affected our study results, because in three of the four comparisons there were no significant differences in the retrieval of specific or categoric memories to helpfulness-relevant and helpfulness-irrelevant cues, and the effect size of the only difference found (i.e., somewhat more specific memories to helpfulness irrelevant cues in previously depressed participants) was small. In future prospective studies, a larger set of theory-driven cue words should be chosen relevant for a special group of patients, such as cue words referring to perfectionism in depression (Clark et al., 1999) or abandonment in patients with borderline personality disorder (Young, 1994; see Crane, Barnhofer, & Williams, 2007 this issue). On the other hand, a strength of the present opportunistic study may be that there were no specific demand characteristics inducing bias in the assessment of autobiographical memories and the endorsement of dysfunctional attitudes or maladaptive schemas. Moreover, classifying the cue words of the AMT, the items of the DAS-A, and the domains of the YSQ with respect to helpfulness proved to be reproducible with a satisfactory inter-rater reliability. Also, the hypothesised association of memory retrieval with schema endorsement was found in two different patient samples and with different measures for the endorsement of higher-order schematic representations. In conclusion, we suggest that it may be worthwhile to study schema activation as one of the factors contributing to the generation of overgeneral autobiographical memories in prospective and controlled studies in various groups of subjects.

REFERENCES

American Psychiatric Association. (1994). *Diagnostic and statistical manual of mental disorders* (4th ed.). Washington, DC: APA.

Arntz, A., Hoorn, M. V. D., Cornelis, J., Verheul, R., Bosch, W. M. C. V. D., & De Bie, A. J. H. T. (2003). Reliability and validity of the Borderline Personality Disorder Severity Index. *Journal of Personality Disorders, 17*, 45–59.

Arntz, A., Meeren, M., & Wessel, I. (2002). No evidence for overgeneral memories in borderline personality disorder. *Behaviour Research and Therapy, 40*, 1063–1068.

Beck, A. T., Ward, C. H., Mendelson, M., Mock, J., & Erbaugh, J. (1961). An inventory for measuring depression. *Archives of General Psychiatry, 4*, 561–571.

Bockting, C. L. H., Schene, A. H., Spinhoven, P., Koeter, M. W. J., Wouters, L. F., Huyser, J., et al. (2005). Preventing relapse/recurrence in recurrent depression using cognitive therapy: A randomized controlled trial. *Journal of Consulting and Clinical Psychology, 73*, 647–657.

Brewin, C. R., Reynolds, M., & Tata, P. (1999). Autobiographical memory processes and the course of depression. *Journal of Abnormal Psychology, 108*, 511–517.

Brittlebank, A. D., Scott, J., Williams, J. M. G., & Ferrier, I. N. (1993). Autobiographical memory in depression – state or trait marker. *British Journal of Psychiatry, 162*, 118–121.

Clark, D. A., Beck, A. T., & Alford, B. A. (1999). *Scientific foundations of cognitive theory and therapy for depression*. New York: Wiley.

Conway, A. R. A., & Kane, M. J. (2001). Capacity, control and conflict: An individual differences perspective on attentional capture. In B. S. Gibson & C. L. Folk (Eds.), *Attraction, distraction and action: Multiple perspectives on attentional capture* (pp. 349–372). New York: Elsevier Science.

Conway, M. A., & Pleydell-Pearce, C. W. (2000). The construction of autobiographical memories in the self-memory system. *Psychological Review, 107*, 261–288.

Crane, C., Barnhofer, T., & Williams, J. M. G. (2007). Cue self-relevance affects autobiographical memory specificity in individuals with a history of major depression. *Memory, 15*, 312–323.

Dalgleish, T., Tchanturia, K., Serpell, L., Hems, S., Yiend, J., de Silva, P., et al. (2003). Self-reported parental abuse relates to autobiographical memory style in patients with eating disorders. *Emotion, 3*, 211–222.

Dalgleish, T., & Watts, F. N. (1990). Biases of attention and memory in disorders of anxiety and depression. *Clinical Psychology Review, 10*, 589–604.

Douma, M. (1991). *The measurement of trait depression. Construction of the Dutch Dysfunctional Attitude Scale (A version) of Arlene Weisman*. Meerssen, The Netherlands: St. Lois Marie Jamin.

Dozois, D. J. A., Covin, R., & Brinker, J. K. (2003). Normative data on cognitive measures of depression. *Journal of Consulting and Clinical Psychology, 71*, 71–80.

First, M. B., Spitzer, R. L., Gibbon, M., & Williams, J. B. W. (1994). *Structured Clinical Interview for DSM-IV Personality Disorders (SCID-II)*. New York: New York State Psychiatric Institute, Biometrics Research Department.

First, M. B., Spitzer, R. L., Gibbon, M., & Williams, J. B. W. (1997). *Structured Clinical Interview for DSM-IV Axis I Disorders (SCID-I/P)*. New York: New York State Psychiatric Institute, Biometrics Research Department.

Giesen-Bloo, J., van Dyck, R., Spinhoven, P., van Tilburg, W., Dirksen, C., van Asselt, T., et al. (2006). Outpatient psychotherapy for borderline personality disorder: A randomized clinical trial of schema focused therapy versus transference focused therapy. *Archives of General Psychiatry*, *63*, 649–658.

Giesen-Bloo, J. H., Wachters, L. M., Schouten, E., & Arntz, A. R. (2007). *Assessment of borderline personality disorder with the borderline personality disorder severity index-IV: psychometric evaluation and dimensional structure*. Manuscript submitted for publication.

Hamilton, M. (1960). A rating scale for depression. *Journal of Neurology Neurosurgery and Psychiatry*, *23*, 56–62.

Harvey, A. G., Bryant, R. A., & Dang, S. T. (1998). Autobiographical memory in acute stress disorder. *Journal of Consulting and Clinical Psychology*, *66*, 500–506.

Jones, B., Heard, H., Startup, M., Swales, M., Williams, J. M. G., & Jones, R. S. P. (1999). Autobiographical memory and dissociation in borderline personality disorder. *Psychological Medicine*, *29*, 1397–1404.

Kremers, I. P., Spinhoven, P., & Van der Does, A. J. W. (2004). Autobiographical memory in depressed and non-depressed patients with borderline personality disorder. *British Journal of Clinical Psychology*, *43*, 17–29.

Kuyken, W., & Brewin, C. R. (1995). Autobiographical memory functioning in depression and reports of early abuse. *Journal of Abnormal Psychology*, *104*, 585–591.

Lau, M. A., Segal, S. Z., & Williams, J. M. G. (2004). Teasdale's differential activation hypothesis: Implications for mechanisms of depressive relapse and suicidal behaviour. *Behaviour Research and Therapy*, *42*, 1001–1017.

Lee, C. W., Taylor, G., & Dunn, J. (1999). Factor structure of the Schema Questionnaire in a large clinical sample. *Cognitive Therapy and Research*, *23*, 441–451.

Maccallum, F., McConkey, K. M., Bryant, R. A., & Barnier, A. J. (2000). Specific autobiographical memory following hypnotically induced mood state. *International Journal of Clinical and Experimental Hypnosis*, *48*, 361–373.

Mackinger, H. F., Pachinger, M. M., Leibetseder, M. M., & Fartacek, R. R. (2000). Autobiographical memories in women remitted from major depression. *Journal of Abnormal Psychology*, *109*, 331–334.

McNally, R. J., Lasko, N. B., Macklin, M. L., & Pitman, R. K. (1995). Autobiographical memory disturbance in combat-related post-traumatic stress disorder. *Behavior Research and Therapy*, *33*, 619–630.

Nandrino, J. L., Pezard, L., Poste, A., Reveillere, C., & Beaune, D. (2002). Autobiographical memory in major depression: A comparison between first-episode and recurrent patients. *Psychopathology*, *35*, 335–340.

Park, R. J., Goodyer, I. M., & Teasdale, J. D. (2002). Categoric overgeneral autobiographical memory in adolescents with major depressive disorder. *Psychological Medicine*, *32*, 267–276.

Power, M. J., & Dalgleish, T. (1997). *Cognition and emotion: From order to disorder*. Hove, UK: Psychology Press.

Ramponi, C., Barnard, P. J., & Nimmo-Smith, I. (2004). Recollection deficits in dysphoric mood: An effect of schematic models and executive mode? *Memory*, *12*, 655–670.

Renneberg, B., Theobald, E., Nobs, M., & Weisbrod, M. (2005). Autobiographical memory in borderline personality disorder and depression. *Cognitive Therapy and Research*, *29*, 343–358.

Schmidt, N. B., Joiner, T. E., Young, J. E., & Telch, M. J. (1995). The Schema Questionnaire: Investigation of psychometric properties and the hierarchical structure of a measure of maladaptive schemas. *Cognitive Therapy and Research*, *19*, 295–321.

Spinhoven, P., Bockting, C. L. H., Schene, A. H., Koeter, M. W. J., Wekking, E. M., & Williams, J. M. G. (2006). Autobiographical memory in the euthymic phase of recurrent depression. *Journal of Abnormal Psychology*, *115*, 590–600.

Van Vreeswijk, M. F., & De Wilde, E. J. (2004). Autobiographical memory specificity, psychopathology, depressed mood and the use of the Autobiographical Memory Test: A meta-analysis. *Behaviour Research and Therapy*, *42*, 731–743.

Watkins, E., & Teasdale, J. D. (2001). Rumination and overgeneral memory in depression: Effects of self-focus and analytic thinking. *Journal of Abnormal Psychology*, *110*, 353–357.

Watkins, E., & Teasdale, J. D. (2004). Adaptive and maladaptive self-focus in depression. *Journal of Affective Disorders*, *82*, 1–8.

Watkins, E., Teasdale, J. D., & Williams, R. M. (2000). Decentring and distraction reduce overgeneral autobiographical memory in depression. *Psychological Medicine*, *30*, 911–920.

Weissmann, A. N. (1979). *The Dysfunctional Attitude Scale*. Dissertation, University of Pennsylvania, USA.

Wheeler, M. A., Stuss, D. T., & Tulving, E. (1997). Toward a theory of episodic memory: The frontal lobes and autonoetic consciousness. *Psychological Bulletin*, *121*, 331–354.

Williams, J. M. G. (1996). Depression and the specificity of autobiographical memory. In D. C. Rubin (Ed.), *Remembering our past. Studies in autobiographical memory* (pp. 244–267). Cambridge, UK: Cambridge University Press.

Williams, J. M. G., & Broadbent, K. (1986). Autobiographical memory in suicide attempters. *Journal of Abnormal Psychology*, *95*, 144–149.

Williams, J. M. G., & Dritschel, B. H. (1988). Emotional disturbance and the specificity of autobiographical memory. *Cognition and Emotion*, *3*, 221–234.

Williams, J. M. G., Healy, H. G., & Ellis, N. C. (1999). The effect of imageability and predicability of cues in autobiographical memory. *Quarterly Journal of Experimental Psychology Section A – Human Experimental Psychology*, *52*, 555–579.

Young, J. E. (1994). *Cognitive therapy for personality disorders: a schema-focused approach. (rev. ed.)* Sarasota: Professional Resource Press.

MEMORY, 2007, 15 (3), 339–352

Psychology Press
Taylor & Francis Group

Overgeneral memory and suppression of trauma memories in post-traumatic stress disorder

Sabine Schönfeld

University of Bielefeld, Germany

Anke Ehlers and Inga Böllinghaus

Institute of Psychiatry, London, UK

Winfried Rief

University of Marburg, Germany

The study investigated the relationship between the suppression of trauma memories and overgeneral memory in 42 assault survivors with and without PTSD. Overgeneral memory (OGM) was assessed with a standard autobiographical memory test (AMT). Participants completed two further AMTs under the instructions to either suppress or not suppress assault memories, in counterbalanced order. Participants with PTSD retrieved fewer and more general memories when following the suppression instruction than participants without PTSD, but not under the control instruction. OGM correlated with PTSD symptom severity, and measures of cognitive avoidance. The results are discussed with reference to current theories of overgeneral memory and its possible relationship with PTSD.

Overgeneral memory was first observed in suicidal and depressed individuals (Williams & Broadbent, 1986). These individuals show difficulties in retrieving specific autobiographical memories in response to cue words, and tend to reply with abstract or general memories (for an overview see Healy & Williams, 1999). For example, instead of retrieving a specific event to the cue *happy*, such as *"Visiting my brother last Sunday"*, they may retrieve a memory of a category of events such as *"Always when I visit my brother"*. This overgeneral memory (OGM) bias has also been found in people with a history of trauma (e.g., Dalgleish et al., 2003; De Decker, Hermans, Raes, & Eelen, 2003; Hermans et al., 2004; Kuyken & Brewin, 1995), and in trauma survivors with acute stress disorder or post-traumatic stress disorder (PTSD) (e.g., Harvey, Bryant, & Dang, 1998; McNally, Lasko, Macklin, & Pitman, 1995; McNally, Litz, Prassas, Shin, & Weathers, 1994). In contrast, patients with other anxiety disorders do not show OGM (e.g., Burke & Matthews, 1992; Wenzel, Jackson, Brendle, & Pinna, 2003; Wessel, Meeren, Peeters, Arntz, & Merckelbach, 2001; Wilhelm, McNally, Baer, & Florin, 1997).

This pattern of findings has led to the hypothesis that OGM may be a reaction to aversive

Address correspondence to: Dr Sabine Schönfeld, University of Bielefeld, Department of Psychology, Unit 11 (Clinical Psychology and Psychological Therapy), PO Box 10 01 31, D-33501 Bielefeld, Germany. E-mail: sabine.schoenfeld@uni-bielefeld.de

The study was supported by grants from the Wellcome Trust, the Daimler Benz Foundation, and the German National Scholarship Foundation. We thank Dr Edward Glucksman for his collaboration. Many thanks to Anke Weidmann for assisting with running the study, to Ed Watkins for his valuable suggestions, and to Michelle Moulds for her concreteness ratings.

This study was conducted as part of the requirements for the PhD dissertation of the first author.

http://www.psypress.com/memory
DOI:10.1080/09658210701256571

life events in that individuals seek to avoid unpleasant memories of such events (*avoidance* or *affect regulation hypothesis*). Williams and colleagues (Healy & Williams, 1999) proposed that OGM is due to disrupted autobiographical memory retrieval. Autobiographical memory is thought to be organised hierarchically, and an intentional search for a specific episode in memory is thought to follow a top-down process (see also Conway & Pleydell-Pearce, 2000). If the end product of this search is a very distressing event, the individual may be motivated to stop the search prematurely at an abstract level. In the long term, repeated premature abortion of the search for specific autobiographical memories may result in an overgeneral retrieval style. A study by Raes et al. (Raes, Hermans, De Decker, Eelen, & Williams, 2003) found preliminary support for the avoidance/affect-regulation hypothesis. Participants who showed a stable tendency to retrieve few specific memories in an autobiographical memory test were less susceptible to negative mood following a frustrating task. Raes et al. (2003) argued that OGM may have immediate benefits for mood regulation but also have negative long-term side effects, such as impaired problem-solving abilities (Dritschel, Kogan,
Burton, Burton, & Goddard, 1998). Watkins (Watkins & Teasdale, 2001; Watkins, Teasdale, & Williams, 2000) further showed that OGM was reduced in dysphoric participants when he induced a specific and concrete (rather than an abstract and avoidant) ruminative self-focus.

However, Philippot and colleagues (Philippot, Schaefer, & Herbette, 2003) have put forward a different view. They proposed that, in order to prevent disruption of ongoing goal-oriented behaviour, the intentional retrieval of specific autobiographical memories requires a concurrent inhibition of the emotional affect that accompanies the respective specific memory. They showed that priming overgeneral memory retrieval leads to an increased emotional reaction in a subsequent emotion induction. Thus, the initial experimental studies of the avoidance/affect regulation hypothesis do not yet show a consistent pattern of results.

Some preliminary correlational data, however, are in line with the avoidance/affect regulation hypothesis. Dissociation, which can be understood as reduced processing of the trauma, was related to OGM in a study by Jones et al. (1999). Similarly, OGM correlated with suppression of trauma memories, current dissociation, and rumination in a study by Schönfeld and Ehlers (2006). Rumination about the trauma and its consequences is thought to be an abstract thinking style, similar to worry, which prevents changes in the trauma memory and maintains problematic appraisals (Ehlers & Clark, 2000). The correlation of rumination and OGM in trauma survivors (Schönfeld & Ehlers, 2006) parallels findings that abstract verbal processing enhances OGM (Watkins & Teasdale, 2001; Watkins et al., 2000).

Furthermore, Kuyken and Brewin (1995) found an association between OGM and intrusions and avoidance in survivors of childhood abuse. This led them to conclude that OGM may be due to a retrieval advantage of the trauma memory over other memories, or due to reduced working memory capacity resulting from intrusive trauma memories. However, other studies suggest it may be the presence of trauma rather than symptoms of stress or level of executive functioning that are related to OGM (Hermans et al., 2004).

In the light of theories of depression, it appears plausible that autobiographical memories of childhood sexual abuse survivors are negatively toned, which may affect all autobiographical memory retrieval. In the case of recently and singularly traumatised individuals, it is less clear why these individuals show overgeneral memory retrieval of non-traumatic (including positive) memories from their past, why the OGM bias is mostly restrained to those with the PTSD diagnosis, and why it is often independent of the degree of depressive symptoms. One explanation may be that people with PTSD not only dwell on their trauma but also on positive events from the past in an abstract ruminative way, focusing on how their life has changed for the worse. In that case, general rumination or thought suppression tendencies would explain the OGM effect and its correlations with such measures.

Schönfeld and Ehlers (2006, 2007) found that OGM in PTSD extended to pictorial cues and involuntary memory retrieval. The latter result is not easily accounted for by explanations that focus on reduced mental capacity due to trauma memories and the individual's avoidant coping responses. The authors therefore suggested that other (additional) inhibitory processes might take place, which are not yet fully understood (Schönfeld & Ehlers, 2006). One possible explanation is that lack of trauma memory integration and its disruptiveness to current goals might motivate the "self-memory system" (Conway & Pleydell-Pearce, 2000) to inhibit the formation of spontaneous memories in general, but without being effective in inhibiting the not-integrated trauma memory, as intended. This would then lead to a vicious cycle of unintentional remembering and unintentional suppression. *Intentional* suppression of the trauma memory might impede emotional processing and trauma memory integration (Ehlers & Steil, 1995), might make the memory more available (Wegner, Schneider, Carter, & White, 1987), and, potentially, might give additional feedback to the self-memory system to continue or even enhance inhibition of both generic and spontaneous memory formation. Thus, OGM in PTSD might partly be the result of a "misguided suppression effect". Disrupted access to the autobiographical memory base may in turn hamper the integration of the trauma memory into the autobiographical memory base, which may lead to poor inhibition of cue-driven retrieval of these trauma memories (Conway & Pleydell-Pearce, 2000; Ehlers & Clark, 2000). Thus, there may be a vicious circle between intrusive memories, thought suppression, OGM, and the inadequate integration of the trauma memory into the autobiographical memory base. Preliminary correlational data by Schönfeld and Ehlers (2006) are in line with this hypothesis.

The present study built on the vicious cycle hypothesis. As a first step we directly manipulated trauma memory suppression experimentally and tested its effect on OGM in traumatised people with and without PTSD. The literature suggests that thought suppression may have paradoxical effects on the accessibility of trauma memories in two ways (Abramowitz, Tolin, & Street, 2001; Wegner et al., 1987). First, there may be an *enhancement* effect, where the to-be-suppressed thought may become more frequent during the attempted suppression itself. This appears to happen particularly under conditions of high mental load (Wegner & Erber, 1992). Second, there may be a *rebound* effect, where the increase occurs after suppression ceases. In PTSD, rebound of trauma-related thoughts after thought suppression appears to be more common than immediate enhancement (e.g., Harvey & Bryant, 1998; Shipherd & Beck, 1999).

In the present experiment, we combined a thought suppression instruction with the Autobiographical Memory Test (AMT) instruction.

We hypothesised that suppression of the trauma memory while doing the AMT would lead to diminished recall of specific memories, and that this reduction in specific recall would be particularly pronounced in people with PTSD compared to those without PTSD. Additionally we hypothesised that OGM would be correlated with measures of cognitive avoidance of the trauma memory, including rumination and abstract thinking about the trauma and suppression of intrusive memories. We further explored whether OGM is associated with general thought suppression tendencies, intelligence, and measures of reduced executive functioning.

METHOD

Participants

The sample comprised 42 assault survivors who had attended King's College Hospital's Accident and Emergency Department, London, 3 to 15 months prior to the study. Participants had replied to a letter that had been sent to all survivors of assault admitted to the Unit during this period of time, informing them about the purposes of the study, and had given permission to be contacted via telephone. Participants were asked about their most severe assault, and answered all questions with respect to this assault. Exclusion criteria were severe head injury during the assault or unconsciousness of longer than 15 minutes, psychosis, and substance dependence (past or present) for more than 3 years. Presence of PTSD and major depressive disorder was assessed with the Structured Clinical Interview for DSM-IV (First, Spitzer, Gibbons, & Williams, 1996). A total of 14 participants met the diagnostic criteria for PTSD. Four participants (28.6%) in the PTSD group, but none in the no-PTSD group, met criteria for major depression, $p = .009$. Table 1 shows demographic characteristics of the PTSD and no-PTSD groups. The groups did not differ in respect to their ethnic group, age, or education. However, there was a higher percentage of women in the PTSD group. The groups did not differ on most trauma characteristics, including a combined assault severity score, which considered the duration of trauma, injuries, number of assailants, and presence of, or threat by, a weapon (see Dunmore, Clark, & Ehlers, 1999, 2001). The only differences were that the assai-

TABLE 1
Demographic and trauma characteristics of the PTSD and No-PTSD groups

Demographics	PTSD (n = 14)	No-PTSD (n = 28)	Statistic	p value
Measure				
Age in years M (SD)	33.79 (13.40)	32.64 (9.52)	$t(40) = 0.32$	.75
Sex n (%)				
Female	10 (71.43)	10 (35.41)	$\chi^2(1, 42) = 4.77$	.05
Ethnic affiliation N (%)				
Afro-Caribbean	6 (42.96)	11 (39.29)	FI = 0.58	1.00
Caucasian	8 (57.14)	16 (57.14)		
Other		1 (3.57)		
Qualification in year M (SD)	11.93 (2.02)	13.73 (4.06)	$t(37.88) = 1.87$	.068
Trauma characteristics				
Type of trauma N (%)				
Physical assault	13 (92.83)	28 (100)	FI	.33
Sexual assault	1 (7.17)	0 (0)		
Time elapsed since trauma (in months)	16.33 (10.75)[a]	16.67 (7.99)[a]	$t(37) = 0.11$	.92
Place of assault N (%)				
At home	4 (28.57)	9 (32.14)	FI = 0.50	.82
Public place	7 (50)	15 (53.57)		
Other	3 (21.43)	4 (14.29)		
Number of assailants N (%)				
One	10 (7.14)	16 (57.14)	$\chi^2(1, 42) = 0.81$	.51
More than one	4 (2.86)	12 (43.86)		
Relation to assailant N (%)				
Unknown	8 (57.14)	17 (60.71)	FI = 6.50	.03
Ex-partner	5 (35.71)	2 (7.14)		
Other	1 (7.14)	9 (32.14)		
Duration of assault N (%)				
5 min. or less	6 (42.86)	16 (57.14)	FI = 1.30	.55
6 to 30 min.	5 (35.71)	9 (32.14)		
More than 30 min.	3 (21.43)	3 (10.71)		
Threatened N (%)				
To be harmed	8 (57.14)	15 (53.71)	$\chi^2(1,42) = 0.05$	1.00
With weapon	4 (28.57)	16 (57.14)	$\chi^2(1,42) = 3.06$	.11
Injuries (more than one possible) N (%)				
None	0 (0)	1 (3.57)	All ns	
Small cuts and bruises	1 (7.14)	3 (10.71)		
Severe cuts and bruises	11 (78.57)	23 (82.14)		
Broken bones	4 (28.57)	4 (14.29)		
Head injury (not internal)	1 (7.14)	3 (10.71)		
Other	2 (14.29)	0 (0)		
Perceived likelihood M (SD)				
To be injured	86.07 (15.71)	61.25 (28.08)	$t(39.35) = -3.67$	.00
To be killed	64.29 (36.53)	38.75 (36.58)	$t(40) = -2.13$	.04
Severity combined score M(SD)	6.29 (1.27)	6.14 (1.11)	$t(40) = -0.38$	.71

[a]$n = 27$.

lant was more likely to be the participant's ex-partner in the PTSD group, and the PTSD group believed to a greater extent that they would be seriously injured or killed during the assault than the no-PTSD group.

Measures

Clinical symptoms. Severity of post-traumatic stress symptoms was assessed with the Post-traumatic Diagnostic Scale (PDS). The

PDS (Foa, Cashman, Jaycox, & Perry, 1997) is a standardised and validated self-report measure of PTSD symptom severity that has been widely used with clinical and non-clinical samples of traumatised individuals. The PDS asks participants to rate how much they were bothered by each of the PTSD symptoms specified in DSM-IV (American Psychiatric Association, 1994) ranging from 0 "never" to 3 "five times per week or more/ very severe/nearly always". Severity of depression and anxiety were assessed with the Beck Depression Inventory (BDI) (Beck & Steer, 1987) and Beck Anxiety Inventory (BAI) (Beck, Epstein, Brown, & Steer, 1988), respectively, standard measures of established reliability and validity.

Measures of cognitive avoidance in relation to the trauma. Two measures of thought suppression were administered. First, *suppression of thoughts and memories about the assault* was measured with the thought suppression scale of the Response to Intrusions Questionnaire (RIQ) (Clohessy & Ehlers, 1999). The questionnaire asks participants to rate how often they use a range of cognitive strategies when they have unwanted memories of the assault. It contains six thought suppression items, e.g., "I try to push them out of my mind", $\alpha = .92$ in this sample. *Rumination* about the trauma was assessed with the Rumination Scale developed by Murray, Ehlers, and Mayou (2002). It contains nine items (e.g., "I dwell on how the event could have been prevented"), $\alpha = .91$.

Second, *general strategies to deal with unwanted thoughts* were assessed with the Thought Control Questionnaire (TCQ) (Wells & Davies, 1994). It consists of five different scales: distraction, social, worry, punishment, and reappraisal. Only the worry, punishment, and reappraisal scales were of interest to the present study (internal consistencies $\alpha = .75$, $\alpha = .76$, and $\alpha = .72$, respectively).

Abstractness of worries about the trauma and about another problem. Borkovec and colleagues (e.g., Borkovec & Lyonfields, 1993) suggested that worrying is a verbal-analytic and abstract way of thinking and a potential avoidance strategy. Stöber and Borkovec (2002) found lower concreteness for topics that people worry about frequently than for topics they worried about less. We therefore assessed the abstractness of the participant's worries with an adapted version of Stöber's problem elaboration procedure (e.g., Stöber & Borkovec, 2002).

The experimenter asked the participant to choose two problems they currently worried about, one of which was assault related and the other unrelated. These problems were written on two different sheets, and for each problem the participant wrote down three possible consequences (e.g., for the assault-related worry: "*I might be assaulted again*", a possible consequence would be: "*I will die and leave my children motherless*"). Two independent raters subsequently gave a global concreteness rating for the three consequences of each of the problems, as well as for the problem itself, on a scale from 1 (abstract) to 5 (concrete) following the guidelines by Stöber and Borkovec (2002). Inter-rater reliability was $r = .79$ (Intraclass correlation).

Some further cognitive and clinical measures were obtained in this sample but will be reported elsewhere.

Cognitive abilities. Verbal intelligence and working memory capacity were assessed to determine to what extent OGM is a function of general cognitive ability. To measure verbal intelligence we administered the Mill Hill Vocabulary Scale (MHV) (Raven, Court, & Raven, 1994). The MHV is a standard measure of verbal intelligence and asks participants to detect the correct synonym in a group of words. We administered set A of the multiple-choice version of the senior form. Working memory capacity was assessed using the digit span tasks (backward and forward) from the Wechsler Intelligence and Memory Scales (Wechsler, 1997).

Demographic variables and trauma characteristics. An adapted version of the Trauma Interview used by Dunmore et al. (1999, 2001) assessed trauma characteristics and demographic information.

Autobiographical Memory Test. This test (AMT, Williams & Broadbent, 1986) followed the standard procedure outlined by Williams (1986) and consisted of 12 words (6 positive and 6 negative), which were given in pseudo-randomised order and with a maximal reaction time of 30 seconds until the next word was given. The words were printed on cards, and the participants were asked to read them out aloud and to recall a specific memory in response to each of these words.

344 SCHÖNFELD ET AL.

The words were chosen from a word pool of non-trauma-related words that had been created for a previous study (Schönfeld & Ehlers, 2006). It included the words used by Brittlebank, Scott, Williams, and Ferrier (1993) and the words from John's word norms for emotionality ratings (John, 1988). These words were rated for imagery, by using the scale and instructions of Paivio, Yuille, and Madigan (1968), and pleasantness by 27 college students and university staff. Three final sets[1] were constructed, and the subsets were matched in terms of emotionality (John, 1988), frequency (Kucera & Francis, 1967), imagery, and pleasantness, with positive and negative words being significantly different from each other in terms of their pleasantness. The three sets were given in counterbalanced order in respect to the three test conditions. The first test was always preceded by three neutral practice words, and the two following tests were preceded by a single practice word. If the participant failed to retrieve a specific memory, he/she was prompted with "Can you think of a particular time?" or "Is there a specific event the word reminds you of?".

The first AMT used the standard instructions developed by Williams and Broadbent (1986, see above). Participants then completed two further AMTs under experimental instructions, a thought suppression (TS) instruction, and a mentioned control (MC) instruction, in counterbalanced order.

Experimental instructions

Thought suppression (TS). The TS condition combined the standard AMT instruction with a thought suppression instruction. After the standard AMT instruction, participants were told:

> However, now we would like you to do something else at the same time. Please try as hard as you can to suppress any thoughts about the assault. It is important that you suppress any thoughts about the assault for the full time of this task. Let us try with one word for practice.

After the practice word, the experimenter said:

> Do you have any questions? Please remember to try as hard as you can to suppress any thoughts about the assault. It is important that

you suppress any thoughts about the assault for the full time of this task.

After every three words, the participants were reminded of the particular task instructions with the prompt "Please remember, try as hard as you can to suppress any thoughts about the assault."

Mentioned control (MC). In the MC condition, the standard AMT was combined with the mentioned control instruction as in Salkovskis and Campbell (1994). This instruction is parallel to the thought suppression instruction in the degree of priming of assault memories, as the word assault is mentioned equally often, while allowing any memory. After the standard AMT instruction, participants were told:

> During this task it is OK to think about absolutely anything, including your assault. It doesn't matter whether a thought about the assault or any other event pops into your mind. During the full time of this task you can remember any event from your life. Let us try with one word for practice.

After the practice word, the experimenter said:

> Do you have any questions? ... Please remember that during this task it is OK to think about absolutely anything, including your assault. It doesn't matter whether a thought about the assault or any other event pops into your mind. During the full time of this task you can remember any event from your life.

After every three words, the participants were reminded of the particular task instructions with the prompt "Please remember, it doesn't matter whether a thought about the assault or any other event pops into your mind. You can remember any event from your life."

Manipulation checks. After six words, and at the end of each experimental condition (TS and MC), the experimenter asked participants how often they had trauma-related thoughts during the respective phase of the AMT (*assault-related thoughts–reported frequency during task*). Furthermore, after each AMT condition (standard, TS, MC), participants completed four visual analogue scales. They indicated how often they thought about the assault (0 "not at all" to 100 "all the time"), (*assault-related thoughts–global rating*) and how anxious (0 "not at all"

---

[1] The list of words and ratings is available from the first author.

to 100 "totally"), happy (0 "not at all" to 100 "extremely"), and despondent (0 "not at all" to 100 "extremely") they felt.

Rebound was tested in two monitoring periods, before and after the first experimental AMT condition. Here the participants were given a counter and were instructed as follows:

Now we will just be sitting here for the next five minutes. During this time, please record occurrences of thoughts about the assault by pressing the button of this counter. It doesn't matter whether a thought about the assault occurs or not; just record the thought if it occurs. It is important that you continue in the same way for the full five minutes. Please leave your eyes open. I will let you know when the time is over.

Procedure

After participants had given informed consent, they received a questionnaire package in the post and completed it on the day prior to the experimental session. The session started with the Trauma Interview, which was followed by two other questionnaires (results of which will be reported elsewhere): the State Dissociation and Self-referent Processing Questionnaires. The experimenter then asked questions regarding general mental health status and general demographic information. After this, the standard AMT was given, followed by the manipulation check ratings and the first monitoring phase. The first experimental AMT (TS/MC) and manipulation check ratings followed. The MHV was administered, followed by the second monitoring phase. Participants then did the second experimental AMT (MC/TS) and manipulation check ratings. The session continued with the Digit Span Tasks and the SCID. Finally, the participants were debriefed about the purpose of this study and reimbursed for their time and travel expenses (on average £25). The sessions were conducted by

graduate psychologists. Figure 1 depicts the exact procedure of the experimental part of the study.

Data analysis

AMT. According to Williams and Broadbent, a memory was defined as specific if it was about an event lasting a day or less, which occurred at a certain place and time even if the subject could not remember when; as extended if it was about an event lasting longer than a day; and as general or categorical if the memory reflected repeated activities or if they were general memories about people or places (Williams & Broadbent, 1986, p. 144). If no memory was given after 30 seconds, this was scored as an "omission". The rater was blind to the diagnosis. For the standard AMT, the main variable of interest was the number of first answers that were general (categorical), which is a commonly used score in OGM research. However, the number of general answers may constitute a somewhat problematic index of OGM in trauma research, as participants may remember the trauma in response to some of the cue words, and trauma memories are by definition specific (if the trauma lasted for less than a day as in the present sample). Therefore, for the main group comparisons, trauma memories were excluded and the ratio of general memories of all non-trauma memories was used as the dependent variable. The results were analysed by analysis of variance (ANOVA) with group (PTSD versus no-PTSD) as the between-subject factor. Pearson correlations were calculated to test the association of performance in the standard AMT (number of categorical answers) and the symptom and avoidance measures. If the variables were not normally distributed, Spearman's Rho was calculated.

The impact of the experimental manipulation on performance in the AMT was analysed with a repeated measures ANOVA with group (PTSD versus no-PTSD) as the between-subjects factor and experimental condition (TS versus MC) as the within factor. The sum of the general memories *and* the omissions was used as the variable of

Session order	1	2	3	4	5	6	7	8	9	10
A	Standard-AMT	Ratings mood and frequency	5 minutes monitoring	Ratings mood and frequency	TS-AMT	Ratings mood and frequency	MHV	5 minutes monitoring	MC-AMT	Ratings mood and frequency
B					MC-AMT			TS-AMT		

Figure 1. Experimental procedure. The Autobiographical Memory Test (AMT) was conducted three times; the standard version at baseline was followed by Thought Suppression (TS-AMT) and Mentioned Control instructions (MC-AMT) in counterbalanced order.

interest in this analysis because it is possible that, in order to comply with the instructions, some participants who could not retrieve a specific memory other than the trauma may have given no answer rather than a general answer. Parallel to the standard AMT, this analysis was done using the proportion of non-trauma answers that were general or omissions, to correct for the possible influence of differential naming of trauma memories in the experimental conditions.

A further ANOVA included order of experimental conditions (TS versus MC first) as a second between-subjects factor to check for order effects. Finally, analyses were repeated with valence as an additional within-subject factor.

Manipulation checks. Manipulation check variables were analysed with repeated measures ANOVAs with group (PTSD versus no-PTSD) as the between-subjects factor and experimental phase (Standard, TS, MC) as the within-subject factor. Possible rebound effects were analysed by comparing the number of assault memories in the monitoring phases with repeated measures ANOVAs with group (PTSD versus no-PTSD) and

experimental condition (TS, MC) as the between-subjects factors and experimental phase (standard, post-manipulation) as the within-subject factor. Results for the rebound check are missing for one participant who aborted the monitoring task because he became too distressed.

An alpha-level of .05 was used for all statistical tests and post hoc tests were Bonferroni-adjusted.

RESULTS

Manipulation checks

The results of the manipulation checks are shown in Table 2. There was no significant group × condition interaction for any of the ANOVAs. The PTSD group reported more assault-related thoughts than the no-PTSD group, for both the number of thoughts during the experimental conditions and the visual analogue ratings completed after each of the three AMT tests. For both measures of assault-related thoughts, there was also a main effect for experimental condition. Participants reported

TABLE 2
Manipulation checks and mood ratings, means (*SD*)

| | PTSD (n =14) | No-PTSD (n =28) | ANOVA | | |
			Group	Condition	G × C
Manipulation checks					
Assault-related thoughts:			$F(1, 37) = 6.62,$	$F(1, 37) = 25.43,$	*ns*
Reported frequency during task			$p = .01$	$p < .001$	
TS	4.00 (4.37)	1.63 (1.96)			
MC	10.07 (9.41)	4.06 (4.43)			
Assault-related thoughts:			$F(1, 39) = 12.44,$	$F(2, 78) = 19.90,$	*ns*
Global ratings			$p < .001$	$p < .001$	
S	65.00 (25.98)	30.00 (32.52)			
TS	35.77 (26.76)	16.43 (22.10)			
MC	58.07 (25.62)	27.32 (31.02)			
Mood ratings					
Despondent			*ns*	$F(2, 78) = 5.61, p = .01$	*ns*
S	58.08 (29.97)	34.82 (32.93)			
TS	39.62 (27.72)	22.14 (27.16)			
MC	48.46 (29.18)	23.21 (27.53)			
Anxious			$F(1, 39) = 17.15, p < .001$	$F(2, 78) = 7.41, p = .001$	*ns*
S	60.77 (24.99)	31.79 (28.19)			
TS	42.31 (27.13)	16.43 (23.72)			
MC	50.77 (26.68)	19.11 (24.80)			
Happy			*ns*	*ns*	*ns*
S	45.77 (33.84)	51.25 (27.68)			
TS	63.08 (26.26)	49.12 (30.31)			
MC	47.31 (31.66)	46.61 (28.25)			

S = standard; TS = thought suppression; MC = mentioned control; *ns* = non-significant.

TABLE 3
Results of the Autobiographical Memory Test (AMT)

	PTSD	No-PTSD
Standard AMT		
Categorical memories		
Negative (total number)	2.50 (1.51)	1.50 (1.48)
Positive (total number)	2.57 (1.65)	2.00 (1.61)
Ratio (positive and negative combined)[1]	0.45 (0.22)	0.30 (0.23)
AMT with experimental manipulation of thought suppression		
Categorical memories and omissions (ratio)[1]		
Thought suppression	0.55 (0.21)	0.29 (0.29)
Mention control	0.47 (0.24)	0.35 (0.28)
Categorical memories (ratio)[1]		
Thought suppression	0.38 (0.25)	0.21 (0.24)
Mention control	0.36 (0.27)	0.24 (0.25)
Omissions (ratio)[1]		
Thought suppression	0.17 (0.14)	0.08 (0.08)
Mention control	0.11 (0.13)	0.11 (0.12)

[1]Proportion of all non-trauma answers.

fewer thoughts about the trauma in the TS condition than in the MC condition and the standard instruction, all $ps = .001$.

The PTSD group reported greater anxiety than the no-PTSD group. There was also an effect of experimental condition on anxiety and despondency ratings. During the standard AMT, participants reported greater anxiety compared to the TS condition, $p = .005$, and greater despondency compared to both the TS, $p = .007$, and the MC conditions, $p = .046$.

The rebound analysis, using the number of assault memories recorded in the monitoring phases after the standard and the first experimental AMTs, showed a trend for an effect of experimental condition (standard versus post-manipulation), $F(1, 37) = 8.29, p = .052$, no main group or experimental condition (TS versus MC) effects, but a trend for a three-way interaction, $F(1, 19) = 3.99, p = .060$. After the MC condition, but not after the TS condition, participants recorded fewer trauma memories compared to the standard AMT condition, and this decrease tended to be more pronounced in the PTSD group.

Standard Autobiographical Memory Test

The results of the standard AMT are presented in Table 3. For the number of categorical memories, the ANOVA showed a trend for a group effect, $F(1, 40) = 3.22, p = .08$. The PTSD group retrieved more general memories than the no-PTSD group.

When trauma memories were excluded from the analysis and the ratio of general memories of all non-trauma memories was considered, the ANOVA showed a group effect, $F(1, 40) = 7.81, p = .049$ (more general memories in the PTSD group).

Table 4 shows the correlations of the number of general memories in the standard AMT with symptom, cognitive avoidance, and executive functioning measures. The table also depicts the group differences on these variables. Overgeneral memories correlated with PTSD symptom severity (total score, reliving, avoidance, and hyperarousal clusters), depression, and anxiety, but not with assault severity. It correlated with verbal intelligence (MHV), but not significantly with working memory capacity as measured by the digit span test. It further correlated with aspects of trauma-related cognitive avoidance, i.e., thought suppression, rumination; and with two of the Thought Control Questionnaire scales, worry and punishment, but not with reappraisal. Overgeneral memory was associated with abstractness (lower concreteness) of worries about the trauma (and consequences), but not of worries about another problem (or consequences).

AMT with and without thought suppression

Table 3 shows the AMT results for the experimental manipulation of thought suppression. The ANOVA showed a significant group effect, $F(1, 40) = 5.50, p = .024$, and a group × condition

TABLE 4

Symptom and cognitive measures in the PTSD versus No-PTSD groups, and their correlation with OGM in the standard AMT

Measure	PTSD (n =14)	Control (n =28)	Statistic	Corr. (r/rho)
Combined assault severity score	6.29 (1.27)	6.14 (1.11)	$t(40) = 0.38$	.02
Clinical symptoms				
PTSD				
PDS-total	27.21 (11.40)	16.71 (14.41)	$t(40) = 2.38^*$	.47**
Re-experiencing	6.62 (3.39)	4.93 (4.31)[a]	$t(39) = 1.29$	.45**
Avoidance	10.79 (6.47)	5.36 (5.88)	$t(40) = 2.73^{**}$	.43**
Hyperarousal	9.79 (3.47)	6.46 (5.17)	$t(36.36) = 2.47^{**}$	.44**
Depression				
BDI	16.64 (11.25)	8.07 (9.25)	$t(40) = 2.63^*$	.32*
Anxiety				
BAI	19.07 (14.22)	8.07 (9.16)	$t(18.57) = 2.63^*$	.31*
Cognitive avoidance measures				
RIQ-thought suppression	13.14 (5.02)	7.36 (13.14)	$t(40) = 3.52^{***}$	.49**
Rumination	15.67 (7.46)	7.25 (5.13)	$t(40) = 4.30^{***}$	.36*
Worry abstractness				
Assault problem	3.09 (1.22)	3.71 (0.92)	$U = 66.5$	−.45*
Assault consequences	3.64 (0.81)	3.47 (1.06))	$t(24) = .44$	−.45*
Neutral problem	3.27 (0.65)	2.52 (1.25)	$t(30) = 2.23^*$	−.03
Neutral consequences	2.91 (0.83)	3.29 (1.26)	$t(26) = 0.89$	−.36
General strategies				
TCQ Worry	12.11 (2.00)	9.57 (2.71)	$t(40) = 2.77^{**}$	.30
TCQ Punishment	11.17 (3.94)	8.86 (2.77)	$t(40) = 2.21^*$	.43**
TCQ Reappraisal	11.00 (2.53)[b]	12.53 (3.90)[a]	$t(40) = 1.29$	−.15
Cognitive ability				
MHV	12.77 (3.83)[b]	17.11 (5.91)[a]	$t(38) = 2.41^*$	−.48**
Digit span forward	9.71 (2.27)	9.61 (2.71)	$t(40) = 0.13$	−.23
Digit span backward	5.79 (2.39)	6.07 (2.84)	$t(40) = 0.32$	−.30

[a] $n = 27$; [b] $n = 13$; *** $p < .001$; ** $p < .01$; * $p < .05$.

interaction, $F(1, 40) = 6.38$, $p = .016$. The PTSD group gave a higher proportion of non-trauma answers that were general memories/omissions than the no-PTSD group in the TS condition ($p = .034$), but not in the MC condition ($p = .162$). There was also a trend ($p = .076$) for the no-PTSD group to have fewer general memories/omissions in the TS compared to the MC condition, with a non-significant difference in the opposite direction for the PTSD group ($p = .108$). Planned comparisons tested whether these group differences were due to general answers or omissions. There was a trend for the PTSD group to have more omissions in the TS than in the MC condition ($W = 1.90$, $p = .059$, no other effects). In the TS condition, but not in the MC condition, the PTSD group had more general memories ($U = 117$, $p = .033$) and omissions ($U = 120$, $p = .036$) than the no-PTSD group. Figure 2 depicts the mean number of omissions and general memories for all test conditions.

Additional ANOVAs showed that the order of the TS and MC conditions did not interact with the experimental condition factor,[2] and that cue valence showed no main effects or interactions with group and experimental condition.

DISCUSSION

The present study investigated the effects of the suppression of trauma memories on autobiographical memory retrieval in trauma survivors with and without PTSD, and explored correlates of overgeneral autobiographical memory retrieval (OGM). The results of the Autobiographical Memory Test (AMT) were largely in line with previous findings that people with PTSD show a

---

[2] When order was included as a factor in the ANOVA, there were no main effects of order nor any interactions with order for both the number of categorical memories and the ratio of categorical memories as a proportion of non-trauma memories.

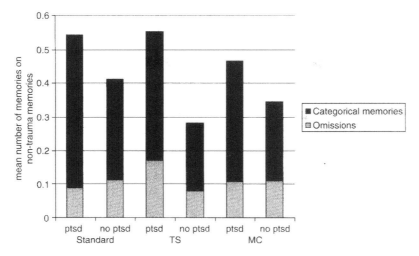

Figure 2. Mean number of omissions and general memories (as a proportion of the total number of non-trauma memories) in the three test conditions of the autobiographical memory test (AMT) (Standard, TS = thought suppression, MC = mentioned control) for the PTSD and no-PTSD groups

bias to retrieve overgeneral memories compared to traumatised people without PTSD (McNally et al., 1994, 1995). PTSD symptom severity was also significantly correlated with OGM.

When participants were instructed to suppress any assault-related thoughts during the AMT, the group differences became more pronounced. Participants with PTSD retrieved more general memories and had more omissions than participants without PTSD. In contrast, when suppression was not required (MC instruction), there was no longer a significant group difference. Within the PTSD group, differences between the TS and MC condition were mainly due to more omissions in the TS condition. This difference suggests that participants followed the instructions because they seemed to prefer not to give an answer than to report the trauma memory, which is specific.

One explanation for the present pattern of findings is that the extent of OGM in PTSD depends on the degree of effortful suppression of trauma-related memories. Degree of thought suppression (RIQ) correlated with OGM. When the experimental task demanded suppression, participants with PTSD clearly had greater difficulties retrieving specific memories than those without PTSD. Overall, the results in the PTSD group are in line with the avoidance hypothesis of OGM (Raes et al., 2003). The trend for fewer general memories/omissions in the TS compared to the MS condition in the no-PTSD group, together with the decrease in anxiety during TS, is in line with Philippot et al.'s (2003) inhibition

facilitation hypothesis. This hypothesis may mainly apply to people without psychopathology. Generally, the susceptibility of OGM to cognitive manipulation is in line with Watkins' findings (e.g., Watkins & Teasdale, 2001).

Thought suppression has been hypothesised to be partly an effortful process (e.g., Rosen & Engle, 1998; Wegner & Erber, 1992). An alternative explanation for the effects of the experimental manipulation is therefore that the thought suppression instruction created a greater task demand for the PTSD group than the no-PTSD group. This may have interfered with the retrieval of specific memories, as people with PTSD generally experience frequent trauma-related thoughts. It is thus possible that they needed more effort to suppress assault memories in the TS condition than the no-PTSD group. We cannot rule out this possibility, as the two experimental conditions were not matched in terms of mental load. The fact that the differences between the TS and MC conditions in the PTSD group were more pronounced with respect to the omissions suggests that the mental load of the TS condition may have played an important role in OGM in this condition. Future studies are needed to clarify the specific task demands and their potential interaction, by carefully considering an adequate comparison task as an additional control condition. Nevertheless, this possibility does not make the results less relevant for everyday life situations, where efforts to suppress trauma-related thoughts and memories may also interfere with the retrieval of specific autobiographical memories in people with PTSD. Digit span as a measure for working memory capacity was not significantly associated with OGM as in previous studies (De Decker et al., 2003), which shows that the connection between different task needs in respect to working memory capacity and concurrent autobiographical memory retrieval may be complex (Williams, personal communication).

The measures of assault-related thoughts during the autobiographical memory tasks that served as manipulation checks suggested that the thought suppression manipulation was successful in both groups. During the TS condition, both groups reported fewer assault-related thoughts than during the MC condition. In line with fewer trauma-related thoughts, they also reported less anxiety in the TS than in the MC condition. Although the PTSD group had more trauma-related thoughts during both experimental tasks, there was no interaction between group and experimental condition; thus, the manipulation did not have differential effects on participants with and without PTSD.

The monitoring phases after the AMT tests did not show an increase in assault-related thoughts after suppression compared to baseline levels after the standard AMT. However, after the MC condition, but not after the TS condition, there was a decrease in assault-related thoughts compared to baseline. This can be interpreted as indirect evidence of a rebound effect. If participants engaged in trauma memory suppression, they did not experience the natural decline of assault memories in the course of the session. However, the small sample sizes in the respective cells warrant only very careful interpretation of these results. Our results are in line with the general finding that immediate enhancement is generally rare or absent in PTSD (Abramowitz et al., 2001), but did not support the hypothesis that a concurrent task can lead to enhancement during thought suppression (Wegner & Erber, 1992).

The study further investigated correlates of OGM in traumatised individuals. In contrast to Henderson, Hargreaves, Gregory, and Williams (2002), De Decker et al. (2003), and Hermans et al. (2004), but in line with Kuyken and Brewin (1995), we found OGM to be associated with symptoms of PTSD, depression, and anxiety, but not with trauma severity. However, trauma severity of a single event may not be comparable to repeated abuse in childhood, which may account for the lack of association in this study.

Verbal intelligence correlated with OGM; however, working memory capacity was not significantly associated with OGM, as in De Decker et al.'s study (2003). In respect to executive functioning, the picture seems more complex, particularly given that in the present study the correlation between OGM and digit span was not trivial. Possibly here, deficits in relation to PTSD are more specific and affect only certain tasks, such as the AMT (see above with respect to the role of mental load).

OGM correlated with cognitive strategies that avoid processing of the trauma, such as thought suppression, rumination, and punishment as a thought control style. In line with a role of rumination in OGM, lower concreteness scores of worry about the assault were also associated with overgeneral memory retrieval (see also Borkovec & Lyonfields, 1993; Stöber & Borkovec, 2002). Only the concreteness of the assault worries, but not of other worries, was related to OGM. It is possible that this effect was mediated by PTSD severity. However, it may also show that it is specifically the avoidance of past events or problems that is associated with OGM, and not so much a general abstract thinking style.

To summarise, this experiment is a preliminary step to support the hypothesis that thought suppression of trauma memories plays a role in PTSD and OGM. At this stage we cannot be certain about the specific mechanisms that are involved in the interplay between thought suppression, PTSD, and OGM. We had hypothesised OGM to be at least partly a side product of thought suppression, which may (1) in the short term, increase general inhibition of autobiographical memory formation via the self-memory system (Conway & Pleydell-Pearce, 2000), and (2) in the long term, prevent trauma memory processing. If the first explanation is supported in future studies, it could be useful to include OGM in cognitive models of PTSD that explain the persistence of symptoms by the lack of integration of the trauma memory into the autobiographical memory base, and emphasise the importance of maladaptive coping strategies (e.g., Ehlers & Clark, 2000)

The study had several limitations. First, due to the mode of recruitment it is possible that the population in this study was biased towards those who were very motivated or very distressed. Second, the PTSD group was relatively small, and the no-PTSD group reported significant PTSD symptoms of moderate severity. This may have reduced the power of the group comparisons. Third, the study did not include non-traumatised or other clinical groups. Future studies including these groups may help to increase understanding of the precise mechanisms between trauma, psychopathology, and OGM. Fourth, as outlined earlier, it would be advisable to repeat the experiment with a control condition that demands comparable amounts of mental load as in the TS condition. Fifth, the correlational data need to be interpreted with caution because they were calculated across groups. It would be advisable to replicate the results with a larger sample to allow more precise predictions about the associations between OGM and the respective measures.

Prospective longitudinal studies and experimental studies are needed to further elucidate the relationship between OGM and PTSD in traumatised populations.

REFERENCES

Abramowitz, J. S., Tolin, D. F., & Street, G. P. (2001). Paradoxical effects of thought suppression: A meta-analysis of controlled studies. *Clinical Psychology Review*, *21*, 683–703.

American Psychiatric Association. (1994). *Diagnostic and statistical manual of mental disorders* (4th ed.) Washington, DC: American Psychiatric Association.

Beck, A. T., Epstein, N., Brown, G., & Steer, R. A. (1988). An inventory for measuring clinical anxiety: Psychometric properties. *Journal of Consulting and Clinical Psychology*, *56*, 893–897.

Beck, A. T., & Steer, R. A. (1987). *Beck Depression Inventory: Manual*. San Antonio, TX: Psychological Corporation.

Borkovec, T. D., & Lyonfields, J. D. (1993). Worry: Thought suppression of emotional processing. In H. W. Krohne (Ed.), *Vigilance and avoidance*. (pp. 101–118). Toronto: Hogrefe and Huber.

Brittlebank, A. D., Scott, J., Williams, J. M. G., & Ferrier, I. N. (1993). Autobiographical memory in depression: State or trait marker? *British Journal of Psychiatry*, *162*, 118–121.

Burke, M., & Mathews, A. (1992). Autobiographical memory and clinical anxiety. *Cognition and Emotion*, *6*, 23–35.

Clohessy, S., & Ehlers, A. (1999). PTSD symptoms, response to intrusive memories and coping in ambulance service workers. *British Journal of Clinical Psychology*, *38*, 251–265.

Conway, M. A., & Pleydell-Pearce, C. W. (2000). The construction of autobiographical memories in the self-memory system. *Psychological Review*, *107*, 261–288.

Dalgleish, T., Yiend, J., Tchanturia, K., Serpell, L., Hems, S., De Silva, P., et al. (2003). Self-reported parental abuse relates to autobiographical memory style in patients with eating disorders. *Emotion*, *3*, 211–222.

De Decker, A., Hermans, D., Raes, F., & Eelen, P. (2003). Autobiographical memory specificity and trauma in inpatient adolescents. *Journal of Clinical Child and Adolescent Psychology*, *32*, 23–32.

Dritschel, B. H., Kogan, L., Burton, A., Burton, E., & Goddard, L. (1998). Everyday planning difficulties following traumatic brain injury: A role for autobiographical memory. *Brain Injury*, *12*, 875–886.

Dunmore, E., Clark, D. M., & Ehlers, A. (1999). Cognitive factors involved in the onset and maintenance of post-traumatic stress disorder (PTSD) after physical or sexual assault. *Behaviour Research and Therapy*, *37*, 809–829.

Dunmore, E., Clark, D. M., & Ehlers, A. (2001). A prospective investigation of the role of cognitive factors in persistent Post-traumatic Stress Disorder (PTSD) after physical or sexual assault. *Behaviour Research and Therapy*, *39*, 1063–1084.

Ehlers, A., & Clark, D. M. (2000). A cognitive model of post-traumatic stress disorder. *Behaviour Research and Therapy*, *38*, 319–345.

Ehlers, A., & Steil, R. (1995). Maintenance of intrusive memories in post-traumatic stress disorder: A cognitive approach. *Behavioural and Cognitive Psychotherapy*, *23*, 217–249.

First, M. B., Spitzer, R. L., Gibbon M., & Williams, J. B. W. (1996). *Structured clinical interview for DSM-IV axis 1 disorders*. Washington, DC: American Psychiatric Press.

Foa, E. B., Cashman, L., Jaycox, L., & Perry, K. (1997). The validation of a self-report measure of post-traumatic stress disorder: The Post-traumatic Diagnostic Scale. *Psychological Assessment*, *9*, 445–451.

Harvey, A. G., & Bryant, R. A. (1998). The effect of attempted thought suppression in acute stress disorder. *Behaviour Research and Therapy*, *36*, 583–590.

Harvey, A. G., Bryant, R. A., & Dang, S. T. (1998). Autobiographical memory in acute stress disorder. *Journal of Consulting and Clinical Psychology*, *66*, 500–506.

Healy, H., & Williams, J. M. G. (1999). Autobiographical memory. In T. Dalgleish & M. Powers (Eds.), *Handbook of cognition and emotion*. Chichester, UK: John Wiley & Sons.

Henderson, D., Hargreaves, I. R., Gregory, S., & Williams, J. M. G. (2002). Autobiographical memory and emotion in a non-clinical sample of women with and without a reported history of childhood sexual abuse. *British Journal of Clinical Psychology*, *41*, 129–141.

Hermans, D., Van den Broeck, K., Belis, G., Raes, F., Pieters, G., & Eelen, P. (2004). Trauma and autobiographical memory specificity in depressed inpatients. *Behaviour Research and Therapy*, *42*(7), 775–789.

John, C. H. (1988). Emotionality ratings and free-association of 240 emotional and non-emotional words. *Cognition and Emotion*, *2*, 49–70.

Jones, B., Heard, H., Startup, M., Swales, M., Williams, J. M. G., & Jones, R. S. P. (1999). Autobiographical memory and dissociation in borderline personality disorder. *Psychological Medicine*, *29*, 1397–1404.

Kucera, H., & Francis, W. N. (1967). *Computational analysis of present-day American English*. Providence, RI: Brown University Press.

Kuyken, W., & Brewin, C. R. (1995). Autobiographical memory functioning in depression and reports of early abuse. *Journal of Abnormal Psychology*, *104*, 585–591.

McNally, R. J., Lasko, N. B., Macklin, M. L., & Pitman, R. K. (1995). Autobiographical memory disturbance in combat-related post-traumatic stress disorder. *Behaviour Research & Therapy*, *33*, 619–630.

McNally, R. J., Litz, B. T., Prassas, A., Shin, L. M., & Weathers, F. W. (1994). Emotional priming of autobiographical memory in post-traumatic stress disorder. *Cognition and Emotion*, *8*, 351–367.

Murray, J., Ehlers, A., & Mayou, R. A. (2002). Dissociation and post-traumatic stress disorder: Two prospective studies of motor vehicle accident survivors. *British Journal of Psychiatry*, *180*, 363–368.

Paivio, A., Yuille, J. C., & Madigan, S. A. (1968). Concreteness, imagery, and meaningfulness values for 925 nouns. *Journal of Experimental Psychology*, *76*, 1–25.

Philippot, P., Schaefer, A., & Herbette, G. (2003). Consequences of specific processing of emotional information: Impact of general versus specific autobiographical memory priming on emotion elicitation. *Emotion*, *3*, 270–283.

Raes, F., Hermans, D., De Decker, A., Eelen, P., & Williams, J. M. G. (2003). Autobiographical memory specificity and affect regulation: An experimental approach. *Emotion*, *3*, 201–206.

Raven, J. C., Court, J. H., & Raven, J. (1994). Mill Hill Vocabulary Scale. In *Manual for Raven's Progressive Matrices and Vocabulary Scales* (1994 ed.). Oxford, UK: Oxford Psychologists Press.

Rosen, V. M., & Engle, R. W. (1998). Working memory capacity and suppression. *Journal of Memory and Language*, *39*, 418–436.

Salkovskis, P. M., & Campbell, P. (1994). Thought suppression induces intrusion in naturally occuring intrusive thoughts. *Behaviour Research and Therapy*, *32*, 1–8.

Schönfeld, S., & Ehlers, A. (2007). *Autobiographical memories in everyday life in post-traumatic stress disorder*. Manuscript submitted for publication.

Schönfeld, S., & Ehlers, A. (2006). Overgeneral memory extends to pictorial retrieval cues and correlates with cognitive features in post-traumatic stress disorder. *Emotion*, *6*(4), 611–621.

Shipherd, J. C., & Beck, J. G. (1999). The effects of suppressing trauma-related thoughts on women with rape-related post-traumatic stress disorder. *Behaviour Research & Therapy*, *37*, 99–112.

Stöber, J., & Borkovec, T. D. (2002). Reduced concreteness of worry in Generalised Anxiety Disorder: Findings from a therapy study. *Cognitive Therapy and Research*, *26*(1), 89–96.

Watkins, E., & Teasdale, J. D. (2001). Rumination and overgeneral memory in depression: Effects of self-focus and analytic thinking. *Journal of Abnormal Psychology*, *110*, 353–357.

Watkins, E., Teasdale, J. D., & Williams, R. M. (2000). Decentring and distraction reduce overgeneral autobiographical memory in depression. *Psychological Medicine*, *30*, 911–920.

Wechsler, D. (1997). *WAIS-III. Administration and scoring manual*. London: The Psychological Corporation.

Wegner, D. M., & Erber, R. (1992). The hyperaccessibility of suppressed thoughts. *Journal of Personality and Social Psychology*, *63*, 903–912.

Wegner, D. M., Schneider, D. J., Carter, S. R. III, & White, T. L. (1987). Paradoxical effects of thought suppression. *Journal of Personality and Social Psychology*, *53*, 5–13.

Wells, A., & Davies, M. I. (1994). The thought control questionnaire: A measure of individual differences in the control of unwanted thoughts. *Behaviour Research and Therapy*, *32*, 871–878.

Wenzel, A., Jackson, L. C., Brendle, J. R., & Pinna, K. (2003). Autobiographical memories associated with feared stimuli in fearful and nonfearful individuals. *Anxiety, Stress and Coping*, *16*, 1–15.

Wessel, I., Meeren, M., Peeters, F., Arntz, A., & Merckelbach, H. (2001). Correlates of autobiographical memory specificity: The role of depression, anxiety and childhood trauma. *Behaviour Research & Therapy*, *39*(4), 409–421.

Wilhelm, S., McNally, R. J., Baer, L., & Florin, I. (1997). Autobiographical memory in obsessive-compulsive disorder. *British Journal of Clinical Psychology*, *36*, 21–31.

Williams, J. M. G., & Broadbent, K. (1986). Autobiographical memory in suicide attempters. *Journal of Abnormal Psychology*, *95*, 144–149.

Subject index